The Nature of Social and Educational Inquiry: Empiricism Versus Interpretation

John K. Smith

University of Northern Iowa

ABLEX PUBLISHING CORPORATION
NORWOOD, NEW JERSEY

Printed in the United States of America.

Library of Congress Cataloging-in-Publication Data

Smith, John K. (John Kenneth), 1942–
   The nature of social and educational inquiry : empiricism vs.
interpretation / John K. Smith.
     p. cm.
   Bibliography: p.
   Includes index.
   ISBN 0-89391-514-9
   1. Social sciences—Philosophy. I. Title.
H61.S5885 1989
300′.1—dc20   89-6613
                                            CIP

Ablex Publishing Corporation
355 Chestnut St.
Norwood, NJ 07648

For my wife, Cheryl

Contents

Preface   *vii*

I   **Framing the Issues**   *1*

The Issue of Method   3
Terms and Terminology   6
The Present Interest in the Discussion   9
The Unity of the Sciences   12
An Outline of the Chapters   14

II   **The Standard View of Science and the Scientific Method**   *17*

The Scientific Method: An Example   18
The Scientific Method: A Description   21
Laws, Explanations, and Theory   31
The Role of Methodology   33
Summary   35

III   **The Origins of the Current Discussion**   *37*

The Development of the Empiricist Approach   38
The Interpretive Reaction   50
The Attempt at Synthesis   57
Summary   61

IV   **The Relationship of the Investigator to What is Investigated**   *63*

Two Examples   64
Two Perspectives   69
Objective and Subjective   78
The Example of the Validity of Measuring Instruments   80
Summary   85

V   The Relationship of Facts and Values   *87*

The Origin of the Issue—The Logical Separation
    of *Is/Ought*   88
Weber—The Separation of Facts and Values   91
Distinct Separation—Inquiry as Value-Free   96
Partial Separation—Values Enter in But Inquiry
    is Still Objective   99
The Inseparability of Values and Facts   103
A Return to the Example of Construct Validity   109
Summary   111

VI   The Goal of Social and Educational Inquiry   *113*

Scientific Explanation   114
Interpretive Understanding   124
Summary   137

VII   The Role of Procedures in the Inquiry Process   *139*

What it Means to be a Person   141
Empiricism and Methods   146
Interpretation and Methods   149
Summary   161

**VIII   Objectivism and Relativism: The Nature of Social
and Educational Inquiry   *163***

Objectivism and Relativism   164
In the End . . .   170

References   *175*

Author Index   *183*

Subject Index   *185*

Preface

About eight years ago I became interested in the increasingly widespread and intense discussion concerning different approaches to social and educational inquiry. My interest was not in the how-to-do-it aspects, since I was well acquainted with the various techniques or practices associated with both the quantitative and qualitative approaches (as they were most commonly called at the time). Rather, to me the most interesting and complex problems were in the area of the philosophical assumptions, or the logics of justification associated with the different perspectives.

My initial review of the literature in this area made it apparent that there was little available on the topic that was of introductory nature. By *introductory* I mean works that were intelligible to someone like me, who was acquainted with the major ideas being discussed in the philosophy of science/social science, but who was not well grounded in these areas. Thus, I was faced with the choice of either reading what little was readily accessible and letting it go at that, or undertaking a more thorough reading of the philosophical literature. For better or worse, I chose the latter course. So began a rather lengthy process of reading and reflection, of which this book is the latest result.

As befits my intention to write an introduction to this topic, I have attempted to address, as clearly and straightforwardly as possible, the major issues involved in the discussion of different approaches to social and educational inquiry. In particular, I have avoided excessive reference to philosophical *isms*, or traditional schools of philosophical thought, and minimized the use of a more technical philosophical terminology. I hope this approach allows researchers to gain a better understanding of the major issues involved in the discussion and, should their interest be further provoked, provides them with a base from which to undertake further reading in the area. Whether or not I have succeeded in accomplishing these goals, of course, remains to be seen.

Although numerous people have both intentionally and unintentionally influenced the development of this book, three colleagues and friends deserve special mention. Jack Yates, Joseph Blase, and Louis Heshusius have given generously of their time to read and critique various parts of the manuscript. Their comments have been invaluable to me. Similarly, I must thank the people at Ablex—the reviewers commissioned by them for their insightful comments and Barbara Bernstein, for her kind and courteous response to my concerns as the manuscript was being prepared for publication. Dean John Downey and Ruth Ratliff of the Graduate College, University of Northern Iowa, also must be thanked for helping me obtain a semester free from my teaching duties so that I could work more intensively on the manuscript.

Finally, above all I must thank my wife, to whom this book is dedicated. She calls herself an editor—but this is at best a thin disguise for colleague and critic. She has not only saved me from committing various grammatical errors in the text, she has continually forced me to clarify my points and state them clearly and concisely. Through it all, she has been my best and most forceful critic.

CHAPTER I
Framing the Issues

Here we touch upon a crucial ambiguity caused by the disparity between
the Anglo-American and the German understanding of the nature of the
social sciences. In the Anglo-American tradition, intellectual disciplines
fall into the trichotomy of the natural sciences, social sciences, and humanities, but on the Continent they are categorized according to the dichotomy between the *Naturwissenschaften* and the *Geisteswissenschaften* (the
expression that was introduced into German as a translation of what Mill
called the "moral sciences"). In the main tradition of Anglo-American
thought—at least until recently—the overwhelming bias has been to think
of the social sciences as *natural sciences* concerning individuals in their social relations. The assumption has been that the social sciences differ in the
degree and not in kind from the natural sciences and that ideally the methods and standards appropriate to the natural sciences can be extended by
analogy to the social sciences. But in the German tradition there has been a
much greater tendency to think of the social disciplines as forms of
Geisteswissenschaften, sharing essential characteristics with the humanistic
disciplines. (Bernstein, 1983, p. 35)

Over the last few years the nature and purpose of social and educational
inquiry have been the focus of serious, sustained discussion among researchers. The terms used to acknowledge this discussion have become
common currency: quantitative versus qualitative, scientistic versus naturalistic, empiricist versus interpretive, and so on. No matter which labels are selected, however, there is still a lack of clarity as to what is involved in this discussion. Accordingly, this book attempts to answer a
number of questions that have a direct bearing on the topic—including,
of course, the following very basic ones: Are the differences between the
two approaches simply ones of emphasis, or are they fundamental differences of kind? Are we engaged in a discussion over different techniques to use to reach the same goal, or are we faced with a situation in
which the goals of each approach are seriously different? More generally, exactly what are the underlying or philosophically oriented issues
of most consequence in this discussion?

As will become apparent throughout this book, the answers to these and other more specific questions are important for various reasons. For the moment, however, two points will suffice to demonstrate this importance. First, in a practical sense, this debate is crucial to the issues of whether or not criteria can be employed—and if so, what these criteria might be—to judge research efforts. The empiricist approach to inquiry has long-standing and generally well-established criteria for sorting out a good study from its not-so-good counterpart. These criteria are largely defined in terms of methods or procedures. As Bauman (1978) notes, this perspective has remained faithful to that 19th century French rationalist tradition that defined "true knowledge as, above all (if not solely), the question of method and of its systematic application" (pp. 15–16).

One major problem involves the extent to which similar methodological criteria can be applied to interpretive inquiry. Can the tenets of validity and reliability, for example, as defined and applied within the empiricist tradition, be somehow translated and/or modified so that they can be used to evaluate interpretive inquiry? Or are the two approaches so fundamentally different in their underlying assumptions that these concepts and the whole idea of methodologically grounding knowledge claims are irrelevant to interpretive inquiry? In other words, the underlying assumptions of the latter perspective on inquiry may mean that no definite criteria and standard procedures can be established.

That these issues have not been resolved is probably most evident—especially from the point of view of interpretive inquirers—in the area of the review of manuscripts for journal publication. For example, in a recent article M. Smith (1987) discussed the problems journal editors and reviewers face in their attempt to judge the merits of interpretive studies. She noted that what may seem a rather straightforward task is actually one of serious complexity because "the body of work labeled qualitative is richly variegated and its theories of method diverse to the point of disorderliness" (p. 173). Whereas her paper makes it clear that interpretive studies must be judged differently from empiricist studies, it also makes it clear that the issue of an established criteria for evaluating interpretive inquiry, whether based on methods or something else, is indeed a problematic one.

Second, in a more general sense, this discussion has consequences for the very interpretation we give to the process of inquiry and the results thereof. Exactly what one makes of a statement such as "the results of research have shown such and such to be the case" may be quite different depending on the tradition within which one is working. In other words, crucial concepts such as truth and validity may be subject to much different characterizations or definitions depending on the approach to inquiry that one accepts. Is social and educational inquiry a matter of the discovery and description of how things really are, or is it a process of constructing realities that depend for their acceptance on considerations of historical time and cultural place? This discussion clearly invokes serious epistemological considerations—particularly in regard to the issue of objectivism versus relativism.

Without a doubt, a discussion of this topic could be approached in various ways, ranging from a review of arguments in philosophy of science/social science to an examination (possibly comparative) of the techniques of the empiricist and interpretive approaches to inquiry. Moreover, the role of advocate could be adopted with the resulting defense of one perspective at the expense of the other.

These possibilities are all legitimate and frequently taken perspectives on this topic. This book, however, takes a different approach, which can be characterized briefly by three points. First, the focus is much more on the logic of justification associated with each approach to inquiry than it is on techniques, or the how-to-do-it aspect. Second, even though various schools of philosophical thought inform the discussion, this book is not a philosophical treatise. The reference to philosophical *isms* and the use of philosophical terminology are kept, as much as is possible, to a minimum. Finally, even though this author finds the interpretive perspective more satisfying, the intent is much less to advocate one perspective over another than it is to present as straightforward a discussion as possible of the underlying issues involved in this discussion. Why this particular approach was chosen, as well as a series of comments to delineate the context of this discussion, constitute the balance of this introduction.

THE ISSUE OF METHOD

Since this book is about alternative perspectives on the study of social and educational life, from the outset it must be clear what is meant by the term *method*. Generally speaking, method may be characterized in at least two ways. The standard, or most commonly encountered, meaning is method as a set of orderly, systematic procedures applied in pursuit of something—in this case, of course, knowledge of the social and educational worlds.

This sense of the term invokes the kinds of how-to-do-it questions found in introductory textbooks to both empiricist and interpretive inquiry. For the former, the discussion generally centers on techniques such as how to sample, perform certain statistical procedures, and design studies. For the latter, the focus is on technical matters such as how to engage in participant observation, analyze field notes, and do member checks. This characterization of method stands behind discussions, very often undertaken in comparison with empiricist methods, of the sets of procedures that supposedly can be employed to establish the major conditions of inquiry, such as validity and reliability, for the interpretive approach (see, for example, Goetz & LeCompte, 1984; LeCompte & Goetz, 1982; Miles & Huberman, 1984a, 1984b). The intent here, of course, is to establish methodologically based criteria that will allow one to confidently sort out the good interpretive study from its not-so-good counterpart.

The second meaning of method is "logic of justification." In this case the focus is not on practice but on the justification given in support of practice. When used in this manner, the term takes on the meaning given it by various scholars such as Durkheim (1938), Weber (1949), and more recently, Kaplan (1964) and Giddens (1976). This characterization of method leads to an interest in some very basic epistemological and ontological questions: What is the nature of social reality? What is the relationship of the investigator to that which is investigated? How is truth to be defined or characterized? and so on.

The claim of this book is that this characterization of method, which involves as it does basic or underlying assumptions, reveals differences of interest and consequence between the two perspectives. Differences in the area of techniques, on the other hand, are less interesting because the focus is on narrower questions such as, Can interpretive inquirers supplement their techniques of description in natural settings with procedures for the quantification of events? or, Can empiricist inquirers supplement their controlled procedures with those of participant observation in ongoing, natural settings? If the issue is conceptualized only at this level, then there is little doubt that the answer to these types of questions is an uninteresting *yes*. In other words, the question of whether each approach can occasionally "borrow" the specific, individual techniques conventionally thought to be associated with the other approach provokes issues of no great concern; the most important issues in this empiricist-interpretive discussion involve the different underlying assumptions of each perspective.

Behind much of the lack of clarity concerning these different approaches to inquiry is a confusion about the relationship between method as technique and method as logic of justification. The point is that the logic of justification does not set detailed, rigid boundaries for the practical application or use of techniques. Researchers who accept the interpretive logic of justification are not prohibited from the periodic use of certain "empiricist" techniques, and of course the situation applies in reverse for empiricist inquirers. Although inquirers of either persuasion may not see the need to borrow a particular technique, they are not restrained from doing so. However, acceptance of the legitimacy of "borrowing" at the level of individual techniques cannot lead to the position—currently very often stated or at least implied (see, for example, Lynch, 1983; Miles & Huberman, 1984a, 1984b; Reichardt & Cook, 1979; Rossman & Wilson, 1984)—that the two approaches are compatible or complementary. An understanding of the major differences in underlying assumptions makes this position untenable.

One complicating factor must be emphasized in regard to this discussion of the two definitions of method. Almost all empiricist inquirers and some, but definitely not all, interpretive inquirers claim that certain systematically arranged and interrelated *sets* of procedures, as opposed to specific or individual practices, will allow inquirers to achieve major conditions of inquiry such as instrument validity and reliability and the internal validity of a study. And, if these conditions can be achieved, they argue, then there is a basis for knowledge claims that goes beyond the tenuous level of "what we might agree upon" to the level of the objective or of that which must be universally accepted. As Bauman (1978) puts it, if inquiry, of either an empiricist or interpretive variety, can be grounded on an objective methodology, then the research "results would be apodictically true; they would, therefore, have to be accepted by all sides" (p. 231).

These systematically ordered sets of practices can, accordingly, be thought of as "linkage" points between the logics of justification and actual practices. How conditions of inquiry are characterized depends on the particular logic of justification one accepts. If one asks, for example, what it means to say that an instrument is valid, the answer depends on how one defines *truth*. The particular definition of *truth*, because it determines how one defines validity, constrains the *set* or *sets* of techniques thought necessary to establish validity. Thus, if interpretive inquirers find the empiricist characterization of validity ill-conceived, it would be pointless for them to employ the latter's overall, systematic procedures in this area. The same applies, of course, in reverse. In short, then, although the two logics of justification differ, this does not rule out occasional "borrowing" of individual techniques. However, the difference between the logics of justification does mean that the two perspectives cannot be considered compatible or complementary—as we shall see, they take quite distinct positions in regard to the nature of reality, the purpose of inquiry, the relationship of facts and values, and so on.

One other theme in the literature that has recently received substantial support requires a brief comment. The argument here is that procedures or techniques can and should be mixed or interchanged because inquiry is a matter of "what works" (see, for example, Cronbach et al., 1980; Miles & Huberman, 1984a; Reichardt & Cook, 1979). The operative criterion seems to be that inquirers can and should undertake whatever procedures work to solve the particular problem at hand. Although this idea is appealing, because it calls forth the image of the educational inquirer using whatever is necessary to solve serious educational problems, it is an oversimplification of the situation.

The problem is that "what works," no matter how expressed, tells one very little about the process of inquiry and about how one is to interpret the results of inquiry. In the absence of knowing the goals one holds for inquiry, the criteria employed for judging results, and so on, what works cannot be some sort of self-evident bottom line. In other words, the interpretation one gives to what works depends on the kind of work one sees inquiry as doing, which in turn depends on the particular ontological and epistemological assumptions one has accepted, implicitly or explicitly, for inquiry. Thus, what works is not a firm foundation upon which to ground a claim that the two perspectives are complementary or compatible.

TERMS AND TERMINOLOGY

One thing that can easily overburden any discussion of these different perspectives on inquiry, especially for those with a limited background in philosophy, is to structure the narrative around the extensive use of philosophical *isms*. Since each perspective has been associated with various long-standing philosophical schools of thought, there is an ever-present temptation to move in this direction. For example, the empiricist approach to inquiry could be discussed with reference to various schools of thought from positivism to logical positivism to realism. A discussion of the interpretive approach to inquiry could be structured around, among other possibilities, phenomenology, hermeneutics, and idealism.

Although there is much to be said for such an approach, the problem is that these schools of thought are not clearly defined and do not possess unambiguous boundaries. The term *hermeneutics*, for example, can include not only Gadamer's (1975) philosophical hermeneutics, but also the very different validation hermeneutics, as elaborated by Hirsch (1967) and Betti (1980). Because the intent of this book is to describe clearly and straightforwardly a number of basic issues underlying each perspective on inquiry, it seems best to *minimize as much as possible* references to philosophical schools of thought and, similarly, to minimize the use of the language common to more purely philosophical discourse.

A somewhat similar problem is that over the years numerous terms have been employed to denote the differences between the two perspectives on inquiry. Rubinstein (1981) lists 12 dichotomies, seen with varying frequency, that encompass some or all of the issues involved in the discussion: objective-subjective, explanation-understanding, observation-interpretation, and so on. Moreover, some terms in the literature, especially those associated with the interpretive perspective (e.g., ethnomethodology, ethnography, symbolic interaction, and naturalistic), denote variations on a general perspective.

Two things can be said about the almost bewildering array of labels that has grown up around this latter perspective. First, even though rarely addressed in detail in the literature, these terms do express variations, often somewhat subtle in nature, on a general perspective. Second, the variations have at their core a great deal in common (for a discussion of this point, see Benton, 1977; Giddens, 1976; Outhwaite, 1975, 1983). This book focuses on the commonality and advances the claim that the important issues, at least at this time, involve differences between, and not within, the two perspectives. Thus, an elaborate discussion of the variations on the central themes is not included here.

One other point must be made in regard to the organization of the following discussion. Just as structuring the discussion around various philosophical schools of thought could obscure as much as clarify, an extensive reference to individual philosophers could tend to have the same result. Over the years numerous people have made substantial contributions to the discussion. To introduce all or even the majority of these individuals in some sort of one-by-one fashion would require a more detailed discussion of their particular positions than is possible or desirable. Thus, although many philosophers will be referred to, many others must by necessity go unmentioned in the following exposition.

Given these limitations, this discussion employs the terms *empiricist* and *interpretive* to describe the different approaches to social and educational inquiry. To refer to the philosophical considerations underlying these approaches, the terms *externalism* and *internalism*, taken from Putnam (1981) but not defined in exactly the same way, are employed. Since much of the balance of this book discusses various aspects of these two philosophical temperaments, it is important to briefly introduce what is meant in each case.

One of the most basic features of an externalist perspective is the idea that reality exists independent of our interest in or awareness of it (see Trigg, 1980—who uses the term *realism*—for a similar discussion of this and the following points). This position holds that social and educational reality is "out there," external to the investigator, existing prior to his or her interest in it, awaiting discovery. Even though externalism accepts that our minds are necessary to conceptualize reality, it does not allow that social reality is mind-dependent—either in the strong sense of being created by the mind or even in the more moderate sense of being irretrievably shaped by the mind. Externalism holds to what can be called a subject-object dualism, or to the position that the mind and the world are distinctly separate entities.

Based on this separation of the knower from what is or can be known, the principal epistemological thrust of externalism is that to know reality is to describe it accurately. To paraphrase Ewing (1974, p. 195), a statement is considered true when it accurately depicts this independent reslity and false when it does not. Truth, in other words, is a matter of the correspondence of our words to reality. Thus, a most significant point for this perspective is that truth has its locus in that independent reality—a reality that can be discovered, given appropriate observational techniques, for what it really is.

Intimately associated with this process of observation is the concept of objectivity. To be objective is to stand separate from, and thereby to be able to describe, reality as it really is. This is the ability to take a "God's eye" point of view (Putnam, 1981), the ability to see the world apart from one's particular place within it. This point of view differs from that labeled subjective because the latter is conditioned or "distorted" by the particular interests and values of the observer (see T. Nagel, 1981, for a discussion of these concepts). For externalism, knowledge can only result from investigations that are cognitive or objective. The process of inquiry and the inquirer must not influence, for whatever reason, the qualities and characteristics of what is being investigated. Externalism holds that the facts of a situation must remain separate from whatever dispositions or values one holds in regard to that situation.

The central feature of the internalist perspective is that what constitutes reality is in a very significant way dependent upon our minds (this is the central issue in what Rescher, 1973, calls conceptual idealism). An immediate implication of this position is that the externalist separation of mind and world cannot be sustained and that the two domains are entangled (a subject-subject relationship as opposed to one of subject-object). The knower and the process of knowing cannot be separated from what is or can be known. Social reality is a constructed reality, the product of the meanings people give to their interactions with others and of the meanings inquirers give to their interactions with subjects and with each other. Thus, whereas externalism attempts to discover and describe an independently existing reality, internalism focuses on our interests and purposes (intentional, meaningful behavior) and engages in what Giddens (1976, p. 162) has labeled the double hermeneutic—the attempt to provide second-order interpretations of the first-order interpretations people give to their daily lives.

Another way to express the implications of reality as mind-dependent is in terms of "theory-neutral data," or data free from a conceptual frame of reference. This type of data, as defined from an externalist perspective, has a self-evident meaning and thereby constitutes the foundation upon which to construct our knowledge. For internalism there are no such "givens," no social and educational data that are resistant to multiple readings and that can accordingly serve a foundational purpose (see Taylor, 1971, on this point). In other words, no descriptions of the world can be offered apart from the describer's particular position in the world. We cannot have a God's eye point of view—as Putnam (1981, p. 50) puts it; we have only the various points of view of various people, which reflect their various interests and purposes.

The most important epistemological consequence of the internalist position is that correspondence is not an appropriate way to define or characterize truth. Even if the idea of an independently existing reality is accepted, our mind involvement prevents exactly what correspondence requires—independent access to both domains of mind and world. In the absence of such access, correspondence—although a natural enough goal—cannot be realized. Given this situation, internalism contends that in the end, what is true is a matter of the internal coherence of our interpretations and a matter of what we can agree, conditioned by historical time and cultural place, is true.

This focus on agreement changes the definitions given to the basic concepts of objective and subjective and also argues strongly against the possibility of separating facts from values. For internalism, objectivity is not a matter of seeing the world as it really is or seeing the world detached from one's particular place in the world. Rather, *objective* is a term that simply refers to the fact that there has been an agreement among inquirers. Likewise, to be subjective is not to represent things as influenced by one's personal taste, personal opinion, or emotive reaction, but, to paraphrase Rorty (1979, pp. 338–339), it is to introduce considerations others find strange or beside the point. If these definitions are accepted and if there can be no theory-neutral description, then the prospect of separating facts from values becomes very difficult to defend. Internalism holds that there are no value-free facts—facts, or what are to count as facts, depend on values. Facts are, in other words, value-laden.

THE PRESENT INTEREST IN THE DISCUSSION

Even though most of the principal ideas involved in this discussion of different perspectives on social and educational inquiry had gained currency by the turn of this century, only in the last few years has the interpretive/hermeneutical challenge to the empiricist approach been taken more seriously. Prior to this time, the dominance of the empiricist perspective was often questioned, but with generally little impact—especially at the level of the practice of inquiry. Interpretive approaches were often seen as useful, primarily to explore a topic and generate hypotheses for more serious and rigorous testing via empirical methods (see Abel, 1948, for a classic statement of this position). The ideal of a science of society modeled on the methods of the natural sciences was—and still is—for most inquirers the only way to conduct social and educational inquiry. There are at least four related reasons why the challenge to this dominant approach is now taken more seriously.

Clearly, the influence of the postempiricist philosophy of science has recently been felt within the social and educational research communities. The beginnings of this movement away from the empiricist image of science are usually traced to the 1950s. Among the many philosophers responsible for this "new" interpretation of the nature and practice of science, one can note Hanson (1958), Polanyi (1958), and Kuhn (1962). To these authors (and, of course, others) can be attributed much of the increased acceptance of the idea that any description of the world must be theory-laden. They have all made the point, in different ways, that observation and even the determination of what is to count as a fact can only be undertaken within a conceptual or theoretical framework. The essential point of the empiricist perspective that there are "givens" or "brute facts"—things that can be discovered and read independent of any particular theoretical perspective and that will thus constitute the basis upon which to found knowledge—has been strongly challenged by this idea of conceptual frameworks.

In particular, Kuhn's (1962) position, based on his interpretation of the history of science, has had a very significant impact on our thinking. In essence, Kuhn's claim is that science does not "progress" in an incremental, self-correcting manner, but rather moves through paradigm shifts. His elaboration of this idea brought to the foreground various questions that empiricism had either ignored or considered settled—questions about the commensurability of different perspectives, about the nature of reality, about the problem of relativism, and so on. In the end, Kuhn and the others have "called the question," not only for philosophers of science but also for researchers, on many issues—including the long-standing one of objectivism versus relativism.

The implications of quantum theory have also provoked numerous questions regarding the nature of scientific investigation. The most well-known example here concerns Heisenberg's uncertainty principle, or indeterminacy relationship (see Wartofsky, 1968, for a brief and clear discussion of this principle). In effect, this principle says that there is an inverse relationship between the precision of measurement of the position and the precision of measurement of the momentum of a particle: The more accurate the measurement of momentum, the less accurate the measurement of position, and vice versa. This point and others from quantum theory, as they have entered discussions of social and educational inquiry, have been generally taken to mean that the act of observation itself influences what is being observed. A basic assumption of the empiricist approach—that something can be known independent of the knower and the process of knowing it (or if not, that the influence can be taken into account)—is called into question by the implications of quantum theory.

Wheeler (1975), in a very interesting and readable discussion of some of these implications of quantum theory, maintains that the observer can no longer be thought of as independent of what is observed. Investigators can no longer think of themselves as standing behind and looking through a plate glass to observe and describe an independently existing reality. Quantum theory has shattered that glass, and the investigator has been "thrown into" the world of the observed. In other words, the observer of reality has become a participant in the reality that is "observed." As is the case with the postempiricist philosophy of science, quantum theory leads to the conclusion that one's choice of what to observe makes a great deal of difference as to what one finds. Description cannot be undertaken outside of a conceptual framework, and investigators can no longer pretend to a God's eye point of view.

A third factor of consequence in promoting this discussion of approaches to inquiry is the direct challenge to the adequacy of the empiricist approach in the social area. Very often this challenge allows that the empiricist perspective is appropriate for the natural sciences but is woefully inadequate for social and educational inquiry. The argument originates, even though it has changed somewhat in nature and tone over the years, with the separation of the natural and social sciences made by Dilthey and others just before the turn of this century.

One of the earliest, most important advocates of this separation, and to this day still one of the most forceful critics of the empiricist approach to social inquiry, is Winch (1958). Much of his discussion is based on the idea that social events are meaningful in a way different from physical events. The implication of this idea is that the study of social life must involve interpreting and understanding the meanings (interpretations) people give to their own activities. Moreover, this task of "making sense" of an activity must take into account the rules associated with that activity. These rules, however, vary from group to group or from context to context, so that the meaningfulness one ascribes to an activity will depend on the context, or the "form of life" within which it takes place.

Winch (1958) maintains that interpretations of social life are not therefore susceptible to the same sort of causal explanation, based on regularities, as is the case for physical events. Social inquiry is not a matter of applying generalizations to particular cases, but must be seen as a process of interpreting the interpretations of others. Because these interpretations are context-bound, the validity of an interpretation cannot be checked by an appeal to universal, invariant, law-like generalizations. Like Kuhn, Winch has raised questions concerning the nature of rationality and concerning the issue of objectivism and subjectivism.

Finally, the discussion has been further provoked by criticism of a more "practical" rather than a conceptual nature. The contention here is that empiricism has not delivered on its promise for the social sciences—an intellectual and practical mastery of the social world similar to what the physical sciences have obtained over the natural world. The crucial test of empiricist social science—the discovery of law-like generalizations that would allow for the explanation, prediction, and control of social events—has not been met. Louch (1966), for example, has argued that social and psychological laws are unavailable to us and what are presently "passed off" as law-like statements are most often only thinly disguised tautologies.

Moreover, for many people, the counterclaim that such judgments are premature, because social inquiry is "young" and will soon find a Galileo or Newton, has recently lost its force. Giddens (1976) and Rorty (1982) have strongly critiqued the idea that a Galileo or Newton will someday arrive to salvage the empiricist approach to social and educational inquiry. To paraphrase Giddens (1976, p. 13), if social science is waiting for its Newton, it is not only a matter of the train not arriving, but of even waiting in the wrong station. Such criticism, held off for many years by the promises of progress based on an increasing technical/statistical sophistication, has recently been more seriously entertained.

THE UNITY OF THE SCIENCES

One interesting and quite complex issue that is very much associated with discussions of different approaches to inquiry is the unity of the sciences. In a general sense this issue can be framed by the following two questions: Is there a unity of the natural and social sciences such that whatever is said about the one applies equally well to the other? Or is there an inherent difference in subject matter, or possibly a different interest taken in the subject matter, between the physical and social domains that makes different sciences necessary? This issue has been long contested.

Comte, in setting forth his positivist philosophy, made one of the most elegant arguments possible for the unity of the sciences (see Simpson, 1969; Thompson, 1975). His analysis of the historical progression of society through stages from theological to metaphysical to positive and his ordering of the sciences based on the criteria of abstractness, complexity, and practical significance led to the conclusion that social science could be and should be modeled on the physical sciences. Even though social science was behind the natural sciences in its development—in part because it was the latest science to emerge—in Comte's view social science, by adopting the forms of explanation, observation, and so on of the natural sciences, would eventually gain a similar intellectual and practical mastery of its subject matter. For Comte, and for others over the years (see, for example, E. Nagel, 1961), there has been no reason to differentiate among the sciences.

The positivist claim for the unity of the sciences was immediately challenged by a late 19th century movement in Germany that attempted to draw a sharp line between the *Naturwissenschaften* (natural sciences) and the *Geisteswissenschaften* (social or cultural sciences). Dilthey, one of the principal exponents of this separation, claimed that the two areas required different approaches because they dealt with significantly different subject matters (see Ermarth, 1978; Hodges, 1944). According to this view, social objects and events, unlike physical objects and events, are constructed by human minds. And since the meaning of social objects and events can only be understood by examining them within their contexts, the approach to the study of these "objectifications" of our minds must be hermeneutical or interpretive. Such an approach is quite different from that used to explain inanimate objects in the natural domain.

Recently the arguments for unity have changed with the advent of the postempiricist philosophy of science. This reinterpretation of the nature of science is based primarily on the idea that both social and physical reality have meaning only when considered within a conceptual framework or theory. Ironically, at least for those long-standing Dilthians, unity is now based on the claim that both the natural and social sciences are hermeneutical or interpretive (see Rorty, 1979; Taylor, 1980). That is, for both sciences the question of what is to count as data cannot be separated from theory; the language for both sciences is metaphorical and not capable of being formalized; and meaning is a matter of theoretical coherence rather than correspondence (see Hesse, 1980, for a discussion of these similarities between the sciences).

Not surprisingly, this claim for unity on a hermeneutical basis has resulted in counterarguments in support of a separation between the sciences. For example, there is the position that social inquiry requires a different approach because it must provide interpretations (by the inquirer) of a world that has already been interpreted (by laypeople). The cultural sciences are involved with what was referred to in a previous section as the double hermeneutic (Giddens, 1976). Natural science, on the other hand, is a case of a "single hermeneutic"—the objects and events under scrutiny do not engage in self- or first-order interpretations. Similarly, there is also the position that the type of understanding necessary to each science is different because of a difference in subject matter. For the sciences of social life, given that values cannot be separated from facts, understanding requires that objects or events be characterized in what Taylor (1980) calls "desirability terms." This level of characterization is not necessary or appropriate for the natural sciences.

In any event, even though the unity of sciences issue is an interesting and important one, an extended discussion of it is beyond the scope of this book. The following chapters focus almost exclusively on a description of two alternative perspectives on social and educational inquiry and only indirectly on the issue of whether the differences discussed apply in the case of the natural sciences. As such, there is no intent to argue that the differences examined in the following chapters constitute a possible way to distinguish the natural sciences from the social sciences.

AN OUTLINE OF THE CHAPTERS

The remainder of this book is organized into seven chapters. Chapter II begins with a description, based on an example taken from medical research, of what can be called the standard or received view of empiricist inquiry. This commonly espoused image of inquiry, which holds strongly to the idea that results can be judged in terms of the proper application of the proper procedures, is the one most frequently encountered in the first chapters of introductory social and educational research textbooks. Since interpretive inquiry has developed principally by rejecting all or most of the crucial elements of empiricist inquiry, the subsequent chapters will make more sense if one clearly understands what is being rejected. There is a great deal to be said for the idea that one must understand the dominant approach if one is to understand the alternative.

Chapter III examines the late 19th century origins of the discussion of the proper approach to social and educational inquiry. Placing the issues in a historical perspective reveals the nature and depth of the distinctions involved. The basic elements of a Comtean positivism (given an externalist-oriented interpretation) are outlined, as is the interpretive challenge to that perspective as posed by Dilthey and others. The intent is to demonstrate that the crucial points that frame our present discussions were well in place by the turn of this century. Weber's attempt to synthesize the two perspectives into a science of society that could take account of value-based meaning is also examined. That he made a monumental attempt to find a *via media*—and more important, that there is good reason to believe he failed—indicates how very difficult it is to bring the two perspectives together.

The first major distinction between the two approaches is the topic of Chapter IV. This discussion focuses on the different answers each side gives to the very basic question, What is the relationship of the investigator to what is investigated? The empiricist side holds to a separation of the two, whereas the interpretive side finds the relationship to be so entangled that no such separation is possible. The different conceptualizations of this relationship are associated with different notions concerning the nature of social reality and different definitions of truth. The chapter closes by applying these different positions to a specific aspect of inquiry, the validity of measuring instruments, and asks this question: Is an instrument or inference judged valid because it accurately reflects an independently existing bit of reality or because it finds agreement? The contrasting answers clearly illuminate a fundamental distinction between the two perspectives.

Chapter V focuses on the relationship of facts to values, a complex topic that can be discussed in terms of three general positions. One position holds that facts can be held radically apart from values. A second position, of a more Weberian-type, recognizes that values enter into the research process but asserts nonetheless that inquiry can still be an objective enterprise. The third position maintains that facts and values cannot be separated and that therefore all facts must be thought of as value-laden. This chapter closes with a return to the example of test validity.

Each side has traditionally taken very different positions on the purpose of social and educational inquiry. Chapter VI examines both positions on this issue and demonstrates how far apart the two perspectives are in this area. The first part of the chapter discusses the empiricist claim that inquiry can result in the scientific explanation and prediction of events. These tasks are accomplished through the discovery of law-like generalizations of a universal or probabilistic nature. The second part of the chapter deals with why the interpretive perspective rejects the idea that law-like generalizations can be discovered. This rejection means that explanation and prediction must also be rejected in favor of the interpretive understanding of the meanings people give to their own actions and activities and to those of others.

Chapter VII returns to the issue of the role of method in inquiry. In this instance the focus is on whether or not it is possible to establish procedures for doing and methodologically based criteria for judging interpretive inquiry. Two different concepts of what it means to be a person are presented to lend context to this issue. These concepts are crucial because they are associated not only with distinctly rival pictures of the nature of human life, morality, and so on, but with the different approaches to inquiry. This chapter also includes a brief reference to what are called norms of agreement as opposed to rules for the discovery of truth.

Chapter VIII integrates the various themes discussed throughout the book and summarizes the differences between the empiricist and interpretive perspectives. The meaning of these differences for the alternative interpretations that can be given to inquiry is discussed. Finally, these issues are examined in light of one of the major philosophical problems of our time—that of objectivism versus relativism.

CHAPTER II

The Standard View of Science and the Scientific Method

> The scientific method is commonly thought to include three major phases. The first step is to formulate a hypothesis, which is a tentative proposition about the relation between two or more theoretical constructs. . . . Suppose a researcher's hypothesis is that teachers will be more likely to implement a new curriculum if it is consistent with their belief system than if it is not consistent. . . . The next phase of the scientific method is to deduce empirical consequences of the hypothesis. . . . For example, the researcher may hear that a new curriculum program is being introduced into a school district. The researcher would deduce that, if his hypothesis is correct, teachers whose beliefs are consistent with this particular program will be more likely to implement each of its features than those teachers whose beliefs are inconsistent. The third phase of the scientific method is to test the hypothesis by collecting data. The researcher would administer measures of curriculum implementation and belief system to all teachers who have been asked to use the new program. . . . If the hypothesis is correct, the belief-consistent teachers should earn higher scores on a measure of implementation than the belief-inconsistent teachers. (Borg & Gall, 1983, pp. 24–25)

The purpose of this chapter is to describe what can be called the standard view of science and the scientific method. The term *standard view* is used to indicate the fact that social and educational inquiry have generally adopted a particular understanding or image of science. Even though at a philosophical level this interpretation has been seriously, and many would add very successfully, criticized by postempiricist philosophers of science, it is still the one presented in the early chapters of most introductory social and educational research textbooks.

This particular image is strongly modeled upon the natural sciences. Since the middle of the 19th century, one of the more persistent themes of the standard, empiricist-oriented perspective on social and educational inquiry has been the need to accept the assumptions of, and borrow the methods thought common to, the natural sciences. This tendency has been sponsored in large part by the obvious inequality of accomplishment between the two areas. The idea has been that if social scientists were to adopt the same or similar sets of procedures as those of physical scientists, they could achieve a similar mastery of their subject matter. In any event, since the interpretive perspective has most often developed in reaction to developments on the empiricist side, an understanding of the issues involved in this discussion of the nature of social and educational inquiry will be greatly aided by an understanding of the standard view of science and the scientific method.

THE SCIENTIFIC METHOD: AN EXAMPLE

The basic elements of the standard view of science and the scientific method can be most interestingly illustrated by beginning with a brief case study of one man's struggle to control what was in his time a deadly ailment (De Kruif, 1932, pp. 88–116). Although this example is not intended to serve as the basis for illuminating all of the complex philosophical issues associated with the scientific method, it does capture that commonly held image of how scientists go about solving problems.

Until the late 1920s, pernicious anemia (PA) was as inevitably fatal an ailment as one could confront. This disease evidenced itself in a thinning of the blood, or the inability of the body to produce sufficient red blood cells. Over the period of a few years this condition would debilitate an individual and eventually result in death. Although doctors in the mid-19th century were aware of the disease, no successful treatment was found until 1927.

The doctor who led the battle against PA was George Minot, a dedicated, highly competent, and detail-minded practitioner. Though associated with various research hospitals in Boston, he was not a research doctor in the sense of spending his time in well-equipped laboratories where it was possible to have more controlled scientific conditions. In fact, his discovery came via his private practice as he worked with the victims of this fatal anemia. His main assets in this fight were his close attention to facts, his use of logical reasoning, and above all, his belief that human beings could master nature.

From the beginning of his career, Minot was particularly interested in problems of the blood. From autopsies of PA victims, he knew that there was a problem with their bone marrow; it would be full of primitive cells that he realized, because of the patient's low count of full-fledged cells, were obviously not developing or being allowed to develop. The question that puzzled Minot was why. Was it a cancer or tumorous condition of the bone? If so, he thought the solution would be long in coming, given the existing state of medical knowledge. However, leaving aside the more complex questions of body chemistry, he systematically began to chip away at the problem.

In 1914 Minot decided to try an operation on a small number of PA patients. Over a 3-year period the spleens of 19 patients were removed. Because of the spleen's role in the storage, formation, and destruction of blood cells, he must have reasoned that a splenectomy might effect a cure. Minot studied these patients carefully, noting their blood counts and monitoring the other symptoms associated with the disease such as tiredness, paleness, and so on. Some of the people initially seemed to improve, but in the end all 19 died. During the same 3-year period, Minot gave transfusions to 46 patients, some of whom received more than one. Almost 50% of the patients showed a temporary improvement, but all died in the end. The best that could be said about the transfusions was that they might extend somewhat the lives of the more debilitated individuals.

As early as 1916 Minot had begun taking detailed notes on the eating habits of his patients—PA victims as well as others. He did not do this because he suspected a direct relationship between PA and diet, but because he thought diet was generally important and he was a thorough physician. He noticed an interesting difference between his PA patients and his other patients. The former tended to eat irregularly, to be "picky" eaters, and to have a preference for butter and other fats.

Minot then began a chain of reasoning that led to a "spark" of insight that apparently characterizes many major discoveries. He knew that PA was found primarily in northern countries, where dairy production was the greatest. However, many people eat large amounts of dairy products without being anemic, and people in these areas obviously eat many other things besides dairy products. On the other hand, he realized, PA had many of the same symptoms as pellagra, which was known to be associated with insufficient consumption of meat. Likewise, he knew that eating liver was beneficial for sprue (a gastrointestinal problem) victims, who were also generally anemic. But it did not make sense to him, since he had already increased the meat in the diet of his patients and this had had no positive effect.

Minot also remembered that he had read that liver increased the growth of rats and raised the amount of hemoglobin in guinea pigs suffering from anemia. He also learned that young lions raised in a zoo on a diet of lean meats were afflicted with rickets and, in some cases, eventually died. But when the cubs were fed liver, fats, and so on, they grew up to be healthy adult lions. There seemed to be a connection between no liver and poor bone development and between liver and good bone development. Possibly the connection might extend to the bone marrow of PA victims. It was worth a try, even though it seemed so unlikely that Minot dared not tell his colleagues or try it out in a hospital.

He began in 1923 by placing 2 private patients on a diet that included a large portion of liver a few times a week. They began to feel better and their condition stayed stable throughout 1924. Minot then added 8 more patients to this group, but he increased the amount of liver to at least one serving a day. By late 1925 all 10 of these people were still alive, feeling very good, and their red blood cell counts had increased. Normally they would have been dead or close to it by this time.

But for Minot this was not proof, and he was far too cautious to be overly enthused. Early in 1925 he increased the number of PA victims on the liver diet to include the hospitalized patients of a colleague. These people also improved and showed increased red blood cell counts. PA victims began to seek out Minot or were referred to his hospital. The liver diet worked on every one of them except for the few who were already too seriously debilitated.

At the American Medical Association meeting in 1926 Minot presented his carefully detailed findings, and as soon as the results could be disseminated, there was no longer any reason for anyone to die of PA. Other researchers carried on the work of Minot, and as a result, it is now known that the cause of PA is the inability of the body to produce a substance in the stomach that allows for the absorption of vitamin B_{12} (found in some types of meat, including liver, and other foods). Normal people absorb about 70% of their daily intake of B_{12}, whereas, in the absence of treatment, PA victims absorb about 2%. At present the disease is controlled by diet and by the injection of B_{12} in combination with the substance.

Although we are principally interested in examining the process in which Minot was engaged, it is worth noting, if ever so briefly, what he did not do. He did not engage the other sources of knowledge commonly noted, such as authority or deductive reasoning based on first principles. That is, he did not retire to his room to contemplate his innate ideas and discover within himself the essence of this medical problem or of medical problems in general. Likewise, even though he may have been a man of deep religious convictions, he did not consider PA to be an inevitable part of God's plan or a way to weed out sinners. He believed, expressing thereby the "scientific spirit" that can be traced back to Galileo and Newton, that an answer could be found by observing the facts and that nature is subject to human mastery.

In a less esoteric sense, Minot simply attempted to solve a problem of intense interest to him by using a particular systematic method—the scientific method. His observations, measurements, and logical reasoning, along with the indefinable ability to ask the right questions, produced a solution that saved lives immediately and laid the groundwork for other researchers to generate more refined insights and treatments. Minot obviously engaged in a scientific approach to his problem, but not in the formal sense often described in textbooks. Practicing scientists generally do not go about the process in a linear, step-by-step fashion. However, at the foundation of what he did is a systematic set of activities based on a way of thinking and a particular way of looking at problems, the major elements of which can now be described.

THE SCIENTIFIC METHOD: A DESCRIPTION

Although exactly what is involved with the scientific approach to problems may vary depending on the particular description offered, in most cases at least five major elements are discussed: observation, description and measurement, inductive generalization, deductive reasoning, and testing. The end goals of this process are, given the desire for intellectual mastery, to explain how the world operates and, given a desire for practical mastery, to relate events in such a way that one can eventually predict that when a particular event occurs under a certain set of conditions, another event also occurs.

Observation

To say that recording experience, or in more common terms, starting with facts, is basic to science poses no major complications on the face of it. The process as engaged in by Minot and other researchers seems to be a relatively straightforward affair: One "takes note" of one's experience with various objects or events, treats them as facts, and thus begins the attempt to explain the world scientifically. However, a closer examination reveals some complications. There is a distinct difference between physically sensing something and observing that same thing—even though this difference does not normally matter to researchers or to people in general as they go about recording and acting upon their daily experiences.

Sensing something may be defined simply as the process of recording impressions in the mind. To observe, on the other hand, means to systematically place objects or events in a given context or to relate them to some preexisting framework. In other words, certain objects or events take precedence over others, depending on the intentions of the observer. The same principle applies to the individual characteristics of an object or event; some may be considered significant, and others may be minimized or ignored. This selectivity allows the observer to find commonality in what may seem to be dissimilar objects or events and to find differences between what may seem to be similar ones.

Observing, then, is more than simply gathering all the data and then allowing them to "speak for themselves." Data do not do this, and a process of selection and interpretation is almost always at work—in fact, *must* be at work. This is because scientific observation must be guided by a tentative hypothesis or some preexisting idea. If this were not the case, the investigator would be overwhelmed with a multiplicity of physical sensations and would be unable to judge which objects or characteristics of objects were relevant to the problem at hand and which were not. However, it must be emphasized that the researcher most often begins with only a tentative hypothesis. In fact, at times these hypotheses are so tentative that they are actually more like suspicions or hunches about the relationship between or among objects and events. Accordingly, the initial ideas that structure observations are almost always modified, changed, and/or elaborated as observations proceed.

Minot presents an interesting example of how observations must be guided by hypotheses—no matter how tentative and/or implicit they may be. As will be recalled, Minot took extensive notes on the dietary habits of his patients. He did not take notes on their reading habits, political preferences, or favorite baseball teams. The reason for this is obvious. He could reasonably infer that diet might be important in relation to PA (and to other diseases for that matter), whereas there was no good reason to believe that the other characteristics might be related to health problems.

It is also interesting to note how Minot was able to combine his own observations and those of others to develop the testable hypothesis that eating liver would have a positive effect on PA sufferers. He took into consideration, among other things, pathology reports on the victims of PA and reports on the diets of young lions with rickety bones. Quite clearly, he was able to do this because he had a tentative hypothesis or initial suspicion that allowed him to sort the relevant observational material from the irrelevant across diverse situations. Whatever else Minot was doing, he definitely was not gathering observational data in an unsystematic fashion—somewhat like a child might collect any matchbook covers that came his or her way. His choice of what to observe and what not to observe was guided, even if not boldly and directly, by his tentative hypothesis.

One particular problem associated with observation is the claim that no two people will observe a situation in exactly the same way. Since our backgrounds, interests, and intentions differ, exactly what is observed in any given situation can differ. In the 1960s, for example, this was a popular theme that found its expression in various areas—that whites cannot understand how blacks experience the world, that men do not see the world in the same way as women, that no individual can truly understand another person, and so on. This was also the point of a rather common classroom "experiment" in which a person runs into the room, fakes shooting the professor, and then runs out. The students, upon being asked to describe the perpetrator, generally presented rather widely divergent descriptions.

To a certain extent, the claim that no two people can see exactly the same thing in exactly the same way is a valid one. In recognizing the validity of this claim, however, the empiricist approach makes a major commonsense assumption in this regard: Although different observers may not agree on all the details of any particular object or event, that object or event will very often create parallel impressions on them. Without this commonality of impressions, or this level of intersubjectivity, which allows for intercommunication, there could be no science (or reasonably orderly daily life, for that matter). All observations would be individually bounded and would have to remain at that level. Simply stated, this concession to common sense presupposes a more or less shared framework that is based on a common language and culture, acquired by a common process of learning and socialization.

Calling attention to this commonsense notion may seem like belaboring the obvious. After all, if a metal bar is heated to a particular temperature and expands a particular amount, two different people will make the exact same observations as long as both know how to read the gauges. To the extent that we deal with situations for which there are more or less precisely quantifiable, agreed-upon standards of measurement and interpretation of those measurements, the issue is latent. But a return to the Minot example demonstrates that for many other situations this is not the case. In addition to quantitative blood counts, the observations he used included such symptoms as paleness and tiredness in his patients and rickety bones in lion cubs. Although Minot did not observe the lion cubs himself, he knew what *rickety* meant, and certainly other physicians knew what he meant by the terms *paleness* and *tiredness*. These are examples of parallel impressions, present because of the common backgrounds of the observers, of things that cannot be or have not yet been precisely quantified.

One further comment about observation is needed. There are, not surprisingly, various complications involved with the process. At one level, especially in the case of the observation of social objects and events, there are problems associated with the "frailties" of the human perceptual system. As is well known, there is always the danger of a lack of consistency, accuracy, and so on in social and educational observational situations. Over the years much time and effort have been devoted to making observations more precise and to ensuring that they are objective. The techniques of test construction, for example, have been central to this effort. At a second level, a major question has been posed as to the relationship of the observer to what is observed. The standard view of science holds to a separation of the two sides, whereas another perspective argues that the observer is very much entangled with the observed. This topic receives extended discussion in a later chapter. For now, the point to remember is that the standard approach to science finds that truth can only be obtained through the precise and objective observation of an independently existing reality or world of facts.

Description and Measurement

The observations of a researcher result in statements that describe and measure objects and events. These statements attempt to fulfill the basic need of science to identify and classify the objects of, and events that take place within, the world—in other words, to discover how things are alike or not alike. This type of comparison enables researchers to discover relationships among objects and thereby make sense of our world. However, this does not mean that researchers describe objects in terms of all their characteristics. It is not an overstatement to say that everything is like everything else in some way or another and different from everything else in some way or another. As with observations, for any given research project a process of selection must take place; certain characteristics are described and others are not.

A descriptive statement is therefore an abstraction because certain characteristics are "abstracted" from their total context. The terms of the statement denote what is important and what is not. This abstracting is what allows inquirers to focus on certain characteristics across objects or events and to pursue the goal of discovering patterns or regularities. For example, Minot may have described the first patient to whom he recommended liver in the following manner: "X seemed more energetic, reported he felt better, and his blood count increased to so many per unit." Certain characteristics were selected as important enough to be formally noted in a descriptive statement. Of course, these characteristics are the points of comparison with patients who had been instructed to eat liver and with others who had not been so instructed. The ability to abstract is crucial to moving beyond seeing the world as a series of discrete events or objects.

Since all descriptive statements are not necessarily true, how do we determine their accuracy? First, we must distinguish between two types of statements—analytic and synthetic. Analytic statements pose no special concern in this regard, since they are true by definition. For example, to say that all triangles have three sides or that the male children of a person's sisters and brothers are that person's nephews are analytic statements. Once you know that something is a triangle, you need not examine it for three sides; once you know a child is your sister's son, you know he is your nephew. The truth of these statements depends on the terms of expression, not on experience.

A statement that goes beyond its subject terms and produces a general implication is called a synthetic statement. The statement "Heavy cigarette smoking causes lung cancer" is synthetic because lung cancer is not part of the meaning of heavy cigarette smoking. The truth of this and all synthetic statements can come only from one source: experience with the objects and events of the world. In other words, these statements must be empirically verified. Of course, the truth of these synthetic statements must always be treated as tentative and subject to modification or even abandonment.

Although synthetic statements are what makes research the empirical business that it is, analytic statements do have importance in the scientific process. At one level, the truths of mathematics and, to a certain degree, geometry are analytic. The statement 2 + 2 = 4, because it can be logically derived from a series of basic premises without recourse to experience or observation, demonstrates that mathematics is analytic. Clearly, mathematics is of immense importance to research. Moreover, such statements may also serve to clarify the meaning of a statement or term by making it more explicit.

The ability to measure certain characteristics of an object and changes in these characteristics is essential to research. Researchers can measure in basically three ways—by classifying, qualitatively, or quantitatively. The most basic level of measurement is classification. With this approach, objects are placed into mutually exclusive categories, and thus an object must be one type of thing or another: male/female, alive/dead, and so on. All scientific areas of study, in their beginnings, struggle at this level. This is often thought of as a necessary "first step" to gain mastery over the complex and unorganized world of objects and events.

As a science develops and becomes more sophisticated, the means of measurement also change—even though classification is never abandoned—and the other two types become important. One of these, called ordinal scaling, is to order objects or events according to a criterion or set of criteria. This familiar process is integral to how we organize many of our day-to-day experiences. Does this taste better than that? Who is the most well-behaved child, the second most well-behaved, and so on? This type of measurement is more precise than mere classification because it supplies more information on a comparative basis. In addition to sorting, objects are now positioned in relation to each other, based on how much of a characteristic they exhibit. If inquirers desire or need to be more precise, however, they must employ units of quantity to examine differences. To know exactly how much more of a characteristic an object has in comparison with another, some standard unit for determining this difference is necessary. For example, we can say that one burner on a stove is hotter to the touch than another, but to do so with greater precision requires a standard unit of quantity, such as temperature in this case. Once standards become established, any further measurement of that characteristic must be referenced to that standard.

The advantage of moving from qualitative to quantitative measurement is an increase in precision. Researchers can then be more precise about how much more or less of a characteristic there is and, more important, more precise about the relationship of characteristics. Minot's measurements of various characteristics is illustrative in this case. First, it is interesting to note that he used all three types of measurements. He used classification when he simply described his patients as alive or dead and qualitative measurement when he described them as having "more energy" and "less paleness." Of course neither of these measures expresses quantity based on a standard measure; they are ordered within the context of either/or and more/less, respectively.

Minot did not present these measurements, in the absence of other data, to his colleagues because they did not establish a precise enough relationship between eating liver and the alleviation of PA. If he had gone before the medical association and said, "If you have your PA patients eat a lot of liver, they will have more energy," one of the first questions would likely have been, "How much liver and how much more energy?" Instead, Minot reported quantitative measures, such as how many servings of what amount (weight) per day or per week and red blood cell counts (energy being difficult to quantify at that time). In this way he was able to state a more or less precise relationship between two factors: If you eat so many servings of liver per week, totaling so many ounces, then your blood count will increase by so many thousands of red cells per unit (at least approximately).

Although the use of quantitative measures indicates more precision and a more mature science, not everything needs to be precisely quantified, and some things seem quite resistant to quantification. In the first instance a high degree of quantification may not take place because the kind of precision that results may not be required. As was noted above, the interests and ultimately the hypotheses of the researcher determine not only what will be observed but the precision with which it will be measured. For example, for most astronomical problems it is sufficient to measure the distance of the sun in miles or even hundreds or thousands of miles—a measurement in inches, even if possible, would be of little use. In the second case, some objects are very difficult to quantify, or, if not difficult, certainly the conventions of measurement for these characteristics are subject to serious disagreement. These problems, to be discussed later, are of particular importance to social and educational inquiry. For example, in educational research, constructs such as intelligence, creativity, or self-concept are constantly subject to discussion in terms of how they are measured and how these measurements relate to their definitions.

Finally, to state more explicitly what has been strongly implied, one of the reasons that precision of measurement is thought to be related to scientific progress is based on our ability to confirm or refute a proposition. The argument can be simply stated: In general, the more precisely measurements are taken and reported, the greater the degree of testability and, hence, the less ambiguity there is in deciding on a proposition. It is more difficult to accept or reject the judgment that this year's earthquake was more intense than the one last year, but less intense than the one the year before that, in the absence of a more precise measurement of the type produced, for example, by seismograph readings. Both the physical and social sciences spend a great deal of time and energy attempting to replace the more vague qualitative measurements with quantitative ones whenever it is appropriate and possible.

Induction and Deduction

How does the researcher go from tentative and often vague hypotheses, which act as guides for observation and so on, to testable, or scientific, hypotheses? Logic—both inductive and deductive—is crucial here.

Induction is often defined in introductory research textbooks as the process by which a researcher produces a generalization on the basis of observing numerous individual instances. Even though the concept poses more complex considerations, such a definition is suitable for present purposes. Everyone engages in the process of inductive reasoning at one time or another. If your car's engine "dies" when you drive through a puddle of water and this happens on repeated occasions, you may be led to generalize the engine will always die when the car is driven through a puddle. Of course, you will not necessarily know how these events are related unless you have some understanding of the workings of the internal combustion engine, but nonetheless you will probably modify your driving behavior on rainy days.

Researchers go through a similar process with one exception: Their observations, descriptions, and measurements of events—because they are based on a tentative hypothesis—are often more directed and systematic. The end result of their efforts is a generalization that is called a scientific hypothesis if it is stated in qualitative or quantitative terms and implies or specifies a test. This statement can be characterized as synthetic because it is based on the observation of facts and its demonstration will require the further observation of the facts. For example, an engineer trying to find out why highways buckle on a very hot summer day may have begun by noting that when concrete is heated, it expands. After a series of similar observations and measurements, he or she could produce a generalization that concrete will always expand when heated. To the extent that it quantitatively states how much heat and how much expansion, this generalization becomes a testable hypothesis that eventually may lead to an answer to the initial question.

The use of induction, however, can be problematic because an inductive generalization cannot be justified solely on logical grounds. This point can be illustrated with a much used example: Because every swan so far encountered in various places and at various times is white, it does not logically follow that the next one observed will be white. In other words, even if all of the previous or individual observations are true, the inference is not necessarily true. In induction, the combination of true premises and a false conclusion cannot be logically ruled out.

One of the ways to overcome this problem of induction is to introduce the idea of probability. Instead of saying that an inductive generalization is totally true, we can say that it is probably true. If an event has occurred repeatedly over a long period of time, the inference is that it is highly likely—highly probable—that it will continue to occur in the future. Both researchers and, for that matter, laypeople are accustomed to judging, based on repeated observations, that even though a regularly occurring particular event may not continue to occur in the future, there is a very good chance that it will.

There is still a problem, however, with this position. Quite simply, accurate probabilities cannot be calculated in reference to events that have not yet occurred or have not yet been observed. If we knew how many black swans and how many white swans existed in the world, there would be no problem. That is, if one knew that there were 10 swans in the world, of which 8 were white and 2 were black, the probability that the next swan one encountered would be white would be 8 out of 10. Unfortunately, the only way to obtain this degree of accuracy is when all possible cases are known. And if all cases were known, inductive inference would not be necessary. In other words, the observation of all possible cases would result in a description of known events rather than an inference about what is unknown or what may occur in the future. Although induction thereby poses some very complex philosophical problems, this situation has not had a paralyzing effect on practicing researchers, who use the process to formulate testable hypotheses and eventually law-like generalizations.

Investigators must also use deductive logic in the effort to verify the correctness of generalizations and their implications. Deduction allows them to specify instances of the implications of a generalization and then submit these instances to testing. This step is important for the scientific process, since the meaning of a hypothesis cannot be truly understood without knowing more precisely what it implies. Deduction is based on the idea that if a class of objects exhibits a particular property, then of course every member of that class will evidence this property. If all concrete expands when heated, then any particular piece of concrete will expand when heated. The movement is from an "if" statement to a "then" conclusion. If a generalization (H-hypothesis) is true, one would then expect the individual event (I-instance) to occur or be present under the specified conditions.

One problem of employing deductive logic is the fallacy of affirming the consequent. If H is posed as true and the evidence shows that I is not the case, H is therefore not affirmed. This is a valid deduction and poses no problem. On the other hand, if H is posed as true and the evidence shows that I is the case, H is not necessarily true. Something else may account for I being the case. The derived implications of a hypothesis can be true, yet the hypothesis can still be incorrect. What all of this means is that hypotheses are never fully proven, even if numerous implications are tested and affirmed. However, this does not mean that subjecting a hypothesis to numerous tests is unimportant. These tests will tell us which particular implications can be sustained and thus will give partial support for a hypothesis.

That induction and deduction are closely intertwined and are integral aspects of the research process can be illustrated by a brief reference to the Minot example. Based on his tentative ideas about the importance of diet in general and the oddness of the diet of his PA patients in particular, he was able to draw together data from seemingly disparate situations to produce the generalization that eating liver might have a positive effect on PA victims. On the basis of this inductive generalization, he deduced that if liver has such an effect, then his subjects could be expected to have increased red blood cell counts, to exhibit more energy, and so on. This type of movement between inductive and deductive reasoning was central to Minot's activities.

Testing

Eventually the derived implications of a hypothesis must be brought to an empirical test or examined in light of the facts. The underlying idea of the test is not difficult to describe: If certain conditions exist, then a particular event will occur. The ultimate type of test is the experimental test, which takes its force from a number of logical canons articulated by Mill. Although Mill discussed various logical canons such as the method of agreement, the method of agreement and difference, the method of residues, and the method of concomitant variation, the one of most concern to us is the method of difference (see Cohen & E. Nagel, 1934, for an extended discussion of Mill's canons).

This canon very often appears in introductory research textbooks under the name "the law of the single variable." Put in its most basic form, this canon says that if two situations are alike in every respect except for a factor that is added or deleted from one situation, any subsequent difference in the two situations must be attributed to that factor. If Minot had had two groups of PA victims who were exactly alike except that one group ate liver and the other did not, any difference in their blood counts could have been attributed to the manipulation of their diet. Of course, for ethical and practical reasons he could not do this in pure form. In most situations, especially social and educational research situations, it is impossible to equalize all conditions across groups or events and then manipulate only one factor.

Does this problem mean that hypotheses cannot be put to rigorous testing? No, this is obviously not the case. By granting certain common-sense assumptions, investigators have learned to live with less than total control. Although Minot was not able to establish a control group (not eating liver) and an experimental group (eating liver) that were equivalent in every other way, he approximated this situation by comparing the PA victims for whom he had prescribed liver with those earlier PA sufferers who had not eaten liver. His concern with equivalence of the two groups was not with all characteristics but was confined to those judged relevant on the basis of his hypothesis and on background knowledge of medicine. What convinced Minot, and later his colleagues, was an accumulation of evidence. In the final analysis, since no sufferer of PA who had started eating the necessary quantity of liver had died from PA, unless already too debilitated, this was considered sufficient to demonstrate his hypothesis.

Although the above discussion obviously does not constitute a detailed discussion of empiricist inquiry, it does provide an outline of some of the elements that are considered most important to this standard approach. Empiricist inquirers must observe and measure objects and events as they exist out there in the world; the process of inquiry itself is "tied together" by the use of both inductive and deductive reasoning; inevitably, hypotheses must be tested against that existing social and educational reality. In order to complete this overview of the standard perspective on inquiry, two more topics must be briefly discussed. The first involves a discussion of the goals of the empiricist approach, and the second attempts to define the role that empiricists have assigned to methodology in regard to achieving these goals.

LAWS, EXPLANATION, AND THEORY

Even though this topic receives extended discussion in a later chapter, it is necessary at this point to say something about the goals or purposes of the empiricist approach. As is commonly noted in introductory courses in social and educational research, one of the basic goals of this approach to inquiry is to discover laws or law-like generalizations. A law-like generalization is a universal (holds at all times and places) empirical statement that describes how the world really operates. Such statements thereby allow inquirers to explain events and eventually to predict events based on the occurrence of other events. These latter tasks, of course, are very much related to a desire to exercise an intellectual and practical mastery over the social and educational worlds. As is discussed in the next chapter, this approach to inquiry was nurtured, if not born, with a strong utilitarian thrust to it.

A law is the crucial element in one of the most commonly acknowledged ways researchers have for generating scientific explanations—the deductive-nomological form. In this form, as articulated by Hempel (1965), the event to be explained (the explanandum) is deduced from a series of premises (the explanans) that contain one or more laws. Symbolically the form is represented in the following way:

L1	L2	. . . . Ln	Laws	Explanans
C1	C2	. . . . Cn	Conditions	

$$E \qquad \text{Event} \qquad \text{Explanandum}$$

The laws in this explanatory framework serve to link together the conditions and the event to be explained. Generally the laws take the form of "Whenever *A* is the case, *B* is the case" or "All *A*s are *B*s": Whenever a body is heated, it expands, or all bodies immersed in water lose weight. Thus, if an event can be subsumed under a law, it is held that researchers are able to explain that event in terms of that law.

A simple example will help clarify these points. The explanation for the expansion of a bridge on a very hot day will take the following form:

All materials (including concrete)
   expand when heated.   L1
The span is made of concrete.   C1
The day was very hot.   C2

The bridge span expanded.   E

The explanation for the expansion of the bridge span is based on a law that links together the conditions and the event. In the absence of this law, the event could not be explained, and we would be left with only three facts: The span is concrete, the day was hot, and the span expanded. This form can also result in prediction: If the span is made of concrete and if today will be very hot, one might predict that the span will expand. If this prediction is not borne out, the accuracy of the reading of the conditions must be checked. If they have been read correctly, then the researcher must think in terms of modifying or even abandoning the initial law-like generalization.

This explanatory form has great force because it is deductive and hence logically conclusive. The event to be explained is implied by the premises and conditions. If the law is correct and the conditions are accurate, the event must follow. In this sense the deductive-nomological form differs from a probabilistic explanation. These latter explanations are based on laws that are less than universal. Instead of "Whenever A is the case, B is the case" or "All As are Bs," the form is, "Whenever A is the case, B is probably the case" or "A percentage of As are Bs."

The following example will illustrate the difference between the two types of explanation:

Persons who drink tap water in country
X have a high probability of getting
parasites.

You drink the tap water in country X.

You get parasites.

Although the form of the two explanations is basically the same, the second type is not deductively conclusive, as is the case for the nomological type. In the probabilistic form the event does not have to follow from the premises and conditions—it is possible to drink the water and not get parasites. In this sense the form is inductive and depends for its explanatory import on the calculation of statistical probabilities. This makes the probabilistic form "weaker," but it is obviously still very useful and very frequently used. In fact, this form is actually the dominant explanatory framework for most social and educational research.

Finally, a brief comment is necessary in regard to theories and their role in science. *Theory* is a term that can have many meanings. In general, however, a theory explains the various regularities observed in the natural or social worlds and helps us to understand those worlds by pulling together seemingly diverse phenomena. Newton's theory of gravitation did this because it explained such diverse things as the falling of a rock, the swinging of a pendulum, the movement of planets, and so on. Hence, theories stand as a sort of overall framework we use to understand the world. Often they are seen, then, as the most general and abstract level at which we deal with reality. In other words, theories are broad-based explanations that tie together laws, hypotheses, and so on.

THE ROLE OF METHODOLOGY

Even though the role of methods in research is discussed at various places in later chapters, at this point it is important at least to introduce the topic. For empiricists, as was briefly noted in Chapter I, true or genuine knowledge is regarded as strongly tied to the proper application of the proper procedures. Such methodologically grounded knowledge, because it is thought to constitute an accurate description of reality, must be accepted by all concerned. In fact, this relation of methods and genuine knowledge is so strong that to deny the results of a properly conducted study is to run the risk of being labeled irrational. Thus, a judgment about the procedures employed for a study is, in effect, a judgment about the findings of that study—not in terms of the importance of the findings, but in terms of whether or not the study presents true knowledge. This qualifier is necessary because findings can of course be considered genuine knowledge but trivial or not worth knowing.

To refer to method in this way is obviously to define the concept in terms of techniques or procedures. For the empiricist approach these procedures include sampling and assigning subjects, designing the study, establishing the reliability and validity of measuring instruments, mathematically transforming observational data, and so on. Because these procedures are basic to any introductory course and textbook in social and educational research, there is no need to elaborate on them as such. What is important is to emphasize the role assigned to them in the inquiry process: These procedures are to protect the research from the particular interests, purposes, and values of the researcher. Methods, in other words, allow researchers to penetrate through the ordinary or everyday level of *how things seem to people* to the level of *how things really are*. The idea is that there is a defined body of procedures or method and, as Rorty (1982) puts it, "that following that method will enable us to penetrate beneath the appearances and see nature 'in its own terms' " (p. 192).

These two levels of *seems* and *is* can be discussed for two types of empirist inquiry. For correlational/descriptive inquiry, the idea is that certain statistical techniques allow researchers to go beyond the seeming relationship among objects or events to the level of whether or not they really are related and to what extent. For example, one might conclude based on day-to-day experiences that there is a strong, positive association between the family background of children and their performance in school—the poorer the background, the poorer the performance, and vice versa. The question is, Is this really the case, or is this conclusion a "distortion" based on the particular observer's values, place in the world, or interests? At the level of everyday discourse and experience there is the ever present possibility that one has allowed one's particular interests and values to bias the results. Accordingly, empiricism calls upon certain statistical techniques to minimize, if not eliminate, the ever possible distorting effects of the observer's subjectivity. Only if the observational data have been properly transformed statistically can the claim be sustained to objective knowledge or to an accurate depiction of the extent to which various things are related.

The same is true for the experimental and quasi-experimental line of inquiry. At an informal or lay level the conclusion that something has an effect on something else cannot be treated as genuine knowledge because, among other things, the finding could easily have been influenced by the individual's particular interests and purposes. For example, a teacher's claim that a reading program he or she developed and "tested" in the classroom resulted in much improved reading performance by students cannot be defended as true knowledge. For obvious reasons, not the least of which is the teacher's possible emotional involvement with the program, this finding can only be given the status of "what seems to be the case." To go beyond this level to that of "what really is the case" requires an investigation with the proper procedures, from design to analysis of the data, properly applied.

This issue of "what seems" as opposed to "what is" and method can be placed in sharper focus by an examination, at each level, of a disagreement over findings. At the level of ordinary, day-to-day discourse, disagreements can of course be resolved, and furthermore, there are norms to guide this process—at least loosely (e.g., a resort to violence is generally considered an inappropriate way to resolve disagreements). Although such agreement often invokes the concept of truth, this concept is defined differently by researchers. For example, two teachers may overcome a previous difference of opinion and come to agree that a particular teaching method is more effective for teaching reading—yet, from a research-level point of view they both can be wrong. The point is that the norms for day-to-day agreement are not the same as the rules for discovering truth. As Bauman (1978) puts it, "The pursuit of true understanding, as distinct from ordinary agreement, must therefore detach itself from everyday discourse and seek its own rules elsewhere" (p. 232). These rules, of course, are ones of procedures or methods.

Disagreements among researchers, then, are not resolved by unmethodical, loosely defined rules for agreement, but rather by a systematic, methodologically grounded examination of reality. This is what is meant, in effect, by the commonly held injunction "that if we disagree, we must return to reexamine the facts of the case." And, as was noted, since the results of the proper application of the proper procedures are considered genuine knowledge, these results must be accepted by all concerned. Researchers, outfitted with the correct method, are thus able to go beyond ordinary agreement and employ a more compelling referent point for resolving their differences.

Therefore, method serves to constrain researchers in the sense that their biases, personal dispositions, values, and so on are not allowed to influence or interfere with the research process and the research findings. These procedures are seen as available to the inquirer prior to the process of inquiry; hence, they are neutral and independent of the process. This idea is what ultimately stands behind the claim of empiricist inquirers—and of some, but certainly not all, interpretive inquirers—that the established rules of procedure must be heeded because they serve as "self-corrective techniques that will check the credibility of our data and minimize the distorting effect of personal bias upon the logic of evidence" (Lather, 1986, p. 65). And of course to the extent that these rules of procedure are in place, there will be compelling methodological grounds for "accepting a researcher's description and analysis" (Lather, p. 78).

SUMMARY

This then constitutes a general outline of the standard view of science and the scientific method—a perspective that, for better or worse, is the one commonly found in introductory research textbooks. The process can be summarized as one of formulating hypotheses, deducing empirically testable consequences from these hypotheses, and then submitting these consequences to testing. These hypotheses must then, of course, be accepted or rejected depending on the results of the tests. As the process goes on over time, the idea is that researchers will develop a body of valid or genuine knowledge—including laws, theories, and so on—of the social and educational worlds.

On the face of it, this seems to be an eminently reasonable way to conduct and to interpret the conduct of social and educational inquiry. However, as noted earlier, this view has been subjected to serious criticism from various quarters. The criticism has been strong enough to provoke a widespread revival of a debate that actually began, in its present outlines, in the late 19th century. We must now turn to this topic of the historical origins of the empiricist-interpretive discussion.

CHAPTER III

The Origins of the Current Discussion

The social sciences, as we know them today, were shaped above all in an encounter with the spectacular advances of natural science and technology in the late eighteenth and the nineteenth centuries. I say this bluntly, in awareness of the complexities which it conceals. It would certainly not be true to say that the successes of men in seemingly mastering nature intellectually in science, and materially in technology, were adopted uncritically as forming a model for social thought. Throughout the nineteenth century, idealism in social philosophy and romanticism in literature, in their various guises, maintained their distance from the intellectual standpoints fostered by the natural sciences, and normally expressed deep hostility to the spread of machine technology. But for the most part, authors within these traditions were as sceptical of the possibility of creating a science of society as they were distrustful of the claims of the sciences of nature, and their views served as no more than a critical foil to the much more influential writings of those who sought to create just such a science. (Giddens, 1976, p. 11)

In the mid-1800s, a substantial concern developed over the inequality of accomplishments between the physical sciences and the social "sciences." The great scientific achievements up to that time in chemistry, atomic theory, mathematical physics, and many other areas provided high standards of comparison against which to measure accomplishments in the social area. Quite simply, physical scientists were intellectually and practically mastering their subject matter in ways not evidenced by social "scientists." Not only were the former producing tangible results, they seemed to know exactly what they were doing and how they were doing it. Understandably, this produced a compelling desire in many social thinkers of that time to find a way to emulate the successes of their counterparts.

Thus, we must give special attention to the work of those social philosophers most responsible for importing the theory of knowledge, or epistemology, and methodology of the natural sciences into the study of social life. The work of Comte and the variations made on it by others probably had the greatest influence on establishing the dominant position of this particular approach within the social sciences.

Although dominant, this point of view was not unanimous. The attempt to borrow from the natural sciences produced an opposing movement based on two counterarguments: One maintained that differences in subject matter require a different methodology, and the other that social research has different aims and therefore requires a different methodology. Either way, both argued that to adopt a natural science model, particularly that of physics, for the study of social life was a grave error. To understand this opposing movement, we must examine the ideas of various people—especially those of Dilthey and Weber—who were probably the most important in developing the foundation for what can be called the challenge of interpretation, or hermeneutics, to empiricist social and educational inquiry.

In any event, by shortly after the turn of this century, the positions on each side of the issue were already well articulated. Regardless of the developments that have taken place since then, our present discussions are still being conducted within the broad context of ideas established at that time. An understanding of the origins of the two traditions is therefore essential to an understanding of the contemporary discussion over method.

THE DEVELOPMENT OF THE EMPIRICIST APPROACH

Although the work of Galileo and Newton in particular was crucial to the development of the natural sciences, neither of them worked out a complete theory of knowledge that grounded the practice of science. The task of building and articulating such a theory of knowledge, one that directly supported what was actually happening in the physical sciences, fell to Locke. Locke is thus regarded as one of the principal elaborators of empiricism—a key tenet of which is the idea that knowledge must be taken from or is based on experience (for a brief discussion of Locke's philosophy, see O'Connor, 1964; Russell, 1945; Yolton, 1977).

In order to tie knowledge directly to experience, Locke first had to reject the idea that there is any such thing as an innate principle. He argued that we simply have no good grounds for believing that a priori knowledge exists. If such innate ideas existed, Locke said, we would expect to see young children using the same rules of logic as adults or, in another example, the same innate moral principles existing in all people. Since neither of these is the case, he concluded that a priori knowledge does not exist. From where, then, does one obtain knowledge? Locke's answer to this question resulted in his famous dictum that the mind is like a blank slate, void of ideas, to be written upon by one and only one thing—experience. Thus, for empiricism, one of the major points is that the only things we can know are the ideas in our minds, and since these ideas come from experience, we can have no knowledge prior to or apart from our experiences.

That Locke was able to develop an empiricist position philosophically—problems and internal contradictions notwithstanding—is important for various reasons. He strongly contributed to a tradition in philosophy that has continued, in one form or another, to this day. This approach, as Russell (1945) noted, is one of the two major trends in Western philosophy—the other being, as will be soon noted, the idealism of Kant (pp. 641–647). Similarly, Locke was successful at his self-appointed task of being an underlaborer who clears the ground and removes the rubbish that lies in the path of knowledge. This clearing of the ground gave the developing physical sciences philosophical support and strengthened the hand of science as the dominant approach to seeking knowledge, so much so in fact that he helped push other sources of knowledge, such as tradition and religious authority, into the background of Western thought (Hull, 1959, pp. 206–207).

Perhaps of greater significance to this discussion of the nature of social inquiry, however, are three other related results. First, because he firmly tied all knowledge to experience and the ability of our minds to combine experiences, Locke both implicitly and explicitly included our knowledge of social affairs with our knowledge of physical phenomena. He applied, and argued we could apply, the same theory of knowledge to both areas. Possibly more important, he brought the empirical process engaged in by physical scientists such as Newton and Galileo into the realm of philosophy. Since philosophy is linked to thought across a wide variety of subjects, empiricism was given the opportunity to expand into other subject-matter areas (Hull, 1959, pp. 206–207).

Finally, Locke contributed strongly to the idea that there is a duality of mind and matter; matter is outside of the mind and stands as a separate reality that exists, whether it is apprehended by the mind or not (see Harris, 1954, pp. 125–139, for a discussion of this point). In other words, the reality that exists "out there" exists regardless of whether or not we presently sense it or have ever sensed it. Even though this dualism poses all kinds of thorny philosophical problems, as a practical matter it has been an accepted position by physical scientists and presents no problems to them in their day-to-day work. For social inquiry, as we shall see later, this duality is also widely accepted, but in this case it presents interesting and serious conceptual and methodological problems.

Positivism

Even though Locke did not necessarily have a direct influence on Comte, the latter's positivist philosophy can be broadly classified as part of an overall empiricist tradition. Comte was not the first to support a scientific approach to the study of social life, but he was certainly the 19th century's most forceful and direct advocate of that idea (see Thompson, 1975, for a discussion of Comte and positivism). He has had, accordingly, a substantial impact on how we conceptualize and seek to perform research on social and educational life. Positivism provided a powerful statement for the unity of all the sciences and thus for the acceptability and necessity of employing the methods of the natural sciences in the study of social affairs.

Comte worked out his positivist philosophy with reference to certain intellectual traditions and political-social conditions in France at the time. It is interesting to review briefly the context within which his ideas developed. Locke had a decided influence on a group of French thinkers known as the Encyclopedists, who were the principal intellectual architects of the French Enlightenment. In their attempt to construct a unified scientific system, these philosophers, who predated Comte by approximately 50 to 75 years, were taken with both the empiricism and the political philosophy of Locke. This philosophy placed a great emphasis on state authority resting on the consent of the governed, on the individual's rights to property, on equality, and so on. The Encyclopedists were definitely anticlerical, hostile to religion, and against the "illusions" of metaphysics in philosophy, and, on the other side, in favor of political liberty, equality, and an empiricist epistemology. In this sense they paved the way intellectually for the French Revolution, which temporarily brought the developing middle class of merchants, manufacturers, and professionals into power (Church, 1974).

The bourgeoisie, however, were not able to consolidate a stable government based on the English model of a liberal-democratic state. In reaction to the Revolution and especially to its excesses, a countermovement in philosophy and social thought developed that expressed little confidence in the liberal individualism of the Enlightenment and focused on the problems of reestablishing and maintaining social order. As Benton (1977) notes,

> The ruling currents in French social thought during the nineteenth century, in contrast to both the Enlightenment and English social philosophy, were preoccupied with the problem of subordination of the individual to the social whole, with the problems of maintaining social order. (p. 26)

Comte's work was thus influenced by two opposing lines of thought in postrevolutionary France. He agreed with many of the ideas of the Enlightenment: its criticism of religion, the need to dispense with the "illusions" of metaphysics, and the need to attempt to unify the sciences based on an empiricist theory of knowledge. Along with the traditionalists, however, he believed that the Enlightenment had brought about an excessive individualism that was leading to a general disintegration of European society. To prevent this disintegration required a return to order and stability, but this could not mean a return to what he called a "retrograde" theological system that was advocated by many conservatives. For Comte,

> [the] only basis of a social construction would be the introduction of a system of beliefs that would put an end to the controversies that were ruining society, but would not be just a replica of an anachronistic theological system . . . science promised such a system. (Szacki, 1979, p. 181)

From its inception, the empiricist approach to the study of society has had a strong underlying practical justification. This "utilitarian thrust"—the idea that the empiricist study of society will contribute to controlled, orderly social progress—has existed to this day as the principal backdrop against which we play out most of our social and educational inquiry.

To support his arguments for this science of society, Comte developed two associated lines of reasoning (Simpson, 1969; Thompson, 1975). The first was an idea borrowed from the philosopher Saint-Simon concerning the law of three stages of society: theological, metaphysical, and positive. Comte theorized that these stages posed an inevitable evolution of the way human beings go about making the world understandable. The first stage involves the search for final causes and an absolute knowledge, followed by the stage in which abstract forces such as nature are seen as most important. During the last stage knowledge is based on science and the scientific method. By posing this progression as inevitable, Comte gave historical sanction to the idea that science must eventually take over as our source for securing knowledge about and for ordering society.

His second line of reasoning concerned a hierarchy of the sciences based on a number of criteria, all of which resulted in the same ordering. The basic criteria were a decreasing degree of abstractness, an increasing degree of complexity, and an increasing degree of practical significance. An ordering based on these characteristics also reflected the historical order in which the various sciences had emerged. The hierarchical ordering was as follows: mathematics, astronomy, physics, chemistry, biology, and sociology (a term that Comte coined). Comte saw mathematics as the most abstract, least complex, and of the least practical significance. He perceived sociology as the least abstract, most complex, and of the greatest practical significance. According to this hierarchy, each scientific area in the progression, even though it has its own subject matter, depends on the developments of the preceding ones; there could be no astronomy without mathematics, and so on.

Comte also argued that there was a break between the inorganic sciences and the organic sciences. In other words, he placed biology closer to sociology than to chemistry. This affinity is based on the idea that we should treat society in a fashion similar to the treatment of an organism—that is, as a system. Like a biological organism, society is a complex system that cannot be understood if it is reduced to simply a collection of component parts. We must pursue social knowledge by focusing on society as a whole and then attempting to understand how the actions of individuals are a part of and/or are constrained by that social whole. This metaphor of society as an organism received, as will be discussed, a more extended elaboration by Durkheim. In any event, given Comte's concern for what he saw as the excessive individualism of his time, it is easy to see why he would argue in this fashion.

The effect of these ideas is not difficult to grasp. Comte's law of the stages seemed to make inevitable the domination of science as an approach to obtaining knowledge. On the other hand, his hierarchy not only tied the social to the physical in terms of epistemology and method, but provided an excellent explanation for why the social sciences lagged so far behind the physical sciences in intellectually and practically mastering their subject matter. In other words, this hierarchical approach has allowed positivists and empiricists to respond that immaturity is the reason for the slower progress.

What, then, were the characteristics of this general positivist school of thought as established in the 19th century, and what methodological procedures did it require? Although positivism allowed that there were some differences between the application of certain aspects of the scientific method in the natural sciences versus the social sciences, such as the ability to exercise control in experiments, these differences were pushed into the background and seen as mere details. Based on the idea of similarity, it was argued that social objects should be treated in the same way as physical objects were treated by natural scientists. From this it necessarily followed that if our knowledge of the natural world was taken from the external appearance of objects as presented to us, the same should be so for social knowledge and social objects. Social knowledge—and Comte and other positivists were well within an empiricist tradition here—must be grounded on observations, and the boundaries of this knowledge were set by the boundaries of our sensory experiences. Certainly, knowledge a priori was specifically ruled out as the basis for a theory of knowledge.

This position was consistent with the empiricist idea that there was a separation between the perceiver and the object perceived, that there was a line between the mind that cognitively apprehended and the matter or object that was apprehended. As with the physical scientist who stood apart from his or her subject, so it was with the social scientist. According to this view, social facts were independent of the observer, and the observer was not a participant in making these facts. In slightly more abstract terms, the knower might combine or analyze sensory experiences, but he or she did not define the facts of any particular situation or give them a reality that they did not already have in and of themselves. Social objects, like physical objects, were considered real in that they existed whether or not we recognized them.

Positivism also argued that social investigation was a neutral activity in regard to values. The social scientist was not to evaluate his or her findings or make normative judgments but was confined to the task of analyzing and reporting what existed. In more common terms, the investigator was to be objective and to prevent bias from creeping into the research process. Positivism went even further than this, however, by saying that statements about values, political judgments, or aesthetics were simply expressions of attitudes and opinions and could not be a part of a positivist approach to knowledge. As was noted in the last chapter, this bias issue and the prospect that bias can be controlled, if not eliminated, by methodology occupy a great deal of the time and energy of social and educational researchers.

Another aspect of positivism was the idea that social science would serve as the basis for social engineering. Positivism required that the knowledge derived from social investigation result in the same or in a similar sort of practical mastery over the social world as the natural sciences were gaining over the physical world. As such, social science was, if not born, certainly nurtured with a distinct utilitarian perspective. This social engineering was not to be comprehensive in scope, but rather incremental. Since the overall goals of society were considered value-laden, or normative, these could not be the province of social science. Immediate problems, given a previous value choice, were thought to be the proper focus for objective analysis and solution.

The desire for practical application and social engineering brought with it a concern for discovering social laws. These laws would, like their counterparts in the natural sciences, state necessary and unvarying relations between and among social objects and events. The discovery of such laws would allow for both the explanation and prediction of phe-nomena. Comte thought that the latter aspect was crucial because it was only through the ability to realize predictions that one could intervene to shape and mold society and thus have inquiry contribute to an orderly social progress. Finally, Comte saw comparison as the best approach to the discovery of laws. He argued that comparisons could be made be-tween the states of coexisting societies and between successive states of societies. He did not, however, elaborate on these more directly meth-odological questions to the same extent as did Mill.

Mill, a contemporary of Comte's later years, extended positivism in at least two ways. He brought the force of positivism into the English-speaking world through his commentary on Comte and through his own works. More important, Mill was one of the first to have taken that theory of knowledge and derived from it certain rules and procedures or methods.

The methodology espoused by Mill is based on two laws that he arrived at by induction: the law of the uniformity of nature and the law of causation. For Mill every event had a cause, and the cause of any par-ticular event was the immediate, unconditional, and always present event that preceded it. He then developed a series of canons of logic that could be used to isolate the cause of a phenomenon—in other words, to discover uniformities that are the laws of nature (Cohen & E. Nagel, 1934).

Even though Mill felt that the canons were difficult to apply to social phenomena because of the latter's complexity, these canons have left a legacy for the way we logically approach doing research. As noted earlier, the canon that has most impressed itself on our thinking, and is explicitly or implicitly a part of the discussion of experimental-type in-quiry in most basic social and educational research textbooks, is that of "differences." Stated simply, this method says that if two situations are alike in all ways except one—a factor added or deleted from one thing or situation—this factor is the cause of any resultant differences between the two situations.

Although causality poses a difficult philosophical problem, at the level of common sense and in much of our social and educational re-search, we employ this concept of cause and Mill's canons of logic. Largely because of his work, experimental and comparative approaches are considered the ultimate forms of empirical inquiry in the social sci-ences. Therefore, Mill strengthened the hand of positivism by devel-oping practical rules and procedures that set the foundation for much of our present-day inquiry of the social world.

Mill and Comte differed in some important respects that should be noted. Mill thought that social laws could be reduced to the laws of behavior for individuals, whereas Comte thought that society was an organism with its own laws (Robinson, 1981; Szacki, 1979). In fact, Comte had little use for psychology because the mind was not directly observable. For him, the attempt to examine the mind introspectively was so much idle speculation. Mill, on the other hand, placed the study of individuals above the study of society in the hierarchy of sciences. He argued that our understanding of social facts depends on the laws of psychology, an area of studies he called ethology. He defined this as the study of the effects of environment on the thoughts, feelings, and behavior of the individual. Although the differences between Mill's and Comte's positions later became quite pronounced in this area, both of them very much accepted the basic agenda of positivism and experimental science. In any event, Mill's psychological method was instrumental in placing psychology on the road to development within the empiricist tradition—just as Comte had done for sociology (Robinson, 1981).

By the middle to late 19th century, an approach to the study of social life modeled on the natural sciences was in the process of being firmly established. The desire to master social life expressed itself in a concern for the discovery of social laws; in the development of a methodology that stressed the observation of experiences, experiments, and comparisons; in the separation of facts from values; and in the separation of the cognizing subject from the object of cognition.

The Development of the Social Sciences

Durkheim, although influenced by both Comte and Mill, was in his own right a very important figure, specifically in the development of sociology, and more generally in the development of social science, along the lines of natural science. His influence was so extensive and significant because he not only wrote about methodology, but also did substantive studies employing that methodology. Durkheim's *Rules of the Sociological Method* (1938) was the first major elaboration of how to conduct sociological research and social research in general. In his books, particularly in his study of suicide, he applied these methods to an examination of social phenomena. By formulating rules and actually putting them into practice, Durkheim produced a substantial legacy, still of major consequence, as to how we think about and perform social and educational inquiry.

Like Comte, Durkheim lived in an era of French history characterized by considerable political and social turmoil. Not surprisingly, Durkheim was also concerned with order in society and the primacy of the social over the individual. He took from Comte the idea of a social science, based on the natural sciences, that would contribute to preventing the breakdown of society. He held that good social science would inevitably yield tangible and practical results, even though researchers need not always and only focus directly on practical problems. Durkheim was also in the Comtean tradition in that he continued to conceptualize society as an organism and even elaborated on this metaphor. On the other hand, he dismissed Comte's three stages of history as metaphysical, since they were not based on empirical evidence.

Durkheim was aware of Mill's work in the area of the logical canons and the latter's argument concerning causality. He agreed with Mill that experiments on social phenomena were difficult to conduct, but in pursuing the comparative method he made at least one of the canons, concomitant variation, an essential part of his methodology. He seriously differed from Mill, as Comte had, on the question of sociology versus psychology. He could not accept the idea that social phenomena could be explained by reducing them to the laws of psychology. On the contrary, he argued persuasively that there was an autonomous realm of the social (society as a whole) that was real in its own right and must be studied accordingly. An example from chemistry illustrates his argument: If a chemist mixes two chemicals, the resultant compound will have characteristics different from those of each of its individual components. A group of people mixed together in a society will likewise produce a reality different from the mere summing of the individual parts that are joined. In presenting this argument, he effectively delineated the subject matter of sociology and gave it a separate status.

One of the most abiding and dominant principles of Durkheim's (1938) theory of knowledge was that social facts are to be treated as things, which he defined as "all objects of knowledge that cannot be conceived by purely mental activity, those that require for their conception data from outside the mind, from observations and experiments" (p. xliii). In this way he was establishing the social as real and external to the individual. Things such as the obligations one fulfills to country or family, the language that expresses thought, the practices of a profession, and laws and customs all existed prior to an individual's participation in them, and they existed whether or not an individual participated in them. These ways of behaving and thinking were external to the individual. In fact the individual might not even be aware of them—at least in terms of details. To Durkheim, social phenomena had the same status as physical phenomena because they were independent of human consciousness and accessible through sensory experience or observation.

He further argued that social facts such as laws and customs had a coercive power over the individual and were independent of the individual will. If an individual conformed to these social facts, their coercive effect was not felt. However, if one attempted to violate them, his or her behavior would be constrained. The method of constraint could range from imprisonment, in the case of a crime, to public ridicule or disapproval, in the case of more minor infractions. Even though we might not be totally aware of all of the rules, there existed outside of us a social reality with the power to constrain us. We were born into this situation, and thus it was independent of us—we did not create it.

The next question was, How do we come to know these social facts? The task of the social scientist was to define these facts and to find out how they came into being and how they interacted with one another to form a social whole. In doing this, the scientist could not deal at the level of common sense, or at the layperson level of discourse. If social science worked solely at this level, it would not be a science. The character of social facts would not necessarily be revealed by common sense. Moreover, what was "common" about common sense might vary greatly even within a single society. Hence, social science had to develop its own language, divorced from a lay language, to define and discuss this social reality, and it had to develop its own method, divorced from everyday approaches to knowledge, to discover that social reality.

Durkheim (1938) then articulated how social scientists were to go about the business of practicing their science: "Our principle . . . demands that the sociologist put himself in the same state of mind as the physicist, chemist, or physiologist when he probes into a still unexplored region of the scientific domain" (p. xlv). This situation involved a number of prescriptions on how social scientists were to investigate their subject matter. First, they were to eliminate all bias, presuppositions, and commonsense beliefs about the investigations, and second, they were to have no emotional involvement with or attitude about the subject. In other words, social scientists were to be neutral and objective like their physical science counterparts. Finally, science was to be strictly confined to what is as opposed to what should be. Social scientists had no business discussing how a society should operate; they should instead discover how, in fact, it did operate. The former could only be considered personal opinion (see Sztompka, 1979).

The next thing was to classify things in terms of their external characteristics as determined through observation. Once a definition was arrived at, everything that conformed to it became a part of that field of study. For example, suicide could be defined as "all cases of death resulting directly or indirectly from a positive or negative act of the victim himself which he knows will produce the result" (Durkheim, 1951, p. 44). The social scientist would then have a defined situation that constituted a field of study and a social fact—that so many suicides occurred in a particular society. This fact would not merely be the sum of individual acts but an independent fact about a particular society. The key point to remember here is that the social scientist had access to these social facts because they were observable—in terms of behavior.

The crucial task for the social scientist was to explain social facts by relating them to other social facts. In the case of this example, the degree of social integration in a society could be related to the rate of suicide, as Durkheim (1951) did in his study. This ability to relate social facts to other social facts is the end goal of social science because it leads to the possible discovery of causes. Durkheim realized, as did Mill, that experiments had limited application to social phenomena. He accepted Mill's definition of cause, that the cause of an event is another event that immediately precedes or accompanies that event. Given this, he applied Mill's comparative method and canon of concomitant variation. Durkheim said that if two events constantly varied together and if we could present ample reasons for this covariation, we had a situation of causation. For example, the greater the amount of social integration in a society, the lower the suicide rate, and vice versa. The technique used was, of course, correlation-type statistics. Actually, Durkheim's use of statistics in this study demonstrated its importance beyond simple counting and tabulation.

A previously mentioned aspect of Durkheim's work requires one further comment. He saw society in organic terms, as a whole with definitive boundaries and a series of functionally related parts. In his view all of the parts of a society were interconnected, and social phenomena could only be completely understood if their functions were defined within the social organism. In this conception of society, Durkheim saw the individual as socially modeled—as the recipient of, not the creator of, social reality. One was born into a society of these interrelated parts and then socialized and educated—or placed under an "unremitting pressure . . . of the social milieu which tends to fashion him [the child] in its own image" (Durkheim, 1938, p. 6).

The basic features of Durkheim's position can be briefly summarized. First, he perceived social science as a neutral, objective, and value-free process. Second, he maintained the dualism of the cognizing subject and the object to be cognized. Social facts were like physical facts in that they were part of a social reality external to us, whether we recognized it or not, and they were facts whose manifestations could be studied by observation and the use of empirical methods. Third, the goal of social inquiry was to use the knowledge obtained from observation to discover reality and find the causes of social phenomena. This required a scientific language, different from a lay language, that would allow us to discover causes and, of course, to produce explanations, predictions, and so on. Fourth, the emphasis was on the individual as constrained by social facts, and much less on the individual as an autonomous, creative being. This idea was related to perceiving society in organic terms as a closed and bounded system.

The development of an empiricist approach to the study of the mind, modeled again on the physical sciences, took place at about the same time as the development of an empiricist approach to the study of society and social life. Both approaches, of course, drew on the same philosophical sources. Robinson (1981) notes in his discussion of the history of psychology:

> Our sense of what an experimental science is and ought to be is taken over, with only the slightest modifications, from J.S. Mill and the general attitude toward the status of science remains the one advocated by Auguste Comte and his positivist disciples. (p. 391)

Even though the discipline of psychology, more so than is the case for sociology, encompasses competing schools of thought such as humanist and Gestalt psychology, the scientific perspective has dominated the field. Certainly this dominance is evident in the case of Anglo-American psychology.

What Durkheim did for sociology, Wundt, probably as much as anyone else, did for psychology. Wundt was certainly among the foremost leaders of the forces that were turning psychology away from such things as introspection and metaphysics and remaking it into a scientific and experimental discipline. For him, a psychology that was directed at the study of what he called the "manifold of consciousness" had to be an experimental psychology. In other words, the study of the mind must address "no more than and only that which is directly reportable as an observation of an internal event . . . a science of the mind can be no more than experimental inquiries into the determinants of thinking, feeling, remembering, etc." (Robinson, 1981, p. 345). There was no room in this formulation for a metaphysics of, or a speculative philosophy of, the mind.

By accepting part of Wundt's agenda for psychology and by rejecting another part, Watson, and of course others, took psychology further in the direction of a natural science. Watson agreed that Wundt, and others such as Titchner, had made the correct start by adopting an experimental approach. He also argued, however, that they had most prominently gone astray by continuing to focus on the mental. For Watson, if psychology was to be truly scientific, it must

> concern itself with the prediction of natural events; a science can study only that which can be observed; mental states and private experiences do

not exist in the world of the publicly verifiable. Behavior alone is the object of a truly scientific study. (Robinson, 1981, p. 407)

Along with Watson, other psychologists, especially Thorndike and Skinner, put a firm scientific, if not scientistic, stamp on the field. This was a psychology free of metaphysical speculation and established very much along the lines of empiricism. This science of psychology was to exhibit the same qualities that characterized the science of sociology: objectivity, practicality, the precise observation and measurement of behavior, an adherence to the logic of analysis as laid out by Mill, and so on.

Similar processes were at work in regard to the study of education. Education did not develop as a discipline in the same sense as the other social sciences. This is reflected in the fact that this field developed primarily as educational psychology and educational sociology. Accordingly, educational inquiry is the application of social scientific methodology to the study of what are essentially social, psychological, and sociopsychological phenomena in an educational context. The forerunners of the scientific study of education were Thorndike in learning, Hall in child development, Watson and later Skinner in behavioral analysis, and so on. From the sociological side, Durkheim included education within his general theory of society and, in doing so, legitimated the methods discussed in his *Rules of the Sociological Method* (1938) as a way to conduct research on various educational problems.

By the turn of this century, the social sciences were well on their way to being modeled on the natural sciences. However, this modeling did not take place without a reaction. It is to this criticism and the demand for a different approach to obtaining social and educational knowledge that we must now turn.

THE INTERPRETIVE REACTION

In the last years of the 19th century a sustained and forceful critique was directed at the positivist theory of knowledge that had come to dominate the study of social life. For philosophers and social thinkers involved in this critical reaction, one of the major shortcomings of this empiricist approach to social inquiry was the "tendency to discuss human behavior in terms of analogies drawn from natural science" (H. Hughes, 1958, p. 37). To treat human social life in this way was to them not only incorrect, but potentially destructive of what is essentially human about us. For example, a common theme in this criticism was that the early sociologists and psychologists were giving too much emphasis to the role of heredity and/or environment as the principal determinants of human action (people as socially and/or biologically modeled) and too little attention to the idea of people as freely choosing, autonomous beings.

The critical reaction to this natural science borrowing began in Germany. Philosophy in that country had not come under the sway of positivist thought to the extent that it had in France and England. German thought was still working with a substantial legacy of the ideas of Kant. We must briefly discuss this idealist-oriented tradition to give some context to the critical reaction of the 1880s and 1890s.

The Kantian Legacy

Kant laid the foundation for what Russell (1945) felt was the second major trend in Western philosophy. We need not discuss at great length or in detail Kant's ideas, which are very complex and at times confusing (see Blakney, 1960, and Wilkerson, 1976, for readable discussions of Kant's philosophy). Our interest is in a few basic points that establish the legacy so essential to the critical reaction to positivism. Among Kant's principal contributions was a counterargument to empiricism's distinct separation of mind and matter, or of subject and object. As noted, one of the tenets of the empiricist position was that all of our knowledge results from sense experience—Locke's blank-slate mind to be written upon by experience. Kant argued that this was not the case, that the mind was not simply a recording device. On the contrary, he believed, there was an intimate relationship between mind and matter. Not only must our knowledge conform to what we experience, but what we experience is shaped by our knowledge.

Kant held that certain preconditions must exist in order for us to make sense of the multitude of experiences we have—or even to have what can be called a meaningful experience. Since these preconditions, which Kant called "categories of understanding," existed prior to our experiences (a priori), they could not be derived from experience or proven to exist based on experience. For example, objects are always seen by us as having location and sequence. These ideas are, in fact, so dominant that it is impossible to think in or of their absence. Other categories of understanding, such as cause, further allow us to organize and make judgments about the experience world. The important point is that these categories of understanding are a priori, and in being so, they tell us not only something about the world but, more important, something about *us* as a part of the world. "What the world is to us is the world as we experience it; our capacities for experience therefore impose a restriction on the *kind* of world *our* world can be" (Warnock, 1964, p. 300).

One might object that this idea is untenable. We cannot simply create the world as we see fit; the world is what it is whether we experience it or not. But here Kant drew an important distinction. He said that there was the world as it appeared to us, the phenomenal world, and the world as it existed in and of itself, the noumenal world. About the latter world, sense experience could supply nothing. About the phenomenal world, however, science could provide us with a true description—at least as it appeared to us. And, it is important to note, the appearance of things of this world would be different if we were different. As Warnock (1964) notes, "for whatever the world may be in itself, it appears to us in the way it does because we are the way we are . . . objects as *phenomena* must conform to our knowledge" (p. 300).

Kant thus posed a challenge to the empiricist separation of mind and matter, and by arguing that a priori concepts exist that order our experience, he was saying that there were limits on the reach of science. In other words, science would not and could not result in a unified view of the world. An acceptance of this view meant that other methods could be utilized to understand what we are all about. It is this legacy that was reworked by the critics, who, maintaining the spirit if not the letter of Kant's work, formulated their objections to a natural science approach to the study of social life. Just as Kant examined the conditions and limits of a science of the natural world, the critics examined the limits and conditions of a science of the social world.

The Critical Reaction: The Challenge of Hermeneutics

In late 19th century Germany a certain amount of disenchantment had set in concerning the idea of orderly social and political progress. The unification of the separate German states (Bavaria, Prussia, and so on) into a more centralized system had not produced the spirit of unity for which many had hoped. Conflict had continued—only now it was among political parties and interest groups. Against this background, the legacy of idealism in German academic thought came to the fore and led to a sustained and sophisticated criticism of the positivist approach to the study of social life. Among the more prominent of the critics was Dilthey.

Even though Dilthey was primarily concerned with the study of history, many of his ideas directly apply to our concern with the study of social and educational life. He said that there was a fundamental difference in subject matter between the natural sciences and the social sciences, or what he called the cultural sciences. This difference meant that there must be differences between the two in regard to the attitudes of investigators, how they do their research, and the goals of their investigations. Dilthey was not opposed to the natural sciences per se; he was only against borrowing their methodology for the study of social life either in a historical or contemporary context.

Whereas the physical sciences dealt with a series of inanimate objects that could be seen as existing outside of us, or with a world of external, objectively knowable facts, Dilthey said this was not the case with the cultural sciences. The subject matter of the cultural sciences concerned the products of the human mind, and these products were intimately connected to human minds (including those of investigators) with all their subjectivity, emotions, and values. From this, Dilthey concluded that society was the result of a conscious human intention and that the interrelationships of what was being investigated and the investigator were impossible to separate. For all people, layperson or social researcher, what actually existed in the social world was what people thought existed. There was no objective reality as such, that is, divorced from the people who participated in and interpreted that reality.

> Dilthey argues that we cannot meaningfully stand *outside* the events and occurrences of life and say with certainty what they signify. What we can know, however, is that historical [and social] events *do* signify things to those who enact them and to those who endure them. (Bergner, 1981, p. 64)

In the social sciences, human beings were both subject and object of inquiry, and the study of the social world was in its essence nothing more or less than the study of ourselves.

A second major thrust of positivism that Dilthey criticized was the idea of causal laws. Dilthey (cited in Hodges, 1944) argued that the search for laws or law-like generalizations was an untenable goal for the social sciences:

> The uniformities which can be established in the field of society are in number, importance, and precision of statement far behind the laws which it has been possible to lay down for nature on the sure foundation of relations in space and the properties of motion. . . . The social sciences are unable to guarantee such a satisfaction to the intellect. (p. 145)

In brief, the complexity of the social world, the variety of interactions in that world, the changes over time, and the differences among cultures would not allow us to establish laws or even law-like statements that would apply at all times and under all conditions.

For Dilthey, the goal of studying society was not to generate laws in the fashion of the natural sciences, but to undertake an interpretive understanding of the individual or the type. In this sense these human studies were descriptive as opposed to explanatory in their intention. Therefore, even though Dilthey allowed that one may engage in generalizations, he thought the real concern of the social sciences was to attempt to generate an interpretive understanding. The crucial concept of understanding—what it means and how an investigator must proceed given this intention—requires examination.

Dilthey posed his most interesting and major contribution to the study of social life with the idea of lived experience and interpretive understanding. He said that there were two ways of experiencing: inner-lived experience and sensory experience. The latter, of course, was the mode used by the physical sciences to build their abstractions and to generate laws of uniformities of nature. The inner-lived experience, crucial to the cultural sciences, referred to that awareness of ourselves and others that was immediate and direct. According to Dilthey, the complex patterns of relationships, values, and features of the mental world, the human-constructed world of mental "objects," were parts of social life. We were aware of this mental world because we were ourselves a part of it through our lived experiences. The imaginative re-creation, or identification, of our own mental life with that of others was apprehended through the "objectifications" of mental life.

Whereas the natural sciences could free themselves from this mental projection because of the inanimate nature of the objects with which they dealt, the human studies depended on this re-creation as the very basis for their approach to knowledge. To return to what was mentioned earlier, the "objects" of the cultural sciences were not physical entities or external processes, but rather manifestations of the mind. Of course, this meant that the subject-object dualism of the natural sciences was not appropriate for the social sciences. Our knowledge of the mental world of individuals and groups in society was based on the lived experiences we shared as a part of that mental world. The task of the investigator was therefore not to discover laws, but to engage in an interpretive understanding, or *verstehen*, of those who were part of the investigation.

The process of *verstehen* involved the attempt to understand others through an interpretive study of their language, gestures, art, politics, laws, and so on. To understand was to know what someone was experiencing through a re-creation of that experience in oneself. To see someone expressing grief provoked an immediate response because the lived experience of another had been internalized in oneself through a re-creation. One lived again the other's experience—this was the essence of understanding. Of course, a degree of empathy or a disposition to re-create must exist. What one understood in this process might be small or even trivial, or it might be complex and deeply rooted, such as a sequence of historical events or the total life of a particular social group.

The more complex the experience, the greater the effort that had to be made to achieve understanding.

Understanding ultimately involved what is called the hermeneutic circle. Hermeneutics originally referred to the interpretation of texts. As Dilthey elaborated the idea, he posed it as a method for the human sciences. One of the crucial aspects of hermeneutics was that a knowledge of context or background was necessary for interpretation. The process becomes circular because every part of a text or a social/historical event required the rest of the text or event to make it intelligible. Likewise, the whole could only be understood if it was undertaken in terms of the various parts or events. Achieving interpretation required a constant movement back and forth between the parts and the whole. There could be no definitive starting point and no definitive ending point for this process. This, then, was to be the method Dilthey attempted to establish for inquiry into human affairs.

The importance of this hermeneutic process was that it pointed up the idea that the meaning of human expression was context-bound and could not be divorced from that context. At this point, however, Dilthey faced a problem he was unable to resolve. If all meaning was context-bound and the interpretation had no absolute starting or ending points, interpretation of meaning could vary. If this was so, could there be any such thing as a correct interpretation versus an incorrect interpretation? Dilthey could find no "norms against which conflicting values could be judged . . . and [he] scorned to appeal . . . to transcendental values of a metaphysical character" (H. Hughes, 1958, p. 199). Contrary to positivism, which had developed standards primarily of a procedural sort against which to judge which research results were true and which were not true (whether they were appropriate standards or not), Dilthey's method led to an apparent relativism that he found unacceptable, but from which he could fashion no escape. This was a problem that reappears not only in Weber's work, but also—as will be discussed in later chapters—is central to our present discussions of alternative approaches to inquiry.

In summary, then, Dilthey provided a strong criticism of the empiricist/positivist school of thought. He did this by posing an alternative to the subject-object dualism of positivism, by criticizing the idea of objectivity, by allowing for no sharp distinction between facts and values, and by stressing that the goal of the human sciences must be understanding rather than laws that lead to explanation and prediction in a natural science sense. As Ermarth (1978) puts it,

> In the human world we do not find the same extreme split between the knowing subject and object known which characterizes the scientific view

of nature. Indeed the traditional dichotomy of subject/object cannot be applied in the same sense as with regard to nature, for in the human world the qualities and attributes deriving from the mental makeup of the observer are not neatly separable from the qualities of what he investigates. The special relation of subject and object in the lived experience of the human world defines both the special efficacy and problems of the human sciences. (p. 99)

What researchers had been able to accomplish in the natural sciences was not possible for the positivists to accomplish in the study of social and cultural life, according to Dilthey.

At about the same time as Dilthey, Rickert made a serious contribution to this critical reaction. He disagreed with Dilthey over the idea that the differences in subject matter between the natural and social sciences was the real issue (see Ermarth, 1978, pp. 185–197, for a brief discussion of this difference). Rickert argued that different methodologies were required because we had different interests in the two areas. In the case of the natural sciences our concern was nomothetic, or with the general and with the discovery of laws. In the social or cultural sciences our interest was ideographic, or with individual events. His main task was to clarify this idea of an ideographic approach to make more precise the concept of individuality.

Rickert's problem in this regard was to determine the criteria or criterion by which the individual event was selected from what seemed to be a formless and inextricable complex whole of events. Out of this mass of social events, how did we select one thing over another for investigation? His solution was to introduce the concept of value-relevance, which became his main contribution to our present concerns over social inquiry. For the natural sciences one selected the common features of objects and in doing so abstracted from the whole with an interest in generalizing. In history and the cultural sciences, our interest in individual events meant that selections made by investigators were based on their values, or made in a context of value-relevance. Furthermore, the cultural sciences had to be concerned not only with what was experienced by people but with what was meaningful to them based on their values.

Rickert's contribution, then, was to bring values into the equation not only as a part of the investigator's work, but as a part of the life of the events studied by the investigator. In this way he posed a challenge to the empiricist idea of a value-free approach to the study of social life in both historical and contemporary contexts.

THE ATTEMPT AT SYNTHESIS

Weber was one of the greatest and most original of the social science philosophers who developed their ideas around the turn of this century. His originality lies in the fact that he attempted—but, one can argue, ultimately without success—to find a middle ground between empiricism and interpretation (see Outhwaite, 1983, and Simey, 1969, for a discussion of Weber's success at finding a *via media* or lack thereof). He accepted much of what Dilthey, Rickert, and others were saying, yet attempted to resolve some of the problems that had plagued aspects of their work. He likewise accepted much of the thinking that had gone into the development of an empiricist-oriented social science, yet he rejected the prospect that only an approach modeled on the natural sciences could be scientific. In other words, he held that the positivists had ignored the need for understanding, whereas the hermeneuticists had ignored the idea of an existent social reality. He thus embarked on the development of a social inquiry that could combine these two aspects.

In his conception of the logic and method of social inquiry, Weber agreed with Rickert that the difference between the natural sciences and the social sciences was not so much one of subject matter as it was one of our interest in the subject matter. He felt that there was nothing about the nature of either social or physical reality that required us to employ only one approach to the total exclusion of all others. Every science could be and had been nomothetic and ideographic in method. However, this did not mean that social science inquiry could be or should be simply modeled on the natural sciences. The reason for this was as follows: The primary interest of social inquiry was in the individual; social science was concerned with the meaningful behavior of individuals engaged in social action. Action, by his definition, was behavior to which individuals attached or assigned meaning and was social because it took into account the behavior of other individuals. Behavior that was merely reactive was not considered a principal concern.

If this was the case, then questions of value-relevance had to play an important part in the entire process of studying social life. What individuals defined as significant must be related to what they valued. Moreover, what social scientists chose to study, because they also were individuals engaged in meaningful behavior, was related to what they valued. This line of reasoning led to a number of conclusions. First, it meant that there was not a determinant starting point for social science in general or for any study in particular. It was acceptable and natural that social scientists should be interested in different things or in the same thing in different ways, according to this idea of value-relevance. In Rickert's world of complexity, this was the basis for the selection of individual events or occurrences. Thus, in Weber's version of social science there was no room for a singular *"objective science of the entire past or of society as a whole"* (Aron, 1970, p. 79). As opposed to Durkheim and a definitive sociology that would determine the system of laws, "Weber opposes to this dogmatism the legitimate multiplicity of approaches and researches, corresponding to the diversity of the spiritual worlds which human societies create" (Aron, p. 79).

Second, this value-relevance brought researchers into an intimate relationship with the world that was the subject of their inquiry. Since researchers were human beings studying the meanings of the social actions of other human beings, they were both the subject and object of their own studies. This viewpoint contrasted sharply with the subject-object dualism of an empiricist social science. Social science actually became a pursuit of self-knowledge—the values, beliefs, feelings, motives, and so on of human beings. Physical scientists did not, of course, stand in a similar relationship to their subject matter given its inanimate nature. For Weber this meant that the major and most important goal was "to achieve *clarity*, clarity about the situations in which men select and act on their values, clarity that helps the individual, in Weber's words, 'to give himself an account of the ultimate meaning of his own conduct' " (Wrong, 1970, p. 11).

It is important to point out, however, that Weber distinguished between using values to determine the choice of what to study and using values to judge the worth of the object of study (this topic is discussed in greater detail in Chapter V). He felt the latter was inappropriate because social scientists could not and should not tell people what they should do, only what they might possibly be able to do given their own values. Once social scientists had chosen their topic, only the facts counted, and personal values should not be masqueraded as scientific facts. The personal character of scientists, their self-restraint and integrity, was crucial in preventing this abuse of position. Although a strict version of positivism would not accede to the need for value-relevance even in the area of problem choice, most versions of this approach have incorporated Weber's distinction and preserve objectivity through the use of proper procedures or methods.

If the prime concern of the social sciences is the subjective meaning of social actors, how are we to understand these meanings? At this point Weber drew on his idealist background, beginning with the idea of *verstehen*. Weber said this aspect of social inquiry made it unique and separated it most from the natural sciences. *Verstehen* allowed us to deal with what was particularly human about our subject matter. Interpretive social inquiry "in contrast with Durkheim's philosophy treats the historical [social] world not as a collection of objects, but as a process of development of human lives" (Aron, 1970, pp. 83–84).

Even though *verstehen* is a difficult concept to define, Weber was able to articulate the concept at two levels. First, there was the Dilthian idea of direct understanding. *Verstehen* in this sense means directly or immediately apprehending a human action such as a gesture or expression, without consciously making an inference based on that activity. In this sense it constitutes a perception of the *what* of an action. Of course, even at this level of understanding, a certain amount of background knowledge is required. An alien from another planet would not have even this direct level of immediate understanding. Likewise, the need for a minimum amount of knowledge separates direct understanding from what we usually think of as intuition.

The second level of *verstehen* is explanatory understanding. This is the level of understanding obtained when we understand the motives and intentions of actors or the meanings individuals assign to their own actions. The *what* aspect of the action is now joined by the *why* of that action. To understand the meanings of another required that one place the action within a context of meaning. In other words, meaning could not be divorced from context. Ultimately, of course, the ability to obtain this kind of understanding is related to the previously made point that human beings were both the subject and the object of social inquiry.

Contemporary social scientists of an interpretive persuasion tend to find many of their roots in this part of Weber's work. For this reason he is often thought of as the originator of interpretive sociology in particular and of interpretive social inquiry in general. However, there is another aspect of Weber's discussion of *verstehen* that is often minimized by interpretivists and, not surprisingly, emphasized by social inquirers of an empiricist orientation.

Weber faced the same problem as Dilthey had: How does one know whether or not the meaning assigned to an action has been interpreted correctly? Or, put more generally, how can one have an objective understanding of the subjective world of meanings and intentions? As will be recalled, Dilthey could find no solution to this problem short of a return to metaphysics. Weber took a different approach that involved a reinterpretation of the idea of causality. He believed that some process of verification must take place. This meant that an investigator had to develop causal hypotheses that could be verified or rejected empirically. By this, Weber did not mean that social science would or even could develop causal laws like the natural sciences, based on concomitant variation, as in Durkheim's version of social science. Weber said that we could only know a small part of reality and that our ability to explain the causal arrangement of events was limited. We could say that something would probably happen if it had previously happened various times in a limited and particular context.

Contrary to the positivists, he held that social reality was far too complex to be brought under a few basic theories and laws. He was concerned about empirical verification, but he did not believe that this was the ultimate level at which to practice science. Even though he has been interpreted in this way, he did not reduce *verstehen* to the status of only generating hypotheses for the more "serious" business of empirical testing. He found the discovery of regularities to be of no value in the absence of interpretive understanding.

Weber attempted to join *verstehen* and his interpretation of causality through the introduction of the concept of the ideal-type (Weber, 1949). The ideal-type in this sense is not an evaluative term, but a descriptive mental construct used by social scientists to make comparisons with reality. For example, to think of the ideal-type teacher did not mean to think of the characteristics of all teachers averaged out to arrive at the definition of the teacher. On the contrary, an ideal-type was constructed as a rationalization: "We bring together characteristics which are more or less evident in different instances, we emphasize, eliminate, exaggerate, and finally substitute a coherent, rational whole for the confusion and incoherence of reality" (Aron, 1970, p. 81).

This rationalization could then be applied to reality and used to uncover the "cause" of social action. However, these ideal-types were not like the laws of positivism because there could be numerous ideal-types constructed—even for more or less the same phenomenon. The only limits were the interests of the social scientists in constructing them. The immense complexity of social reality meant that there could be more than one way to approach it. Ideal-types were to be meaningful explanations, and the course of action specified for a particular group of social or educational actors had to allow not only for the behavior these people might possibly exhibit under certain circumstances, but also for the motives or meanings they assigned to their own actions.

Finally, Weber lodged his argument for the objective understanding of subjective meanings within a particular theory of history. For Weber, objective understanding was possible (or eventually would be possible) because capitalism brought with it the inevitable need for rational-instrumental reason and action. As Western civilization became increasingly rational-instrumental, general agreement would inevitably be reached as to the ends of human action. And once these ends were agreed upon, then the issue for social science was one of choosing the means to achieve these ends in the most effective and efficient way. As Bauman (1978) puts it, "The historically produced ascendance of rationality has supplied the missing foundation for universal agreement as to the interpretation of human action" (p. 85). Accordingly, this last stage in the "development of historical relativity . . . [brings about] . . . at long last, its own demise" (p. 85). This theory of history is a crucial element in Weber's attempt to avoid Dilthey's problem of relativism.

Thus, Weber articulated the three major methodological principles of value-relevance, *verstehen*, and the ideal-type, and tied them to a theory of historical inevitability, in his attempt to develop a middle ground between the two perspectives on inquiry. He thought the externalist-oriented tenets of positivism could not adequately account for our ability to act intentionally and ascribe meaning. Likewise, he felt the internalist-oriented tenets of Dilthey and others lacked a sufficient respect for and understanding of social reality as an existent reality and resulted in the impossibility of objective understanding. His failure to establish convincingly this *via media* is evidenced by the fact that his theory of history has not been realized and that social and educational inquiry is far from a unified, agreed-upon endeavor. Actually, one can argue that his work unintentionally contributed to continuing the differences of opinions and perspectives as to the nature of inquiry. The immense richness and complexity of his writings has allowed proponents on each side of the discussion to draw, either directly or indirectly, on his work as they have built and defended their respective positions.

SUMMARY

By shortly after the turn of this century, most of the points of contention that fundamentally differentiated and still differentiate the two perspectives on social and educational inquiry were already well developed. This is not to say that the 20th century has produced only a stale rehashing of these positions. In terms of philosophical arguments this is clearly not the case. However, the broad, general principles associated with each approach have remained basically the same over the years. In other words, the logic of justification developed by the early positivists is really not so very different from the one accepted by contemporary researchers of an empiricist disposition. Similarly, the logic of justification put forth by the early idealist- or internalist-oriented critics of positivism is very much like the one employed by researchers of an interpretive persuasion.

In social and educational inquiry we are therefore faced with two approaches. In terms of basic assumptions, or logics of justification, they are fundamentally different. Although there are, of course, many different ways to compare the two logics of justification, it seems appropriate to examine the differences between the two in major areas. The first area centers around a discussion of the relationship of the investigator to what is investigated and, in the process, also addresses how each side answers the traditional philosophical questions concerning the nature of reality and what is to count as truth. The second area involves the crucial topic of the relationship of facts to values—a discussion that must then engage the all-important concepts of objectivity and subjectivity. The purpose of social and educational inquiry, or what researchers and others expect will result from the process, is the third topic of interest. Finally, because the issue of the procedures for doing research is an ever present point of concern among inquirers, the position each side takes on the role of methods within the inquiry process must be examined.

CHAPTER IV

The Relationship of the Investigator to What is Investigated

> To the ordinary person, raised in the tradition of Western empiricism, physical objects usually seem to exist "by themselves" out there in time and space, appearing as disparate clusters of sense data. So, too, social objects appear to most of us as *things*: land, labor, capital; the working class and the employing class; the state and the superstructure of ideas, philosophies, religions—all of these categories of reality often present themselves to our consciousness as existing by themselves, with defined boundaries that set them off from other aspects of the social universe. However abstract, they tend to be conceived as distinctly as if they were objects to be picked up and turned over in one's hand. (Heilbroner, 1972, p. 9)

One of the major themes developed in the last chapter was the relationship of the investigator to what is investigated and the different assumptions regarding that relationship. The position that is generally the basis for empiricist approaches to social and educational inquiry is that of separate entities—the investigator on the one side and the world of things that exist independent of the investigator on the other side. These objects or things exist "out there" regardless of whether or not they are presently experienced or have ever been experienced. Accordingly, this position allows the researcher to stand apart from that reality, adopt the role of neutral observer, and thereby investigate social reality in very much the same way as physical scientists investigate the natural world.

For the interpretive approaches to social and educational inquiry, this notion, often referred to as subject-object dualism, is unacceptable as a basic starting point for the study of social and educational phenomena. Social reality is a constructed reality, based on the meanings people (including researchers) give to their own intentions, motives, and actions and those of others. Interpretive-oriented inquirers therefore see themselves in a different relationship to their subject matter than do their empiricist counterparts. For the former, what is studied is not "out there" independent of the inquirers. On the contrary, inquirers, both in their day-to-day lives and as professionals, are thoroughly and inseparably a part of what is studied. This is often described as a subject-subject relationship as opposed to a subject-object dualism.

Very much associated with these different relationships of the investigator to what is investigated are different ontological and epistemological positions. For empiricists, social and educational reality is thought of as an independently existing reality. "Things" like social class, moral stages of development, self-concept, intelligence, and so on are conceived of as independent and separately existing entities. From the interpretive perspective, social and educational reality is not independent of our interests and purposes, but is rather the product of the formative activities of our minds—in other words, reality is the interpretation. Finally, each side defines or characterizes truth in a different fashion. For empiricists, truth is a matter of a correspondence between our words and that existent reality. To speak the truth is to describe accurately how things really are. For the interpretive approach, truth does not have this external referent, but is rather a matter of socially and historically conditioned agreement. Truth is, in other words, a label given to those statements with which one can agree.

TWO EXAMPLES

The following two examples serve to set the stage for this discussion of the two different ways in which the relationship of the investigator to the investigated can be conceived.

The Discovery of Pulsars

In 1967, using a recently constructed radio telescope designed for sensitivity to weak radio signals, Dr. Anthony Hewish and his research student, Jocelyn Bell (now Dr. Burrell), discovered the existence of pulsating radio sources, or pulsars (see F. Smith, 1977, pp. 1–9, for a more complete discussion of this discovery). Shortly after recordings began in July of that year, Bell noted that they were receiving large signal fluctuations that would repeat over several days. Because these signals looked very much like the kind of interference sensitive radio telescopes can pick up from such things as passing cars, Hewish initially dismissed them as unimportant. However, since the signals continued to appear on and off for the next few months, he was forced to reject the possibility of simple interference. In November, by recording the signals at a different speed, he found that they were receiving a series of astonishingly rapid and regular pulses. Quite clearly, something previously unknown had been discovered. The problem was that no one had a very clear idea of what it was.

During the next few months, Hewish discarded the possibilities that the signals were of human origin or that they came from an extraterrestrial civilization. When he published his findings, he noted that the source was outside the solar system and was most likely produced by a condensed star such as a white dwarf (a star, originally the size of the sun, that has collapsed to about the size of earth). Other radio and optical astronomers around the world immediately began to search for similar pulsing signals, and theorists began to try to explain what was producing them.

Although much of the initial work favored the idea that the pulsing came from conventional white dwarfs, overlooked by many was a paper by Dr. Franco Pacini, who argued that a rotating neutron star could produce such an energy source (a neutron star, originally about three times the size of the sun, is one that has collapsed to as little as 15 miles in diameter). This paper, along with one by Dr. Thomas Gold, which appeared shortly after the discovery, set out the theory that linked pulsars with neutron stars.

The confirmation that the signals are produced by neutron stars came with the discovery of pulsars in the Vela and Crab Nebulas. These sources had pulse periods, based on rotations of up to 30 times a second, which were not possible for a white dwarf. The faster spin, caused by the more condensed nature of the object (as with the faster spin of a skater when the arms are tucked in), meant that the signals were coming from neutron stars. In 1969 other astronomers, by photographing the pulsar in the Crab Nebula, noted that pulsars also had an optical pulse. Hewish and Bell had discovered a new and significant object out there in the physical world—one that resulted in a Nobel prize for Hewish.

Except to those who enjoy the "if a tree falls in the forest does it make a sound" type of discussion, the use of the term *new* to describe this discovery indisputably means "recently added to our stock of knowledge" and not that pulsars are "new" in the sense that they did not exist prior to the moment the pulses were recorded. No sense of intellectual disquietude is provoked by the assumption (even though this must remain an assumption, since it cannot be proven—at least scientifically) that pulsars were there long before they were experienced, are there now, and will be for a long time in the future, even if astronomers no longer focus their telescopes on them. This situation illustrates the thinking employed by scientists, and by most laypeople for that matter, in their approach to physical objects and physical processes. Quite simply, the idea is that physical objects and processes have an existence in and of themselves that is independent of human interests in and experiences of them.

Very much a part of this assumption of object independence is the idea that should an investigator decide to study the qualities and characteristics of pulsars in greater detail, the inquiry can proceed (if done properly) without influencing the object of study—at least in any way that makes a difference or a difference that cannot be accounted for. Inquiry, from this perspective, is dedicated to providing as accurate as possible a description of the object and/or process under investigation. An astronomer, in a further study of pulsars, can "stand aside" and take on the classical role of observer in order to record the characteristics of pulsars. In fact, this perspective holds that the line of separation between the researcher and the research process on the one side and the object investigated on the other side is absolutely crucial if science is to tell us how things really are out there in the natural world. (As will be recalled from Chapter I, some theoretical physicists, such as Wigner, 1967, and Wheeler, 1975, argue that quantum theory calls this separation into question. Others, however, such as Trigg, 1980, hold that quantum theory need not alter this relationship of separation.)

Within the same general context, it is also clear that physical objects (humans excepted) are not thought of as self-constituting or self-defining. Physical objects do not ascribe meaning to their own existence, make intentional choices based on values and preferences, or react to what scientists say about them (they are not reflexive). Should an investigation lead to a change in the description of, for example, the rate of spin of pulsars, it would be quite acceptable to attribute this change to an increased precision of measurement and/or some physical occurrence. Certainly, the change would not be attributed to an intentional choice by the pulsars to adopt a different rate of spin or to the pulsars' reaction to what scientists may have said about them. In other words, we think of physical objects and processes as having a certain determinate or "fixed" character: The world of the ancient Greeks is the same as the world of today—the difference in the way we describe it simply means we know more in the sense that our descriptions are closer to the way nature really is.

The principal point of this example is that the physical sciences are concerned with the accurate description of a physical reality that is seen as existing independent of the investigator and the process of investigation. To the extent that the social sciences have been modeled on the physical sciences, social inquiry is similarly directed at describing an independently existing social reality. However, the acceptance of this subject-object dualism, which has posed few problems over the years for the physical sciences, has been and still is a central issue in any discussion of the nature of social and educational inquiry. An examination of the nature and implications of the debate can begin with the following example.

The "Discovery" of Childhood

Although it is impossible to date the "event" precisely, sometime around the 15th century childhood was "discovered." Ariès (1962), in his study of the history of Western family life, argues that childhood did not exist in the Middle Ages. Of course, this does not mean that there were no small human beings who, if they survived, would grow to become more or less standard-size people. Rather, Ariès's point, particularly in regard to the 11th and 12th centuries, is that people "did not dwell on the image of childhood, and that image had neither interest nor even reality for them" (p. 34).

The evidence Ariès (1962) drew upon for this contention comes from various sources. In the paintings of that time, young people were apparently perceived by artists as miniature adults. These "children" were portrayed with the facial features and body structure of adults. From other sources Ariès found that these smaller beings dressed in clothing styled the same as that of adults, participated in adult games and social situations as adults, and were not protected from such "vices" as alcohol and sex. Furthermore, and especially important to understanding the other evidence, the literature of the time reflects little emotional attachment to these smaller beings—even to the point, in some cases, that whether they lived or died seemed to provoke no great concern. As Montaigne (cited in Ariès) said, "I have lost two or three children in their infancy, not without regret, but without great sorrow" (p. 39). That he is imprecise about the number is interesting.

By about 1600, the concept of childhood was well on the way to being established. A group of moralist reformers, concerned with what they felt was the anarchy, corruption, and evilness of society, led a movement to separate and protect these smaller beings from the excesses of adult society. The motivating idea was that young people were in a state of innocence and that if this quality could be nurtured, a more moral society would eventually result. With the French Jesuits and other religious orders leading the way, the idea of education or schooling as a means for protecting the young from adult life took hold, books were expunged of indecencies, clothing specially designed for young people became common, and so on. In other words, a group of people intentionally began to act toward, and interact with, these smaller beings as if they had characteristics distinguishable from those of adults. A particular image of childhood, as defined by certain qualities and characteristics, came to be thought of as a social reality.

Each of these two examples illustrates, in the first instance, the discovery of a bit of reality—physical in the first example and social in the second—with its qualities and characteristics. Based on the comments made in regard to the pulsar example, a number of questions can be raised about the discovery of childhood. The possible answers to these questions dominate the discussion in the balance of this chapter.

Whereas we may assume that pulsars existed prior to and exist independent of our interest in and experience of them, can the same assumption be made in the case of childhood? In other words, is the term *discovery* as used in the case of childhood somehow different? Does *discovery* in this sense mean a reality that is made or constructed, based on intentional, meaningful behavior, as opposed to *discovery* in the sense of "to find"? If this is so, then clearly the reality of childhood is mind-dependent in a much more significant way than is the case for the reality of pulsars.

Similarly, whereas we generally accept that the study of pulsars both allows and even requires that the investigator adopt the role of observer—standing apart from what is investigated—is the same separation possible for inquirers in their investigations of childhood? Or do the latter participate, through interpreting the interpretations of others (as Ariès interpreted the interpretations of the Jesuits), in constructing reality, as opposed to describing a preexisting and independently existing reality? Also, whereas an investigation of pulsars need not take into account the possibility that pulsars are self-defining or self-constituting, can the same be said for the study of childhood? Since it is based on interpretations, the study of childhood might well have to be concerned with the question of reflexivity. Finally, any change in our description of pulsars, assuming no physical event has caused them to change, will be due to the fact that more precise measurement or greater insights have allowed us to know more about them. In this sense, the pulsar of today is the same as the pulsar of years ago—the difference is that we have gotten nearer the essence of pulsars or closer to how they really are. Is this situation the same for childhood, or does a change of description mean that we have constructed, based on different interests, purposes, and values, the reality of childhood in a different way?

Ultimately, these and similar questions are very much a part of the broader issue of the relationship of the investigator to what is investigated. In the case of social and educational reality, is this relationship one of separate entities (subject-object dualism), or is it one of interdependence (subject-subject relationship)?

TWO PERSPECTIVES

Probably the best way to discuss the issues of the relationship of the investigator to what is investigated and the nature of social reality is in terms of the two quite different intellectual or philosophical temperaments that were briefly summarized in Chapter I—externalism and internalism. A brief examination of the general outlines of each perspective will help clarify both the nature of these issues and their implications for the different approaches to social and educational inquiry.

Externalism

One of the most important tenets of an externalist perspective is that the object of investigation must stand separate from the investigator. As Urban (1949) put it, from this general perspective "it is scarcely understandable how one can call that knowledge at all in which knowing makes any difference to the thing known—in which the thing known is not wholly other than the knower" (p. 16).

Clearly, this position entails various commitments of significance. First, there is the idea that reality is mind-independent beyond anything more than the obvious point that minds are necessary to conceptualize reality (by definition only minds can do so). Second, this mind-independent world of things or objects is susceptible to being described "as it really is." For externalism, then, truth is a matter of the correspondence between our words and these external, independently existing things. Truth is, in other words, a judgment taken in reference to whether or not a description accurately reflects or mirrors reality. Finally, common to this perspective is what Putnam (1981) calls a "God's eye" point of view (p. 50)—meaning that we are able to stand apart from and thereby apprehend the world from no particular place within it. These elements require elaboration.

At a minimum, externalism holds to a line of separation between the investigator and what is investigated. Two separate entities are involved—the investigator (our minds) on the one side and the investigated (the world of objects) on the other side. Reality is accordingly given the status of existing external to and independent of us; it is out there, whether presently experienced or even not yet experienced. Without a doubt, the position that mind and world are intertwined, in any significant sense of the idea that reality is mind-dependent, is unacceptable to an externalist perspective.

Externalists stress this point because they hold that any claim to know something must depend on there being something to be known. This something must exist before any attempt is made to know it. What is known cannot be thought of as something that has been brought into existence by the activity or process of knowing. If this were the case, externalists would argue, one could no longer talk about knowing, but rather would have to revert to the level of supposing or imagining. Therefore, to talk sensibly about knowledge or to claim that one possesses genuine knowledge, as it might be called, requires that what is investigated remain untainted by the investigator and the process of investigation. Trigg (1980) has well summarized this situation:

> There are endless complications when the activity of scientists itself affects the object of investigation, and even then their task is to understand the nature of reality concerned apart from their interference. . . . any blurring of the distinction between the investigator and his method of research, on the one hand, and the object of study on the other, will merely make the investigation pointless. (pp. 93–94)

Very much associated with this last point is a problem of obvious consequence for social and educational inquiry—that people are self-defining and act intentionally. Whereas physical scientists can pursue their inquiries with no concern that the object of their study will process information and act accordingly (or will "act back on them" in a conscious way, so to speak), such is not the case for social scientists. In other words, the study of social and human reality must ultimately take into account that the investigator stands in a reflexive relationship to the subject matter. *Reflexivity*, as loosely defined in this case, means that people can and very often do react to, and even change their thinking and behavior as a result of, what investigators say about them, to them, and/or do in relation to them.

Within the externalist perspective, as broadly defined here, two different solutions may be offered. The first, which is distinctly of a behaviorist orientation, posits that this aspect of intentionality (and the mental in general) is of no concern, since the interest of social science is only in overt or observable behavior. The second solution holds that methodological techniques of various kinds, such as social desirability scales, certain types of "indirect" observational procedures, and various statistical procedures, allow the social scientist to minimize the problem very much. The influence of the investigator and the process of investigation on the object of study can be, if not eliminated, certainly taken into account, through the use of sophisticated research procedures.

At this point a most important issue arises. The externalist position must address the prospect that the subject matter of social and educational inquiry—meanings and intentions—seems to "exist" in a way different from the subject matter of the physical sciences. When one talks of physical things like pulsars, there is no difficulty in accepting the idea of independently or separately existing entities—minds on the one side and the world of physical objects and processes on the other. However, as one attempts to focus on such "things" as the working class, childhood, social integration, and self-concept, it is clear that these things are not, like pulsars, dimensional in time and space. In contrast to our thinking about physical objects, it is difficult to sustain a conception of the social and human as things that can be "picked up and turned over in one's hand" (Heilbroner, 1972, p. 9). Social and human objects are more like instruments of our thoughts, or hypotheticals that have no "real" existence in and of themselves. Thus, this major approach to social and educational inquiry must justify, to the extent it desires to remain in concert with the physical sciences, that there truly can be a separation between the investigator and the object of investigation.

The key to understanding this issue, as foreshadowed in the quotation by Heilbroner, is to realize that social scientists have simply come to treat these instruments of our thoughts as realities in themselves. Whether one calls this reification, hypostatization, or something else is of no consequence. What is important is that the practice of empiricist social inquiry is based on a commitment to what Spencer (1982) calls an operative realism. He argues that abstractions such as interaction, cooperation, and competition are treated as if they were realities that are independent of the constraints of any particular time and place. As he notes, "The ontology of these pure theoretical statements . . . ascribes a real status to abstract, or ideal entities" (p. 126). In other words, a dualism of subject-object requires, to paraphrase Rorty (1979, p. 30), that the reference is not to how people feel, but to feelings as self-subsistent entities—free of people in the same sense that a universal is free of an instance.

This position, though often criticized as a "fallacy of misplaced concreteness," is supported by some sophisticated reasoning. As may be recalled, Durkheim (1938) argued forcefully and very effectively that social facts are to be treated as things. Such social facts as obligations, laws, and customs, he said, exist prior to one's participation in them and exist whether or not one participates in, or is even aware of, them. They are therefore external to and independent of any one individual and outside of individual consciousness. Moreover, social facts are general in society because they exist over and above any individual manifestations. Finally, these facts, according to Durkheim, have a coercive power in that they constrain us to act in certain ways. Even though his argument clearly has some weaknesses (see Keat & Urry, 1975, pp. 81–90, for a concise discussion of these weaknesses), the important point is that the externalist position of treating the social as things is not based on whim or on an unthought-out fancy.

Given the externalist idea that social reality can and must be thought of as external to and independent of us, it is important to note how this point is related to the issue of how investigators judge some statements about social reality as true and others as false. In other words, for the empiricist approach, how do investigators determine what is to count as knowledge or what is to count as truth?

For most externalists (and for most laypeople, even though they do not employ the same terminology), the answer is that they have accepted what is called the correspondence theory of truth: A statement is true when it corresponds to that independently existing reality and false when it does not (see Ewing, 1974, p. 193). Even though the correspondence theory has numerous complexities at the philosophical level, these need not be introduced for our discussion of research practice. For our purposes, it is sufficient to note that, for externalism, a true statement is one that accurately describes what is really out there, whereas a false one has in some sense distorted that reality.

Crucial to the idea of correspondence is that judgments about the accuracy of statements are the product of observation. If one wants to judge the truthfulness of the statement "the cat is on the mat," the process involves observing the mat to see whether or not the cat is there. If it is, the statement is judged true, and vice versa. Although the observational process engaged in by researchers is of course usually much more complicated, similar criteria are used to judge the truth of statements made about social and physical reality. To liberally paraphrase Rorty (1979, p. 334), this discovery that the cat is on the mat embodies the essence of our notions of contact with reality, truth as correspondence, and accurate representation. This is the standard against which other discoveries, such as that of a new "law" of social behavior, of the moral stages of development in children, or of quantum indeterminacy, are compared in terms of objectivity.

In reference to our examples at the beginning of this chapter, astronomers will continue, through the use of observational techniques, to sort out statements that accurately correspond to the qualities and characteristics of pulsars from those that do not. Likewise, it is presumed that social investigators, using their particular observational techniques, similarly will be able to sort out statements that accurately describe the qualities and characteristics of childhood from those that do not. And, should disagreements among inquirers occur in either case, the referent point for resolving these differences is further examination and reexamination of what exists out there. Thus, for externalism, truth has its source in an independently existing reality—one that we can describe, given the proper methods of study, for what it really is.

Much of what has been discussed to this point, from the example of pulsars to the ideas of reality as mind-independent and truth as correspondence may seem to be little more than common sense. This is not surprising, since these beliefs are integral to many of our ordinary, everyday activities and judgments. They are so important to us, in fact, that we usually consider anyone who does not agree with them to be, at a minimum, eccentric. The point is that externalism as a basis for scientific inquiry is very much related to, and gains force from, this commonsense perspective. Externalist assumptions constitute the framework within which the practice of investigation of the physical world and of most investigation of the social and educational realms is undertaken. MacKinnon (1972), using the term *scientific realism* to denote what we have discussed as externalism, has concisely summarized this situation:

> The scientist in his ordinary practice accepts and affirms propositions as true in a correspondence sense and as statements of what obtains in reality. In this sense, science as practiced necessarily entails a functional realism. This realism is functional inasmuch as it has a definite function within science. Without it there could be no truth claims, and without truth claims there would be no science. (pp. 57–58)

Internalism

The position that treats social reality as mind-independent and accepts a correspondence theory of truth is not the only basis for investigative efforts. There has been a serious internalist challenge to externalism. Internalism, in broad terms, is based on the very different assumption that social reality is, in a very significant sense, mind-dependent and that the idea of truth is ultimately a matter of socially and historically conditioned agreement. Furthermore, this position holds that we cannot take, or even imagine how we could take, a God's eye point of view. We can have "only the various points of view of actual persons reflecting various interests and purposes that their descriptions and theories subserve" (Putnam, 1981, p. 50).

The basic idea of the internalist perspective is that one cannot "talk of knowledge in any intelligible sense if the supposed object is wholly independent of the knower—in which there is not in some way and in some degree mutual involvement of mind and object" (Urban, 1949, p. 16). According to this perspective, the mind plays a foundational role in the shaping or constructing of social reality, and therefore what exists is not independent of, but in a very significant sense is dependent upon, our minds.

To understand more fully the idea of mind-dependence, we can apply to this discussion of internalism some of Rescher's (1973) comments concerning what he calls "conceptual idealism." Rescher argues that although physical things exist independent of us, their reality as it is for us is mind-dependent. The mind does not create the world of objects but, through its determining categories, shapes or constructs that reality. This shaping is based on our interaction with the environment through the use of conceptual schemes or frameworks. These frameworks are a priori, if not in the Kantian sense as innate structures of the mind, certainly in the sense that they must be in place before one can have a meaningful cognitive experience. Rescher's conceptual idealism (and our internalism), if applied to social inquiry, would acknowledge that physical beings exist independently and would focus on how we interpret what these physical beings say and do. Mind-dependence here does not mean that the mind "creates" what people say and do, but rather that how we interpret their movements and utterances—the meanings we assign to the intentions, motivations, and so on of ourselves and others—becomes social reality as it is for us. In other words, social reality is the interpretation.

An obvious and immediate implication of the internalist position of mind-dependence is that the two elements of mind and world are entangled. The knower and the process of knowing cannot be separated from what is or can be known. Social reality is not something that exists external to or independent of us; rather it is a reality that is humanly constructed or shaped through social interactions. This constructed reality is a product of the meanings people give to their interactions with others and of the meanings social investigators give to their interactions with subjects and with each other. Inquiry is a matter of interpreting the interpretations of others.

Hence, there is a major difference between the two perspectives—with definite implications for the practice of, and the interpretation given to the results of, research. Externalism argues for an independent reality and a social science that attempts, through the use of proper procedures, to discover and describe that reality and our relationship to it. Internalism takes a much different tack: It focuses on the interests and purposes of people, or on our intentional, meaningful behavior, including that of investigators, and then attempts to examine how we construct and continue to reconstruct social reality, given these interests and purposes.

Another important way to express the implications of social reality as mind-dependent is in terms of the idea of "presuppositionless knowl-edge," or "data free from interpretation." From this perspective there can be no such thing as "brute data" upon which to found knowledge or to verify our propositions. Brute data, as defined by Taylor (1971), is "data whose validity cannot be questioned by offering another interpre-tation or reading, data whose credibility cannot be founded or under-mined by further reasoning" (p. 8). There are, as such, no self-evident givens in the sense of social and educational data that are resistant to multiple readings. The reason for this situation, as it relates to Rescher's (1973) position of conceptual idealism, is that the shaping of reality by our minds prevents independent access to any reality there may be, and hence theory-free observation is not possible. Thus, from this internalist perspective, we must again take heed of the point that a God's eye view is not possible—all we can have are the various points of view that reflect the interests and purposes of various people.

The differences between the mind-involvement of the internalist ap-proach and the dualism of the externalist approach result in markedly different ways of looking at the nature of inquiry. For the latter, reality exists in and of itself, external to and independent of the investigator. The process of inquiry is thought of as one that seeks to discover aspects of this reality with its qualities and characteristics. Childhood, thought of in this way, is an independent and external bit of reality, similar to physical reality. Inquiry discovers and describes for us, presumably with increasing accuracy over time, the qualities and characteristics of childhood. Just as pulsars, though only recently discovered, have "al-ways" existed with certain qualities and characteristics of size, location, and so on, so too childhood, with certain qualities and characteristics such as stages of moral development, has "always" been out there, even though only recently discovered. Moreover, knowledge in this sense has a linear, developmental aspect to it—we come to know increasingly more about things over time.

The internalist perspective adheres to a different line of reasoning. Childhood exists, but only in the qualified sense that it is a socially con-structed reality. Of course, this does not mean that the actual physical beings are constructions of our minds. What it does mean is that child-hood is real only to the extent that it is a function of our intentional and meaningful behaviors as these are played out in social interaction. And this reality varies with time and place: The reality of childhood in the 1980s is different from the reality of childhood in the 1960s, the reality of childhood in the United States is different from the reality of childhood in Japan, and so on. Childhood—and the same holds for other social and human "things" we study such as social class and self-concept—has the reality it does for us because of the meaning it has for us as we act out our daily lives in concert with others. Recalling Ariès (1962), if people (including investigators) did not act intentionally and meaningfully toward younger physical beings in ways different from how they intentionally and meaningfully act toward other physical beings, childhood could easily have no reality or have a different reality for us.

The investigation of childhood, then, does not lead to increasingly accurate depictions of a bit of external reality. Our knowledge of childhood is not linear in the sense that the present builds on the past as we move toward some sort of final depiction of the essence of childhood. On the contrary, these inquiries participate, through their interpretive nature, in the continuing process of constructing and reconstructing the reality of childhood as it is perceived at any given time and place. From an internalist perspective, social investigation must be thought of as a process of interpretation, based on one's interests and purposes, of the interpretations of others, based on their interests and purposes, which in turn act back on one's own interpretation, and on and on. This poses a circle of interpretation (an expression of what is called the hermeneutic circle), which, as Dilthey noted, can have no fixed beginning or ending points. Thus, for internalism there is no independent reality that is susceptible to increasingly more accurate description, but, to paraphrase Pinkard (1976, p. 172), the reality itself is the interpretation or the reality is established by the interpretation.

The most important epistemological consideration associated with this internalist position is that correspondence is not an acceptable way to define or characterize truth. This argument begins with the point that even if there is an independent world of objects out there, our mind-involvement prevents exactly what correspondence requires—an independent access to both domains of mind and world. Or, put differently, "we have no access to 'the world' as an undescribed or unperceived entity, and therefore we cannot compare our descriptions of the world with the world itself" (Meiland & Krausz, 1982, p. 13). Even though correspondence may be a natural enough desire or hope, in the absence of such independent access, it is an unfulfillable one. Given this situation, internalism contends that what is true about the social world is ultimately what we can agree, conditioned by time and place, is true. Inherent in this position is the idea that at certain times and in certain situations, agreement will be greater in degree and extent than at others.

Very often, a coherence theory is advanced as a major alternative to the correspondence theory. A coherence approach allows that a statement can be judged true if it is connected to and consistent with other statements in a system or scheme. Although philosophical difficulties abound in regard to some of the basic elements in this approach, the general idea is that the statements must be not only consistent with one another, but must also stand in some form of dependent relationship. The important thing to note for our purposes is that, even though most often associated with an internalist perspective, coherence is also accepted and considered important by externalists. Yet, in the end, a fundamental difference exists between each side as to the actual role of coherence.

This difference is revealed as soon as one examines the issue of what statements are supposed to cohere with. If, to be judged true, a statement must only cohere with other statements, then, "it is logically possible for there to be any number of internally coherent systems of beliefs, and since there are no external criteria for choosing among them, it cannot be known which is the 'right' one" (Grayling, 1982, p. 137). Given this view, as Russell (1912, p. 196) noted, there is no way for the coherence theory to sort out the truth from a consistent fairy tale. To avoid this problem, one can argue that at least one statement in a scheme must be judged true on a different basis.

At this point the two perspectives part company. Externalism must hold that at least one statement in the scheme refer to extralinguistic facts or is true in a correspondence sense. This statement then will serve as an Archimedean point or as the foundation for the whole scheme (see Hempel, 1965, pp. 40-42, for a discussion of this idea). Internalism must hold that all we can do is construct coherent schemes that become reality as it is for us. Since social reality is mind-dependent and there is no external referent, any statement accepted as the basis for constructing a scheme (or any scheme itself for that matter) is true only to the extent we are able to agree it is true.

Finally, the difference between the two approaches is also apparent in how each proposes that disagreements are to be resolved between or among investigators. From an externalist perspective, the acceptance of the correspondence theory means that differences can be resolved by an appeal to that independent reality. If we disagree about the relationship of age and moral development during childhood, we can appeal to the facts to resolve the problem. In this sense, the properly done study will produce results—a knowledge of how things really are—with which all reasonable or rational people must agree (not to agree in the face of the facts is to run the risk of being called irrational or stubbornly subjective). For internalism, no such verification procedures are possible. If we disagree about the interpretation given to the qualities and characteristics of childhood, we can only attempt to convince others that our interpretations are adequate or that our construction of reality (based on our interests, purposes, and values) makes sense. In the end, the resolution of differences can only come via a constant dialogue within which appeals are made to a common understanding.

OBJECTIVE AND SUBJECTIVE

Before discussing how these two perspectives lead to significantly different points of view in regard to one of the most important aspects of social and educational inquiry—that of establishing the validity of measuring instruments—the very commonly employed terms *objective* and *subjective* must be discussed. Even though these terms have been mentioned only infrequently up to this point, a discussion of the different ways they can be conceptualized is very much associated with the previously discussed differences as to the nature of social reality, of truth, and of the relationship of the investigator to the investigated. Let us first examine how these terms are conceptualized from an externalist perspective and then note how they must be reconceptualized from an internalist perspective.

From an externalist point of view, *objective* can be thought of as having its referent in what is external to or outside of us. T. Nagel (1981), for example, has noted that the essential aspect of objectivity is a sense of externality and detachment:

> The attempt is made to view the world not from a place within it, or from the vantage point of a special type of life and awareness, but from nowhere in particular and no form of life in particular at all. (p. 208)

The crucial assumption here is that everything is something in and of itself—beyond any one particular (group or individual) point of view. Objectivity is therefore a matter of detaching oneself from one's particular circumstances and seeing or representing things for what they really are. This is very much what Durkheim (1938, p. xiv) meant when he said that the social scientist should take on the perspective of the chemist or physicist and thereby be neutral and guard against presuppositions.

Subjective, not surprisingly, is defined very differently from *objective*. Instead of a focus on an external referent, attention is directed at what is internal to us. To be subjective is to see the world based on one's particular place in it. This is why, if one is accused of being subjective when objectivity is required, it is usually a charge of a "failure to maintain the necessary detachment or distance."

One major problem that externalism faces in regard to these definitions is that the same individual is the source of both objective and subjective points of view. The issue, then, is how to keep the two sides separate. More pointedly, the specific task is to ensure that the distorting threat of one's subjective side does not interfere with one's objective side, which attempts to represent the world as it really is. The proper methods, and of course the detachment gained through their proper use, are absolutely crucial in this regard. As T. Nagel (1981) puts it, "If there is a way things really are, which explains their diverse appearances to differently constituted and situated observers, then it is most accurately apprehended by methods not specific to particular types of observers" (p. 209). Objectivity requires a process of observation and analysis that is not "observer-specific," a process that can be interposed in the same way between any and all observers and what is observed. Measuring instruments or tests, for example, must be designed such that they can be read in the same way by anyone, at any time, regardless of the individual situation.

The internalist objections to the preceding definitions can be illustrated by asking a question inspired by Rorty (1979): In just what sense were the moral stages of development in children out there awaiting discovery (and accurate description) before anyone thought of doing so? If the traditional definitions of *objective* and *subjective* are to be preserved, the answer must be "in the fullest and most straightforward sense" (p. 334). Of course, as discussed, this answer can only arise out of a characterization of social inquiry as a process of discovering what exists prior to and independent of our interests and purposes. From an internalist perspective, such a conceptualization of social inquiry is unacceptable because social reality is a constructed reality. This position means that the traditional definitions of, and the type of distinctions drawn between, *objective* and *subjective* must undergo a significant change.

The crux of the issue from an internalist point of view is that correspondence and the God's eye view are not possible—we simply cannot have independent access to both domains of mind and world. Thus, no description can be offered that does not reflect the makeup of the describer and his or her particular position in the world. Any definition of *objective* that is framed in terms of the accurate description of an external referent cannot be sustained.

Rorty (1979) has presented different definitions of *objective* and *subjective* that are much in line with an internalist perspective. Rather than defining *objective* as the "accurate representation of what is out there" and *subjective* as the "result of what is inside us such as emotions, place in the world, and so on," Rorty considers the former to be a matter of what we can agree upon and the latter to be a label given to points of view that are "strange" to us. In Rorty's terms, "Objectivity [is] . . . a property of theories which, having been thoroughly discussed, are chosen by a consensus of rational discussants" (p. 338). (Of course, from his perspective what is to count as rational is a result of discussion, persuasion, and so on; there can be no neutral arena we may enter to sort out disagreements.) By contrast, to be subjective is a matter of bringing into the discussion considerations "which the others think beside the point" (p. 339). For a consideration to be subjective, in this sense, is simply for it to be unfamiliar.

Thus, for the internalist, who believes that any description offered is theory-dependent or based on particular interests and purposes, the only usable definitions we can have for the terms *objective* and *subjective* must involve, respectively, what we can agree is pertinent to the issue at hand and what we find to be beside the point.

THE EXAMPLE OF THE VALIDITY OF MEASURING INSTRUMENTS

An example focusing on one of the most crucial aspects of social and educational inquiry, the attempt to establish the validity of measuring instruments, will both expand upon and illustrate the practical consequences of many of the points made above (see J. Smith, 1985, for a more extended discussion of test validity). For the conventional or externalist approach to the practice of social and educational inquiry, the validity of measuring instruments, or the validity of the inferences one makes based on these instruments, is an indispensable element in any attempt to secure knowledge about the social world. Most social scientists of an externalist/empiricist persuasion would agree that in the absence of instruments or interpretations of results that can be considered valid, we would have no way (at least in a foundational sense) to discover and describe how the social and educational worlds really are. Validity is therefore worthy of examination in light of the two different positions discussed concerning the nature of reality, of truth, and of the relationship of the investigator to what is investigated.

The Empiricist Approach to Validity

Since validity is a complex and often confusing concept, we must briefly examine how, in the standard empiricist view, validity is supposed to be established. We will focus on the idea of construct validity, which can best be defined by paraphrasing two questions from Cronbach (1971, p. 446): Does the test measure the attribute it is designed to measure? Are the descriptions offered by the results of a test true in terms of the construct?

Establishing construct validity must obviously begin with a construct or hypothetical possibility, a process that is inductive (Cronbach & Meehl, 1955, p. 292). Social scientists develop generalizations based on observations of people doing certain things in certain ways under certain conditions. These generalizations, stated in what is considered to be a context-free scientific language (as opposed to a context-bound lay language), become constructs that are intended to explain the results of the observations. After the construct is formulated, instruments are developed to measure the attribute posed by the construct. At this point one must be concerned with how accurately this instrument will measure the designated thing or attribute.

To respond to the question of accuracy requires, at one level, theory and, at a second level, strategies of confirmation and discrimination. Theory is the foundation upon which are built hypotheses about behavior and the relationships among behaviors that can be empirically examined or verified—most often with the use of standard correlational techniques. Should positive correlations result (as predicted, by theory) between measurements taken with the instrument and those taken on some other variable, this would be considered at least one bit of support for the validity of the test or for the inferences it allows. Should no correlation of consequence result, presuming the evidence was collected and analyzed with the proper methodological procedures, we could either (a) accept the evidence and then modify the instrument and construct or (b) reject the evidence, perhaps by turning it into a hypothesis for further investigation, and preserve the original construct and instrument. In addition to these confirmation strategies, one must also employ a discrimination strategy to demonstrate that the measure is not substantially related to measures of other theoretically distinct constructs. Such evidence is considered essential to eliminate counterinterpretations of the particular measure one is attempting to validate.

The process of validation does not end with merely one or two attempts at empirical confirmation or discrimination. Hypothetically, the process is endless, involving a continual accumulation of evidence and a continual refinement of theory and constructs. If the instrument endures throughout this process, it may be judged provisionally valid, that is, valid within particular contexts until better theory and new evidence, or possibly more accurate instruments, bring about a change in judgment. In any event, to the extent that an instrument gains evidential support, it is considered capable of yielding data that permit valid, sound, or accurate interpretations.

Externalist Interpretation

To examine the assumptions underlying the conventional approach to validity, we must first inquire into the meaning given such basic terms as *accurate* and *sound*. When these terms are used to describe instruments and, more important, the data and interpretations of data derived from instruments, in essence questions of truth are being introduced. Validity is above all epistemological in import; how it is conceptualized will determine the basis of what will count as social facts and for the ability to make and defend as true any statements about the social and educational worlds. For this conventional approach to validity, *true* is defined in correspondence terms: A description is true if it corresponds to or accurately reflects the way things really are; an inaccurate or untrue description is a distortion of reality. A valid instrument is thought of as one that yields accurate descriptions of some independently existing attributes or characteristics, whereas an invalid instrument distorts what is being measured.

Just as externalism poses a separation of mind and world, conventional validity holds that an instrument and the attribute being measured are two independently existing items. An accurate instrument serves only to reflect, more or less accurately, an object. Certainly this perspective cannot entertain the notion that a test participates in constructing the reality of an object or attribute. If this were the case, social inquirers espousing this approach would violate one of their basic premises—that an investigation can be undertaken without influencing the subject of the investigation. To paraphrase Trigg (1980) again, this perspective must hold that any blurring of the line between the investigator and his or her instruments on the one side and the object of investigation on the other side would make the attempt to establish construct validity pointless. Social scientists, with their measuring instruments, would actually be participating in constructing reality rather than in discovering and describing a reality that preexisted their interests and efforts. For externalism and the conventional approach to validity, this prospect is unacceptable.

A crucial point here is that the use of the term *accurate* in the context of the conventional approach to validity implies that there is something to be accurate about. To make judgments about accuracy, one must believe that a bit of reality can be known as it really is (independent access). To say that a scale accurately measures what it intends to measure, such as the moral stages of development in children, is to accept that such stages exist and can be known independent of our interests and dispositions (objectively). In the absence of these beliefs, *accurate* would have to be reconceptualized as a matter of internal consistency and connectedness. An accurate statement could only be one that was consistent with and connected to other statements. This absence of an independent, external referent entails a situation that the externalist approach to validity finds difficult to accept.

This need to keep the instrument and object separate is clearly demonstrated by the fact that the conventional approach to validity must reject a statement such as "Intelligence is just whatever a Stanford-Binet Scale measures." Other objections aside (Cronbach, 1971, p. 482), the major problem is that such a statement espouses a breakdown of the line of separation between the test and what is measured. The ultimate implication here is that intelligence is defined by the scale. To accept this position would be inconsistent with the basic tenets of the conventional approach to validity. That is, if what is measured is defined by the instrument, it would be pointless to even ask the traditional question of whether the test accurately measures the attribute it is designed to measure. The instrument would of course do so simply by definition. In other words, an instrument could not be in error about what it constructs or defines. Although social scientists may disagree about the version of reality constructed by the instrument, this is far different from a judgment of validity in terms of accuracy or distortion.

The second relationship of importance to this analysis is that of the investigator to the measuring instrument. Since the process of establishing validity is an evidential one, it must depend on observation. The referent for judging valid instruments or valid interpretations of data must be reality itself and not how one defines or constructs reality given particular interests and purposes. Even though value considerations are involved with the social use of an instrument, questions of how well it measures an attribute or object are statistical/technical ones and relate strictly to our cognitive sides (Messick, 1980). For the conventional approach, the process of establishing validity must then be divorced, or even protected, from the unwarranted intrusion of our subjective sides, or from the investigator's particular interests and purposes. Instruments that accurately measure what they are designed to measure are those that "see" the world from no particular place within it (objectively).

Internalist Interpretation

If social reality is mind-dependent and true implications are those we can, however temporarily and incompletely, agree are true, construct validity must be seen in a rather different way. Whereas an externalist perspective holds to the independence of the instrument from the attribute or object measured, the internalist position finds this separation impossible to accept. For this latter position, an instrument does not simply reflect or mirror reality but contributes to constructing or defining social reality. Social scientists, then, through the use of their measuring instruments, are actually participants in the process of making social reality rather than discoverers of the qualities and characteristics of an independently existing reality.

The traditional question of whether a test measures the attribute it is designed to measure makes little sense from an internalist perspective. If a test participates in constructing reality and is part of an internally consistent scheme (coherence), then every instrument is by definition valid—if *valid* is defined as measuring what the test is supposed to measure. In the absence of an independently existing external referent to which we have independent access, the idea that a test can be invalid in the sense that it distorts reality is a very difficult idea to put in focus.

To ask if a scale measures what it is designed to measure can only be seen as a question of internal agreement, not as one that can be answered by an appeal to an external reality. In other words, it is impossible, given this perspective, to answer any question regarding accuracy or distortion (as traditionally defined). An instrument can only be invalid if it is inconsistent with other parts of a scheme and, more important, if the version of reality constructed by that scheme—of which the instrument is a crucial part—is one that finds little agreement. From an internalist perspective, valid scales are ones that find agreement, and vice versa.

If validity hinges on agreement, then the issue of the basis for such agreement is very important. At the heart of the internalist conceptualization of validity, at least for professional social inquirers, may very well be the question of the hierarchy of academic influence. The extent to which a test is seen as valid and is generally used has little to do with accuracy and very much to do with who is able to convince others to accept a particular version of reality. Agreement cannot be "obligated" by an appeal to an external referent or to the facts—facts that must be accepted by all rational discussants—since there are no unconceptualized or theory-free facts to which we have independent access. Rather, agreement is a result of coming to share similar values and interests through, in the best of possible situations, open dialogue and justification.

To state quite bluntly the differences between the externalist and internalist interpretations, it is one thing to say that a test is valid because it provides an accurate reflection of, for example, the attribute intelligence; it is quite another thing to say a test is valid because it defines or constructs the reality of intelligence in a way that is generally acceptable to a number of people based on their shared interests, purposes, and values. Depending on the position one takes, the epistemological significance of construct validity is quite different—with, of course, quite different implications for the meaning of truth claims about social and educational reality.

An internalist perspective must also result in a significantly different interpretation of the relationship of the instrument to the investigator. The cognitive-normative division of the externalist approach, typified by statements such as "Even though I do not like it, I must accept the facts" or "Even though we may disagree about the social use of a test, we must agree (based on a technical assessment of the facts) that it allows for valid inferences," cannot be sustained. The problem again is that such a division requires a belief that there are independently existing facts to be technical about and that to be technical is to adopt that God's eye point of view (objective in the traditional sense). If one holds, to the contrary, that all descriptions must be undertaken within a context or within a conceptual scheme, then the cognitive-normative split becomes fuzzy at best. Instrument development, as well as the use of that instrument, depends on the conceptual scheme or on the interests and purposes of the developer. This particular aspect of the validity process is discussed in the next chapter.

SUMMARY

What is apparent from this examination of the different perspectives of externalism and internalism is that we have at least two different ways to conceptualize the relationship of the investigator to what is investigated. The externalist position maintains that social reality is an existent reality—external to and independent of us. The mind, or the investigator and the process of investigation, is thought of as separate from the world of objects, or what is investigated. Truth in this case means a correspondence between our words and those external things. Truth therefore finds its source in an external reality to which we can appeal, in a methodologically sound manner, to resolve our differences.

From an internalist perspective, social reality is mind-involved, since our minds construct social reality as it is for us at any given time and place. This construction of social reality is based on a constant process of interpretation and reinterpretation of the intentional, meaningful behavior of people—including researchers. Because any description we undertake is dependent on interests and purposes and because social reality is, or is established by, the interpretation, there can be no separation of investigator and investigated. Truth is a matter of social agreement or of coming to "see" the world in a similar way based on similar interests and purposes. Any resolution of differences is (or at least should be) a question of dialogue and justification. Our appeal is not to an external reality, but to what "makes sense" given these various interests, purposes, values, dispositions, and so on. The relationship is one of subject-subject as opposed to the dualism of subject-object.

Finally, it is clear that these two different perspectives lead to different interpretations for one of the most crucial aspects of inquiry. The conceptualization we give to the construct validity of measuring instruments depends greatly on the philosophical temperament one accepts. The empiricist approach to validity, based on an externalist perspective, defines validity in correspondence terms: A valid instrument or inference is one that accurately reflects or measures an independently existing bit of reality. From an interpretive/internalist perspective, validity is a matter of agreement conditioned by time and place. Instruments participate in constructing reality as it is at any given time and place.

CHAPTER V
The Relationship of Facts and Values

Understood in a sufficiently wide sense, the topic of fact and value is a topic which is of concern to everyone. In this respect, it differs sharply from many philosophical questions. Most educated men and women do not feel it obligatory to have an opinion on the question whether there is a real world or only appears to be one, for example. Questions in philosophy of language, epistemology, or even in metaphysics may appear to be questions which, however interesting, are somewhat optional from the point of view of most people's lives. But the question of fact and value is a forced choice question. Any reflective person *has* to have a real opinion upon it (which may or may not be the same as their notional opinion). If the question of fact and value is a forced question for reflective people, one particular answer to that question, the answer that fact and value are totally disjoint realms, that the dichotomy 'statement of fact *or* value judgment' is an absolute one, has assumed the status of a cultural institution. (Putnam, 1981, p. 127)

A second major theme that emerged in Chapter III concerned the relationship of facts and values in the process of social and educational inquiry. This relationship has been conceptualized in basically three different ways. First, there is the position most particularly associated with a logical positivist logic of justification and the related behaviorist procedures for inquiry. This approach accepts what Thomas (1979) calls a "radical heterogeneity of fact and value" (p. 118). The realm of "what is," which is responsive to our objective or cognitive side, is seen as quite separate from the realm of "what should be," which is responsive to our subjective side. Social and educational researchers, at least when acting in a professional capacity, must confine themselves to dealing at the level of what is. Given the proper application of the proper procedures, factual statements (i.e., statements expressed in a neutral or scientific language that have a determinate truth status) can be made at this level. Even though this idea of a radical separation is now explicitly argued with decreasing frequency, it is still at least implicitly a part of the logic of justification employed by many inquirers of a strongly empiricist persuasion.

The other two positions reject the notion of radical heterogeneity and hold that values are a part of the process of social inquiry. After this initial agreement, however, they very significantly part company. One position advances the idea that social and educational inquiry is inevitably normative—that such inquiry is in its very essence a normative process. From this perspective, it is not possible to draw a line of separation between where the object under study "leaves off and where we begin" (Bellah, 1981, p. 5). "Social facts" do not and cannot exist apart from values, since the latter act to determine what are to count as the former. Because the process of inquiry cannot be divorced from the normative commitments of the inquirers, advocates of this position often hold that social inquiry is better thought of as "moral inquiry." This perspective on the issue finds its adherents among many, but not all, inquirers of an interpretive persuasion.

The third position is one that is accepted by most empiricist inquirers and by some inquirers of an interpretive persuasion. In this instance the basic idea is that even though values enter into the inquiry process, the process can still be considered objective (as the term is defined within an empiricist perspective). A number of arguments have been made in defense of this contention. For example, a common line of reasoning in this regard holds that although a researcher's values determine what problems he or she considers important for study, these values can and should be prevented from influencing the solutions to problems (Kaplan, 1964, pp. 370–397). Or, in another example, it is often argued that even though values are a part of social inquiry, an explicit recognition by the researcher of his or her own values will allow for objectivity (Myrdal, 1944, pp. 1035–1064; 1958).

The discussion of these three different conceptualizations of the relationship of facts and values is the principal focus of this chapter. However, before we turn to this topic, it will be helpful to review the logic behind the separation of *is* from *ought* and then to examine briefly the most important and famous argument of all on the separation of facts and values—the one advanced by Weber.

THE ORIGIN OF THE ISSUE—THE LOGICAL SEPARATION OF *IS/OUGHT*

The issue of the relationship of facts and values can best be understood if one has a prior understanding of the logical separation, which became firmly established only in the last century, between the realm of what is and the realm of what should be. A simple example will illustrate what is involved with this logical separation. In the 1950s J. Robert Oppenheimer, in reflecting on his role as director of the Manhattan Project, voiced concern that he was responsible for the deaths of so many people killed by the first atomic bombs. Given a "scientific" and, for that matter, a commonsense approach to this situation, two separate questions can be asked: *Did* Oppenheimer feel guilty about his role in the project? and, *Should* he have felt guilty about his role in the project?

To find an answer to the first question, which is a "what is" question, one can review Oppenheimer's public and private writings, interviews he may have granted, and so on. To the extent that a specific instance is found in which he said, "I feel guilty," one can conclude in a definitive way (that is, make a statement with definitive truth status, verified by observation) that "Yes, he felt guilty." The answer to the second question, in contrast, depends on one's response to a different type of evidence. If someone says that Oppenheimer should have felt guilty, can this contention be supported by referring to his statement that he felt guilty? Logically this is not possible, since whether he should or should not have felt guilty cannot be logically derived from the question of whether he did or did not feel guilty. Put in more general terms, the point of logic here is that one cannot deductively arrive at a conclusion as to how people should feel or behave based on how they actually feel or behave. The two realms of *is* and *ought* stand (as far as logic is concerned) on either side of an "unbridgeable gulf." Thus, any answer given the "should" question, at least in this case, must involve factors such as a discussion of Western cultural traditions and Judeo-Christian ethics.

The reason for this unbridgeable gulf is that we have come to accept certain rules in the area of deductive logic, the most important of which is that nothing can be added to the meaning of a proposition—one can merely make explicit what the proposition implies. Let us consider why the following example violates this rule.

1. All members of a society profit from public schooling.
2. Hence, all ought to support public schooling.

Even though the conclusion may well seem to follow from the premise, this is not the case. Since the premise is in the *is* form and the conclusion is in the *ought* form, the latter, instead of only making explicit what is implied in the premise, actually adds meaning to it. As another example more clearly demonstrates, what one does and what one should do can be quite different things—at least logically.

1. Teachers who physically beat their students get them to learn more.
2. Hence, teachers should physically beat their students.

Even if the premise were true, most of us would find it difficult to accept the second statement as a logical conclusion. In this case, and in all others with an *is* premise and an *ought* conclusion, it is clear that the conclusion contains more than can be deduced from the premise.

Historically, this logical separation of *is/ought* did not become firmly established until well into the 19th century. As long as agreed-upon premises in the *ought* form were available, as derived from religious revelation in particular, the fusion of *is* and *ought* posed no significant problem. Only when an empiricist approach to knowledge began to take hold, as discussed in Chapter III, and inductive reasoning began to dominate was it possible to consider restricting *is* questions to one side of a line of separation and *ought* questions to the other side. As Brecht (1959) put it:

> Only when in the seventeenth and eighteenth centuries religion and science began to separate, when the scientific capabilities of intuitive reason were critically examined, when consequently the afflux of first principles or premises in Ought-form was petering out, and scholars could turn only to inductive reasoning for help, only then was the time ripe for the emergence of a maxim that insisted on the strict distinction between Is and Ought all across the board of science and that meant also in the process of inductive reasoning. (p. 200)

As with other major changes in the development of ideas throughout history, this maxim, as Brecht (1959, pp. 191–200) further notes, did not seize the "collective intellect" all at once. Even though various philosophers, such as Kant and Mill, had made a tentative separation of *is* and *ought*, it was not until well into the last century that the distinction became firmly established. Among the first to distinguish between the two elements, particularly as far as the development of social inquiry is concerned, were Simmel and Rickert. Both of them argued strongly that an examination of what is (the province of science) cannot set norms or tell us what we ought to do. Simmel (cited in Brecht) bluntly captured the thrust of their arguments when he said that the scientist must "sever the scientific task, which is merely to state empirical and hypothetical realities impartially, from the normative one, which is to mold reality practically, and that means aiways onesidedly" (p. 217). These points subsequently became so well established that Weber, writing only a few years later, felt no need to discuss at any length the logical status of *is/ought*.

He was able to accept this logical separation as virtually a given and directly focus on the relationship of facts and values within the process of social investigation.

WEBER—THE SEPARATION OF FACTS AND VALUES

No serious examination of the relationship of facts and values within social and educational inquiry can be made without referring to the work of Weber. In 1904 (1949), he published a major article on this topic entitled "Objectivity in Social Science and Social Policy." This article, which was written to describe the editorial policy of a journal (*Archiv für Sozialwissenschaft und Sozialpolitik*) of which he had assumed coeditorship, has been so influential that an extended examination of it is required.

One of the main purposes of the *Archiv*, Weber (1949) said in the article, was to educate about, and provide criticism of, practical social problems and social policy. This task was to be undertaken in a scientific manner, or with the use of the empirical method. He then asked whether the stated purposes and method were compatible. In the following questions he revealed his line of thought in this regard:

> What has been the meaning of the value-judgments found in the pages of the *Archiv* regarding legislative and administrative measures . . . ? What are the standards governing these judgments? What is the validity of the value-judgments which are uttered by the critic, for instance, or on which a writer recommending a policy founds his arguments for that policy? In what sense, if the criterion of scientific knowledge is to be found in the "objective" validity of its results, has he remained within the sphere of *scientific* discussion? (pp. 50–51)

After posing these questions, Weber (1949) then moved to a brief discussion of the logical fusion of *is* and *ought* (although with a slightly different terminology than is employed above) and how the development of a distinction between the two realms had been hampered by the ideas of natural law and of an evolutionary principle. In the first case, what was considered normatively right was thought to be identical with the "immutably existent," and in the second instance, it was considered identical with the "inevitably emergent" (pp. 51–52). Weber, drawing from the work of Simmel, Rickert, and others, dismissed this fusion and made a distinction between what he called existential knowledge, or knowledge of what is, and normative knowledge, or knowledge of what should be. Given this separation, he then stated his major premise: "It can never be the task of an empirical science to provide binding norms and ideals from which directives for immediate practical activity can be derived" (p. 52).

Weber (1949) added a very important qualification that must be clearly understood. The issue was not that social science must abstain completely from value judgments or that values could never be a part of any scientific discussion. Rather, Weber's concern was to examine how social science could deal with such judgments. As he put it, "it is certainly not that value-judgments are to be withdrawn from scientific discussion in general simply because in the last analysis they rest on certain ideals and are therefore 'subjective' in origin" (p. 52). On the contrary, the real problem, he said, is "the meaning and purpose of the scientific criticism of ideals and value-judgments" (p. 52).

To make sense of this question, Weber (1949) introduced the idea of the difference between means and ends. He said that ultimately we want something either for its own sake or because we see it as the means by which we can obtain something else that is more highly desired. In the second instance, scientific analysis becomes important and the proper relationship of such an analysis to value judgments, at least from Weber's point of view, can be clearly seen.

> The question of the appropriateness of the means for achieving a given end is undoubtedly accessible to scientific analysis. Inasmuch as we are able to determine (within the present limits of our knowledge) which means for the achievement of a proposed end are appropriate and inappropriate, we can in this way estimate the chances of attaining a certain end by certain available means. In this way we can indirectly criticize the setting of the end itself as practically meaningful (on the basis of the existing historical situation) or as meaningless with reference to existing conditions. (pp. 52–53)

An example will help clarify Weber's reasoning on the difference between means and ends. Suppose one adopts, in the standard *ought* form, the following rule of conduct: All teachers should treat each child as an individual. Whether or not this is an end that all teachers should strive for cannot be directly answered through scientific analysis. Taken strictly in terms of a goal, any judgment here is a choice between competing values, a choice that science cannot directly make for us. What science can do, however, is to determine the means appropriate for achieving a goal once it has been chosen. In other words, if one's goal is to treat children as individuals, a scientific analysis can instruct one on how to behave interpersonally, how to structure a classroom, and so on to reach that goal. Through an analysis of various possible patterns of interaction in classrooms, the question of means appropriate to the end can be examined. This type of analysis might even lead to the conclusion that because of the nature of classroom life (Weber's "existing conditions"), there are no means available to reach the chosen end.

Weber (1949) also argued that there are three other ways, in addition to helping us find the appropriate means for reaching a goal, in which science can deal with questions of values. First, scientific analysis can help a person realize that to take a particular action (or to take no action, for that matter) implies that one accepts certain values and rejects others; the cost of striving for a particular desired end is the loss of other values. Second, it can give people an "insight into the significance of the desired object" (p. 53), thereby increasing our ability to understand rationally the ideals for which we strive. Finally, it can certainly analyze, particularly in terms of internal consistency, the ideals that we think important to us. The crucial point is that science can clarify the basic premises from which a person derives his or her desired ends.

Even though Weber (1949) thought that a scientific approach can assist us in various ways in the area of values, he did not believe that science can apply the results of such analyses. He held that human dignity lies in the fact that people are able to ponder and choose from among values according to how they view the world and according to their own conscience: "An empirical science cannot tell anyone what he *should* do—but rather what he *can* do—and under certain circumstances—what he wishes to do" (p. 54).

Up to this point Weber's arguments on facts and values seem clear enough. The definitive distinction Weber accepts between the two sides makes it easy to understand why he is often referred to as the father of value-free social science. However, to leave Weber at this point would be to oversimplify. Some of his other thoughts are not only more complex than is readily apparent, but are very possibly contradictory.

In discussing the importance of values in our lives, Weber (1949) said, "Certainly the dignity of the 'personality' lies in the fact that for it there exist values about which it organizes its life" (p. 55). A variation on this theme is stated in more universal terms in the following quotation:

> The fate of an epoch which has eaten of the tree of knowledge is that it must know that we cannot learn the *meaning* for the world from the results of its analysis, be it ever so perfect; it must rather be in a position to create the meaning itself. It must recognize that general views of life and the universe can never be the products of an increasing empirical knowledge, and that the highest ideals, which move us most forcefully, are always formed in the struggle with other ideals which are just as sacred to others as ours are to us. (p. 57)

These quotations, and the earlier ones about values as a part of scientific discussions, indicate that Weber wanted to emphasize that people (including social scientists) are much more than simply "scientific" beings. For Weber, our ideals, or our values—not the accumulation of empirical knowledge—were what gave meaning to our lives.

What do these views on the importance of values mean for the social scientist? As noted in Chapter III, Weber (1949) accepted that values determine, or are inherent in, the social inquirer's choice of what to study: "Those highest 'values' underlying the practical interest are and always will be decisively significant in determining the focus of attention of analytical activity in the sphere of the cultural sciences" (p. 58). In other words, social scientists will only study something to which they attribute cultural significance. More important, Weber said that one must accept that "all knowledge of cultural reality . . . is always knowledge from *particular points of view*" (p. 81). A conservative interpretation of this statement is that Weber did not find the line between facts and values to be as distinct as some of his earlier comments seem to indicate. One might even interpret this and other comments to imply that there can be no facts without values—thereby very much blurring any distinction between the two sides.

At any rate, values are, at least at the point of problem selection, part of the process of social scientific inquiry. Weber (1949) also acknowledged the fact that he could not "deny to . . . contributors the possibility of expressing in value-judgments the ideals which motivate them" (p. 59). How, then, can we determine when we have "crossed over" from fact to value or from an analysis untainted by values to one of evaluation? Weber said that two fundamental imperatives must be followed in this regard.

First, social scientists must keep both themselves and others informed as to their own standards for judging reality—standards from which their value judgments are derived. Second, "it should be constantly made clear to the readers (and—again we say it—above all to oneself!) exactly at what point the scientific investigator becomes silent and the evaluating and acting person begins to speak" (p. 60). He believed the confusion of these two aspects was both common and very damaging to scientific work. However, it must be noted that his arguments were directed at the muddling of the two sides and not against a straightforward introduction of the social scientist's own ideals—at least at the proper point—into the discussion. Ultimately, for Weber, even though values are essential for asking the questions, the analysis—if properly conducted by an investigator who is openly responsible and sufficiently self-aware to remain detached—can be scientific and result in "a universally valid answer to a question which is itself inspired by a passionate interest" (Aron, 1967, p. 196).

One other point about Weber's work, discussed in Chapter III, must be repeated here. His discussion of the possibility of factual answers to value-charged questions must be understood within the context of his theory of history. As will be recalled, Weber held that the capitalist stage of Western civilization had inevitably brought with it the dominance of the ultimate value of rational-instrumental thought and action. In other words, the "ends" in his "ends-means" distinction would no longer be as diverse as they once had been. All other values had been or were being pushed into the background by the ultimate, universal value of technically oriented, rational, and instrumental human activity. Thus, for Weber, "the prevalance of this unique type of human action has made an objective social science a realistic possibility" (Bauman, 1978, p. 75). In other words, the ends are in place, the means can be empirically analyzed, and facts can be held separate from values.

At this point it is important to note that some people hold that Weber was unable to sustain his position either conceptually or in terms of his own studies. In the first instance, Simey (1969, pp. 69–87), for example, has noted that Weber was unable to convincingly establish a middle ground between the subjectivism of interpretation and the objectivism of empiricism. In the second case, Strauss (1953, pp. 52–59) has pointed out that Weber employed numerous value-laden terms, such as *laxity* and *absolutely unartistic* without specifically recognizing that he had "crossed over" to the side of making value judgments. The point is, according to Strauss, that given Weber's position, these terms cannot be included in the scientific analysis side of the discussion. More recently, Bellah (1981, pp. 7–10), arguing in a similar vein, said that Weber's ethical commitments not only determined the substantive questions he asked, but also influenced his analysis from beginning to end, making it impossible to know where Weber's subject matter left off and where Weber began. From Bellah's point of view, Weber could not abide by his fundamental imperative concerning the separation of facts and values.

The ideas Weber put forth in the *Archiv* article, and less directly in other writings (1946a, 1946b), have been very important to our thinking about the fact-value issue. That his thinking on this topic may be contradictory in some places is likely; that it is complex is certain. In fact, his work is so complex and broad in sweep that different interpretations of it are possible. For example, at one level he can be read as an advocate of a distinct separation between facts and values. He viewed the investigative process as scientific to the extent that investigators were able to separate their investigative side from their evaluative side. Yet, at another level, this separation appears much less distinct in that he saw values as deeply involved in, if nothing else, the selection of problems. Some of his comments could easily lead one to conclude that facts and values do not at all comprise distinct realms.

In any event, advocates of each of the three conceptualizations of the relationship of facts and values—distinct separation, partial separation, and inseparability—have been able to draw in varying degrees on Weber's work to support their positions. The discussion must now turn to these three conceptualizations and to how they are related to the different perspectives on social and educational inquiry.

DISTINCT SEPARATION—INQUIRY AS VALUE-FREE

Of the three basic conceptualizations of the relationship of facts and values, the one that holds that the two realms are or can be distinctly separate (a radical heterogeneity), thereby allowing inquiry to be completely value-free, is the least able to withstand serious scrutiny. Yet, this weakness notwithstanding, the idea that there can be a dichotomy of "either statement of fact *or* value judgment" has had a strong influence on the nature of inquiry and, for that matter, on our everyday thinking. As Putnam (1981) noted, this idea "has assumed the status of a cultural institution" (p. 127).

At a more philosophical level, the fate of this idea of a strict fact-value separation has been tied to that school of thought known as logical positivism. When the latter appeared convincing, the dichotomy seemed very reasonable; but as logical positivism suffered a very serious decline, so too did the argument for a distinct separation. At the level of the practicing researcher, any continued allegiance given to such a separation owes a good deal to the influence of behaviorism. This approach is based on a rejection of the mental, a focus only on observable behavior, and the use of methods that are purely objective (B. MacKenzie, 1977, refers to the latter as "methodological objectivism"). This combination of conditions held out to investigators the possibility that their work could stand completely apart from value considerations.

Logical positivism was most influential as a philosophy of science from the 1920s to the 1950s. For the most part, it arose as an attempt to refine the ideas that scientific authority must be based on empirical purity and logical reasoning and that there was a unity of all sciences. The crucial feature of logical positivism was that two elements—our perceptions and logical reasoning—were all that was required for science and for the possibility of obtaining genuine knowledge. The former element meant that scientific activity could only be based on what was available to our senses. The latter one required that science must be principally inductive.

Given these points, logical positivism set forth three major injunctions. First, science was to operate with a strictly physicalist or behaviorist language and method. Anything to do with intentions, purposes, and introspection was pushed aside in favor of the observation and description of physical movement. Second, all metaphysical terms (which were considered terms of transcendental speculation) were to be eliminated from science. Third, any statement that was not verifiable empirically was not only unscientific, but meaningless. In other words, unless a statement could be expressed in physicalist terms such that it could be empirically verified, it was considered, at least by the more aggressive logical positivists, as nonsense. Under this stricture a statement such as "I acted because in the depths of my soul I felt it was the right thing to do" is not only unverifiable empirically (i.e., it cannot be judged via observation as true or false), but it is also cognitively meaningless.

By advocating these points as fundamental, logical positivism was making the sharpest possible distinction between the realms of facts and values. The basis for this distinction was that factual statements, formulated of course in a physicalist or behaviorist language, addressed publicly observable events and were thereby subject to verification via observation, measurement, and empirical analysis. Value-laden statements, those expressing the goodness, badness, and so on of things, were not susceptible to such verification. Since *verifiable* was considered equivalent to *cognitively meaningful*, value judgments could not claim this latter status and were consigned to the level of emotive expressions. Value judgments had absolutely no place at all in scientific activities, and likewise scientific analysis had nothing to say about value judgments. For logical positivism, the gap between what we do and what we should do was unbridgeable.

Shortly after these ideas were proposed, they began to undergo modification in a number of areas. For example, the requirement of verifiability was narrowed to include only the logical possibility of verification, and not necessarily actual empirical verification. Later, when it was accepted that no proposition could be completely verified, the less rigorous idea of testability, or confirmability, was substituted. By the 1950s, this kind of back-pedaling notwithstanding, the movement began to "break-up and disappear as a recognizable philosophical tendency" (Putnam, 1981, p. 184). The reasons for this breakup, and the arguments directed against logical positivism, were many and varied. The most telling point was that the criterion posed by logical positivism—that cognitive meaning could only be associated with what was verifiable (in one form or another) by empirical means—was self-refuting. In other words, the criterion itself was not empirically verifiable. Many logical positivists recognized this point and attempted to avoid its implications by arguing that the criterion was only a proposal, but their arguments did little to prevent the decline of the movement.

Of direct interest to the fact-value issue is that logical positivism was unable to resolve the problem of developing and employing a physical-ist or behaviorist language. To hold facts separate from values, one must express the former in behaviorist language, whereas the latter would be expressed in the abstract terms of "good," "bad," and so on. The prob-lem was (and is) that advocates of this perspective were not able to de-velop such a language. As Rorty (1979) put it, "We have not *got* a lan-guage which will serve as a permanent neutral matrix for formulating all good explanatory hypotheses, and we have not got the foggiest notion of how to get one" (pp. 348–349).

The problems associated with a physicalist language are most clearly evident when one attempts to describe social situations. A simple exam-ple will illustrate these problems. Suppose an investigator said, "The teacher was insensitive (acted as such) to the needs of the child." Leav-ing aside the problem that *needs* is a fuzzy concept at best, what is one to make of the term *insensitive*? Is it a purely descriptive term that indicates a factual state of affairs and that has no connotation of how teachers should or should not act? Clearly, a good argument can be made that the expression has a value or evaluative aspect to it. An attempt to define *sensitivity*, if the term is to have any descriptive force at all, must be made in relation to a conceptual scheme that inevitably includes consid-erations of what is good and bad behavior for teachers. If this is so, then a term will "describe," or give a different "fact," depending on the con-ceptual scheme one possesses; one has access to the term and what it purports to describe only through a framework of values. Thus, insensi-tivity as a factual state of affairs presupposes values, and different values may lead to different factual states of affairs.

In response to this point, advocates of a strict fact-value distinction might argue that they recognize the problem and would not use the term. Many terms become "value-contaminated" through their use in ordinary discourse and must therefore be avoided. This argument, how-ever, is not thought to be a very convincing one. First, even the strictest logical positivists cannot avoid using such terms in their daily interac-tions. One simply cannot describe human social life as nothing more than the movement of physical bodies through time and space. Second, even if such descriptions could be produced, we would consider them inadequate. To remain at the level of "the teacher moved back two paces as the child approached from the left" tells us nothing of serious impor-tance about teachers and students. Banning the use of terms such as *in-*

sensitive, considerate, and *aggressive* when they are called for, given one's conceptual framework, would impoverish description—at least the describer could be accused of being superficial and "insensitive" to the situation (Putnam, 1981, pp. 138–139).

These kinds of terms demonstrate how unclear the fact-value distinction is once we look at it in regard to real-life and real-language situations. The sharp distinction of fact and value is very difficult to uphold when the "facts" are on the order of "the teacher was insensitive" or "the child was considerate." These statements are not framed in a strictly physicalist or behaviorist language, and no one seems to know how they ever could be translated into such a language. The factual status of the terms contained in them depends on values or a conceptual scheme.

Arguments such as these have contributed to the breakup of logical positivism, the disaffection with behaviorism among researchers, and the much decreased allegiance to the idea that facts can be held distinctly separate from values. Many researchers, as a result, have been drawn to a position that acknowledges the role of values but still maintains that research can be objective.

PARTIAL SEPARATION—VALUES ENTER IN BUT INQUIRY IS STILL OBJECTIVE

In contrast to the position that social and educational inquiry can be based on a distinct separation of facts and values is the position that accepts values as a part of the process of investigation. This acceptance notwithstanding, however, advocates of this approach do not concede that social inquiry is thereby unscientific. On the contrary, they believe that values have, or can be given, an objective basis. To discuss this position, we must examine the work of one of its most distinguished exponents—Kaplan (1964, see especially pp. 370–386). His arguments on this topic, which are frequently cited by various empiricist and some interpretive inquirers, deserve an extended review.

Kaplan (1964) dismisses any attempt to make a radical separation between facts and values as undesirable, if not impossible. He said the idea that science must take a "hands-off" attitude toward values eliminates the possibility of affirming values through science and, hence, the possibility of enriching our lives through knowledge and experience (p. 371). His principal thesis is that

> not all value concerns are unscientific, that indeed some of them are called for by the scientific enterprise itself, and that those which run counter to

scientific ideals can be brought under control—even by the sciences most deeply implicated in the value process. (p. 373)

In other words, even though the introduction of values into the inquiry process can interfere with its scientific character in many ways, values can enter in, given appropriate controls, in ways that will prevent their interference.

The major threat values pose to the scientific nature of inquiry is the possibility of provoking bias. As Kaplan (1964) defined the term, *bias* means an "adherence to values of such a kind or in such a way as to interfere with scientific objectivity" (p. 373). Bias, for example, would be evident in any situation in which one believes something to be true solely on the basis of one's values. In this instance, the motivation to believe something results from factors outside the actual process of inquiry rather than from what the inquiry, per se, tells us.

In developing this point, Kaplan (1964) made an important distinction between motives and the purposes of inquiry (and of the inquirer). Motives involve the relationship of the inquiry/inquirer to that general flow of events of which they are a part. Motives may include the inquirer's feelings of loyalty, desires for personal gain, the "spirit of the times," and so on. Purposes, by contrast, are related to particular problems of interest and can involve a series of "internal" matters such as the extent to which the event is subject to certain laws or how well the explanation covers similar cases. Based on this division, bias is a problem of the "intrusion of motives, which are extra-scientific, on the fulfillment of scientific purposes" (p. 374).

Kaplan (1964) pointed out, however, that simply because social scientists have motives, which they must have because they are human beings, does not mean bias is automatically present. The crucial factor is how the study is conducted: "Everything depends on the conduct of the inquiry, on the way in which we arrive at our conclusions" (p. 375). To Kaplan, this means not only adherence to proper procedures, but also a commitment on the part of the individual inquirer in particular and the profession in general to maintain an "open mind" and to resist bias wherever it might be encountered. Although bias cannot be eliminated, it can in this way be taken into account and canceled out. The inquirer and the process of inquiry can thus avoid arriving at conclusions prior to and/or independent of the evidence.

Can values be a part of the scientific process in ways that do not result in bias? Kaplan posed this question and discussed a number of possibilities. First, values can enter into the inquiry process by being the subject matter of scientific investigation. Bias need not be involved here, since the scientific questions raised can be confined to the presence or absence of particular values in any given situation and not to the worth or validity of those values. This crucial distinction was taken from the work of E. Nagel (1961), who differentiated between "characterizing value judgments" and "appraising value judgments" (pp. 494–493). The former means to affirm what particular values are held or not held (and to what extent) by the subjects of an inquiry, whereas the latter process involves judging whether those particular values are good or bad. Both Kaplan and Nagel argue that one can characterize or describe without engaging in evaluating or appraising. As Kaplan (1964) put it, "We can judge that something conforms to a certain standard without making *that* standard our own, even though the judgment may presuppose our own standards of what conformity is" (p. 378). Although recognizing that this distinction is often a difficult one to make because of the normative ambiguity of the language of social science, Kaplan maintains that it is one that must and can be made.

The second way that values enter into the scientific process is that they constitute the ethics of the profession. In this sense they do not provoke bias, but actually operate to work against it, if not eliminate it. To be a scientist is to make certain value commitments. For Kaplan (1964), science is a calling, as opposed to an occupation, which means that one must make an emotional investment in it. This investment requires that the scientist have a passion for the truth: "The scientific habit of mind is one dominated by the reality principle, by the determination to live in the world as it is and not as we might fantasy it" (p. 380). More specifically, the scientist must submit to the facts and accept whatever judgment they may bring. The ethics of this calling demand that one resist those "external" considerations that can lead to bias. Although Kaplan admits this is an ideal version of scientific behavior, he believes it is nonetheless a goal toward which scientists, if they are truly scientists, must strive. Kaplan also commented on the metaprofessional ethic, which encompasses not only the actual conduct of inquiry, but also the context of those pursuits. This ethic requires an adherence to the values of freedom of inquiry and expression: Scientists must attempt to preserve the conditions under which science can flourish. As Kaplan summarized this point, "that a scientist has values does not of itself imply that he is therefore biased; it may mean just the contrary" (p. 381).

As was noted in the discussion of Weber, values also enter into science as the basis for the selection of problems. Kaplan (1964) very much agrees that a scientist selects problems for a reason(s) and that the reason(s) is inevitably related to that scientist's values. However, simply because problem choice is not based solely on some sort of "advancement of knowledge" consideration does not automatically mean that bias is involved. The distinction between choosing a problem and prejudging its solution is again, for him, a valid one to make. Thus, "values make for bias, not when they dictate problems, but when they prejudge solutions" (p. 382).

In addition to the three ways in which values can enter the investigative process without provoking bias, Kaplan also discussed the relationship of values to meaning and of facts to values. Both topics are important in their own right and also because the arguments advanced in this discussion provide crucial support for his previous analysis. Kaplan accepts that values are determinants of the meanings given to events and phenomena. The potential danger to science in this regard is that the meaning of something will be based on how any particular observer or interpreter happens to conceive of it. Different values result in different meanings, and this opens the door to an "endless subjectivity" that must be unacceptable to the scientific process. His solution to this problem is to emphasize that the meaning of an act must be examined in terms of the values of the actor and of those who interact with him or her. In other words, meaning depends on the subject's values, not on those of the inquirer. Scientists can study, in an objective manner (as with values as subject matter), the values people hold and how these values relate to the meanings people give to their actions and activities. To do so, however, does not require appraisal on the part of the investigator.

In his discussion of the relationship of facts and values, Kaplan (1964) posed what he called the "central issue in the question of whether science ought to be, or can be, value-free" (p. 384). This issue centers around the idea that if values enter into the "determination of what constitutes a *fact*" (p. 384), then it may be inappropriate to hold that a realm of facts exists separate from a realm of values. If such a distinction is impossible to maintain, then the idea that social inquiry is not objective, but very much normative, may make more sense.

The critical question here is whether values are important only for problem selection or whether they are inevitably entangled with any conclusions an investigator reaches. Kaplan (1964) put this point as follows: "What is at stake here is the role of values, not in our decision where to look but in our conclusions as to what we have seen" (p. 384). The basis for this concern is that he has accepted the premise that the facts do not speak for themselves and the corollary that "data are the product of a process of interpretation" (p. 385). This position entails the obvious danger that there may be no such thing as facts per se—things that the scientist must be "humble before . . . submitting his will to their decision" (p. 380). And if there are not independent facts, then what we call "facts" might be what anyone wants them to be, given his or her particular values. There is the possibility of an endless "subjectivity"—a situation in which one interpretation vies with others and there are no independently existing facts to which one may appeal to separate correct from incorrect interpretations.

Kaplan's (1964) response to this dilemma is contained in some of his earlier comments. Accepting the general thrust of an externalist position, he said, as previously quoted, "the scientific habit of mind is one dominated by the reality principle, by the determination to live in the world as it is and not as we might fantasy it" (p. 380). This implies a belief in a realm of facts external to and independent of any individual and/or collective interest or purpose. Even though the facts do not speak for themselves, they must be listened to, and even though data require interpretation, "there is some sense in which the materials for the process are 'given' " (p. 385). In other words, a realm of facts exists that, although dependent on our values in one sense, is independent of our values in another sense. Kaplan summarized this position as follows:

> The most basic point, perhaps, is that even though values are not *sufficient* to establish facts it does not follow that they are therefore not *necessary*. The ultimate empiricism on which science rests consists in this, that thinking something is so does not make it so. (p. 386)

In summary, advocates of this position start from the premise that it is both undesirable and impossible to exclude values from the process of inquiry. They agree with Myrdal (1944) that such an attempt would constitute a "hopeless and misdirected venture" (p. 1043). Accordingly, the task is to give values an objective basis or objective grounding. In this way, science can include values, yet remain free of that bias or subjectivity that would distort inquiry. For Kaplan (1964), and those who find his arguments persuasive, the principal issue of methodology is not whether values enter into the inquiry process, but which values enter in and how our values can be empirically grounded.

THE INSEPARABILITY OF VALUES AND FACTS

For advocates of this third position any separation of facts from values is not only impossible to maintain, but it would be undesirable even if it could be made. In the first instance, the claim is that facts are presupposed by values or that there can be no facts without values. In the second instance, the argument is that values, which for empiricist inquiry pose a threat to be controlled for, are actually the very substance of interpretive inquiry.

To examine the contention that facts and values cannot be held separate, let us return for a moment to one of the major points made by Kaplan (1964). Even though Kaplan holds that values are a part of the inquiry process, he still maintains the idea of a realm of facts as distinct from a realm of values. When he said that values enter into what constitutes a fact, he did not mean they "completely or totally constitute it." He was thereby able to claim that even though facts do not speak for themselves, they must be listened to, and that even though data require interpretation, some sense of "givenness" is involved. The problem with Kaplan's position, at least as advocates of fact-value inseparability would argue, is that one cannot specify at what point the facts stop being "heard," or their "givenness" ends and the inquirer's interpretation begins. Putnam (1981) succinctly captured the essence of this position when he noted that the "distinction is at the very best hopelessly fuzzy because factual statements themselves, and the practices of scientific inquiry upon which we rely to decide what is and is not a fact, presuppose values" (p. 128).

To hold that a distinction exists between facts and values requires one to accept, at least to some degree, such externalist assumptions as reality as mind-independent and truth as correspondence—assumptions that are obviously unacceptable to internalists. For externalists, a statement of fact is, by definition, a statement of how something really is—independent of our interests in or dispositions about that something. To believe that it is possible to have statements of fact, one must hold that things exist in and of themselves and accordingly can be known in that way (the "givenness" of Kaplan). Only to the extent that we assume we are able to discover an independently existing reality and describe it in an appropriately neutral or nonevaluative language can we make sense of a distinction between facts and values. To paraphrase Rorty (1979, p. 364), only if we hold to the idea that an independent reality exists that can be discussed in a value-neutral vocabulary, does the idea that we can be "knowers of facts," on the one side, separate from "choosers of values," on the other, look plausible.

Internalists make a series of assumptions, as previously noted, that are incompatible with the prospect of a fact-value distinction: social reality as mind-constructed; truth as socially and historically conditioned agreement. The internalist position further holds that we cannot adopt a God's eye point of view (Putnam, 1981, p. 50) and the needed value-neutral language with which to elaborate it. On the contrary, all we can have are the various points of view that depend on the values and interests of the various people from whom they issue. Any language employed to discuss these particular points of view must be laden with the values and interests of the describer(s). Values quite simply determine and are ultimately entwined with what we hold to be statements of fact and even with what is to count as a fact. Since we cannot "get outside" of ourselves or our own particular positions in the world to undertake neutral description, there is therefore little prospect that the facts of a case can be divorced from the values of that case. These points can be elaborated and clarified with a series of examples.

Putnam's (1981, pp. 139–141) example of a fictitious group, the super-Benthamites, is a good place to begin in order to point out the differences between the two perspectives. This example focuses on whether people who agree on all of the facts can still disagree on values or if their disagreement on values means that their description of the facts must also be different. In other words, what is to count as a fact presupposes values.

Imagine the super-Benthamites are a group of people who believe that one should always act to maximize the greatest happiness of the greatest number. In any situation in which they know this will result (assume they are very good at predicting the consequences of their actions), they will even undertake acts we would find barbarous, such as torturing people. To us, accordingly, the morality of the super-Benthamites is unattractive and may even be considered warped.

Superficially this seems to be a situation in which both sides can agree in the cognitive area of facts but not in the noncognitive area of values. Let us suppose, however, that the super-Benthamites realize that their goal of greatest happiness for the greatest number requires them to tell lies on occasion and that doing so is not considered dishonest in any pejorative sense of the term. Over time the term *honest*, even as used by them in a *descriptive* way, would come to have a rather different meaning for them than it does for us. To say "John is an honest person" or "that was an honest act" would mean one thing to them and possibly quite another to us. Their vocabulary for describing the social would simply be quite different from ours.

> In short, it will not be the case that we and the super-Benthamites 'agree on the facts and disagree about values.' In the case of almost all interpersonal situations, the descriptions we give of the facts will be quite different from the description they give of the facts. (Putnam, 1981, p. 141).

The same reasoning can be applied to the classic example of the "good Nazi." Kaplan (1964) employed this example to illustrate the difference between "characterizing judgments" and "appraising judgments." According to Kaplan, we can judge that someone is a good Nazi without believing that being a Nazi is a good thing: "We are saying only that certain characteristics are present in that instance without committing ourselves to whether they are worthy of approval" (p. 378). He also noted that this distinction, although not absolute but relative to context, is one that is both appropriate and sensible to make. However, upon closer examination this seemingly benign distinction brings with it a series of complications—particularly in regard to the idea of "relative to context."

The key assumption here is that fact can be held separate from value. That is, we have one vocabulary to elaborate our values and another, which is neutral-descriptive, for statements of fact. By definition the latter vocabulary must be contextless or free from anyone's particular value dispositions, interests, or purposes—if the fact-value distinction is to seem plausible. Accordingly, to accept this interpretation of the "good Nazi" example as telling, one must hold that a disagreement about values (different contexts) will not influence an agreement on the facts. In other words, value differences about Nazism notwithstanding, a Nazi and an anti-Nazi would be making the same description or presenting the same "facts of the case" when they characterize "X" as a good Nazi. This is really not the case.

When the Nazi states that "X" is a good Nazi, he may well be describing "X" as someone who has energetically contributed to the purification of the race. When the anti-Nazi says that "X" is a good Nazi, he may be stating the fact that "X" has systematically murdered non-Aryans. One person's description of a good Nazi (fact) is not, given different values, the same as the other person's description (fact). This is because the context of values within which the description is undertaken has a direct influence on what is to count as a fact or a factual description. According to this position, one cannot describe without first having—either explicitly, but more likely implicitly—a framework of appraisal. This view obviously contrasts with Kaplan's position that one can undertake to characterize a situation or activity independent of or separate from a context of values. The point is, from this perspective, all social description of consequence is value-impregnated at all levels— that of the subjects, the investigators, and the readers.

One final example will serve to lend force to this conceptualization of the fact-value issue. Isaiah Berlin (see Bhaskar, 1979, pp. 75–78, for a discussion of this famous example) noted that, among other possibilities, there are at least four ways to characterize or describe what happened in Germany under Nazi rule: (a) the country was depopulated; (b) millions of people died; (c) millions of people were killed; and (d) millions of people were massacred. There is little doubt that all these characterizations describe, at one level or another, the situation. Of the four, the last one, which uses the term *massacre*, is clearly the most value-laden or most evaluative. However, this characterization is also the one that most adequately (in the sense of precision and accuracy) characterizes the situation—at least for those who hold a certain value position in regard to what happened. In fact, for those who find the Nazis' actions deplorable and barbarous, this is the only adequate description of the situation.

Therefore, the adequacy of one's characterization in this case, or in any case of consequence, depends very much on values or on how one appraises that situation. A term like *massacre*, to borrow from Putnam's (1981) analysis of the term *considerate*, is a "very fine example of the way in which the fact/value distinction is hopelessly fuzzy in the real world and in the real language" (p. 139). Characterization and appraisal, fact and value, cannot be neatly separated with the former reserved for our cognitive sides and the latter confined to our normative sides.

One objection, which harkens back to the section on a distinct separation of facts and values, must be noted. One could argue that two people who hold radically different value positions could still agree that the first characterization ("the country was depopulated") describes the situation. Thus, the facts of the case could be held apart from the values of the case. However, this argument fails to take into account the idea of "adequate" description. It is always possible to prise facts away from values if description is reduced to a series of very narrow statements—a good Nazi would only be described in terms of physical movements in time and space—that thereby seem to "bathe in the atmosphere of value-neutrality" (Taylor, 1973, p. 170). However, employing this behaviorist language results in a very shallow and inadequate description. Such depictions, because they are impoverished in terms of substantive meaning, cannot be the basis for social and educational inquiry. That is why the separation of facts and values is considered undesirable by interpretive inquirers. Their point is that social inquiry that accepts such a separation cannot be adequate to its subject matter.

Finally, this section can conclude with an examination of two major points, mentioned in the last section, both of which concern ways to prevent a collapse of the fact-value distinction. First, one way to protect inquiry from this collapse is to accept what might be called a protective concession. As will be recalled, values can enter into the process in the sense that social inquiry presupposes at least one major value—truth. The desire for truth brings with it other related values, such as the integrity of the investigator and the desire to avoid bias. These values do not pose a danger to objectivity but are instead conducive to the ability of social inquiry to engage in an objective examination of the social world. This line of reasoning also includes Kaplan's (1964, pp. 379–381) ideas about science as a "calling" as opposed to an occupation.

As long as truth is defined in a way considered virtually self-evident by its advocates (that is, as a mirroring of an independent reality), this argument appears reasonable enough. If, however, one holds that it is unacceptable to characterize truth in correspondence terms, that truth is a question of agreement based on dialogue among people who hold different interests and values, then the argument that science values truth does not tell us very much of interest. Truth cannot be, in Putnam's (1981, p. 130) terms, the "bottom line"; what is crucial are the criteria one uses for judging truth. Unless one specifies the criteria employed for judging results, for how objectivity is defined, what procedures are thought acceptable for inquiry, and so on, to say "I seek the truth" or "Science values the truth" is to do little more than make a formal statement.

Putnam (1981) has succinctly summarized this line of argument:

> If the notion of comparing our systems of beliefs with unconceptualized reality to see if they match makes no sense, then the claim that science seeks to discover the truth can mean no more than that science seeks to construct a world picture which, in the ideal limit, satisfies criteria of rational acceptability. (p. 130)

However, exactly what is considered rationally acceptable, or what criteria are employed for such judgments, is of course a question of values. The bottom line is this: How we go about constructing the reality of social and educational life depends on what we consider reasonable—which of course means that our constructions are based on our interests and values. In the absence of truth as correspondence, this protective concession does not prevent a thorough penetration of inquiry by values.

The second line of reasoning also accepts that values cannot be held separate from the inquiry process, but then goes on to claim that objectivity is still possible to the extent that inquirers freely and fully admit their values to all concerned. In doing so, both the inquirers and the readers will be "put on guard." This very popular and influential position can be primarily attributed to Myrdal (1944): "There is no other device for excluding biases in social sciences [or any other] than to face the valuations and to introduce them as explicitly stated, specific, and sufficiently concretized value premises" (p. 1043).

This position sounds very reasonable; however, it rests on the premise that one is fully aware of and can precisely state one's values, that values, as a product of the conscious mind, cannot influence in an unconscious way. The idea that one can be fully aware of one's values, that they can be held out for "objective" examination, does not do justice to the complexities of the human mind. Moreover, such a disclosure of values also implies that inquirers can know precisely when they have been rational as opposed to rationalizing. In other words, there would be no difficulty in answering a question such as, Did I interpret the event in that way because that was the way it really happened, or did my values unconsciously creep into the analysis? And, if there were no difficulty, the whole fact-value issue would be meaningless, since objectivity would be self-evident. As Bauman (1978) puts it, "Paradoxically, *a truly objective understanding would be accessible only in conditions which do not require it: which do not posit such an understanding as a problem*" (p. 231; also see Bhaskar, 1979, pp. 70–73, for a similar discussion of this point).

A RETURN TO THE EXAMPLE
OF CONSTRUCT VALIDITY

In the last chapter we discussed how the different perspectives on the relationship of the investigator to what is investigated result in different interpretations of the relationship of the inquirer/instrument to what is measured. Let us now consider a second major relationship—that of the inquirer to the instrument. As was briefly noted, the perspective that holds to a separation of facts and values finds that even though values are important for judgments about the social use of a test, the development of a test is an objective process. On the other hand, the position that regards facts and values as inseparable holds that both the development and use of an instrument depend on the interests, values, and purposes of the people involved. These differences must be examined in order to illustrate some of the more practical consequences of the different stances taken in regard to the relationship of facts and values.

In conventional terms, the process of establishing the validity of a test, because it is an evidential process, must depend on observation. The referent for judging valid instruments or valid interpretations of data must be reality itself and not how one defines or constructs reality given particular interests or values. In other words, even though value considerations are involved with the social use of an instrument, questions of how well it measures an attribute or object relate to our cognitive sides. The process of establishing validity must thus be divorced, or even protected, from the unwarranted intrusion of our normative selves. Instruments are valid if they accurately measure what they are designed to measure—they "see" the world from no particular place within it.

According to this view, investigators are able to separate questions of validity into cognitive and normative through the use of method, or statistical-technical procedures. Adherence to proper method constrains our normative or valuing tendencies and thereby allows us, at least in principle, to develop instruments that will reflect without distortion the object being measured. This is considered possible, since these procedures are thought to stand above or apart from the particular interests of any individual and/or group; they are neutral and nonarbitrary. As such, instruments developed with the proper technical procedures can be seen as products of our objective sides. The results obtained with such tests must be accepted (at least by all "rational" people) at the cognitive level—even though we may disagree about acting on them for normative reasons.

To maintain this balancing act between the cognitive and the normative requires the acceptance of externalist assumptions. Unless one confers upon the social the status of an independently existing reality and holds that facts are separate from values, this separation of cognitive-normative begins to slip out of focus.

An internalist position, which holds that facts are determined by values, will result in a significantly different interpretation of the relationship of the investigator to the instrument. The cognitive-normative division, typified in statements such as "Even though I do not like it, I must accept the facts," or "Even though we disagree about the use of a test, we must agree that it allows for valid inferences," cannot be sustained. Again, such a division requires that one hold that there are independently existing facts to be technical about and that to be technical in this sense is to be objective (God's eye point of view). If one holds, to the contrary, that all descriptions must be undertaken within a context or within a conceptual framework, then the cognitive-normative division becomes an artificial one at best.

The implications of this situation can be seen if one asks, How is it that inquirers come to agree that some tests are valid and others are not? From an internalist perspective, an instrument or inference attains the label valid because the version of reality it participates in constructing is normatively acceptable to those who do the labeling. Agreement about validity results because inquirers happen to share a similar view of the world; that is, they hold similar values or have similar interests and purposes. Ideally, such a shared view results from a process of justification and persuasion within the context of a free and open dialogue; realistically, such agreement may depend on social power arrangements as much as anything else. Either way, the point is that to reject a separation of facts and values is to reject the notion that measuring instruments can be developed objectively or free from normative considerations. Even though the context for decisions concerning instrument development differs from that of decisions regarding instrument use, both types of decisions are normatively based, or presuppose a framework of values.

SUMMARY

The relationship of facts and values has been conceptualized in three ways. The idea of a distinct separation and of inquiry as completely value-free, although a widely held position at one time, is at present the least acceptable and defensible of the three. Even though some inquirers still hold to this position, its credibility has decreased because of loss of interest in logical positivism and the decline of behaviorism and behaviorist methods as a basis for conducting inquiry.

The position that values are a part of the inquiry process but that inquiry can still be objective is the one espoused by empiricists and by some interpretive inquirers. According to this view, even though values pose a constant threat of bias, this threat can be controlled by conducting inquiry in the proper manner—including the adherence of the inquirer to the value of seeking the truth. Ultimately, the central claim here is that one can characterize an event or situation without appraising or evaluating that situation or event.

The position of many interpretive inquirers is that any distinction between facts and values is at best "hopelessly fuzzy." There can be, in other words, no facts without values, and different values can actually lead to different facts. Thus, a solid line of distinction cannot be drawn between fact and value and between characterization and appraisal. Although this is a problem for empiricists—one they attempt to resolve through proper methods—the inseparability of facts and values is the essence of interpretive inquiry. For this reason many people think social and educational inquiry should be thought of as moral inquiry.

CHAPTER VI

The Goal of Social and Educational Inquiry

Two rival perspectives have been dominant in the social sciences. . . . Numerous debates as to the methods and explanatory goals of the social sciences are involved, more or less directly, in these perspectives. But in large measure, the debate between objectivism and subjectivism has centered on the relationship between explanation in social sciences and the models of explanation that have come to dominate the physical sciences. The issue has been, essentially, whether the format of natural science explanation is appropriate for the task of understanding meaningful human behavior. Objectivists, influenced in the main by positivism, have for the most part advocated a unity of scientific method: a methodological monism that considers the 'thing language' of natural science to be applicable to any subject matter. Subjectivists are uniformly hostile to the doctrines of positivism, and argue, primarily, that because of the meaningful character of human actions and products their explanation requires a unique approach, and results in different forms of knowledge. This essentially philosophical dispute has had significant practical consequences, because the conduct of social scientific inquiry as well as its final product have been substantially affected by the orientation of its practitioners. (Rubinstein, 1981, p. 9)

From the empiricist perspective, the goal of inquiry is the scientific explanation and prediction of social and educational phenomena. Such explanation and prediction are based on the idea that given a law and the presence of the appropriate conditions, we can conclude that an event occurred or must occur. This approach is known as the covering-law model of explanation. Crucial to this model is the assumption that inquiry must result in the discovery of laws. Laws are by definition statements of either universal invariant relationships or, as is more common to social and educational inquiry, probabilistic relationships between observable event and properties. Because these laws are stated in a neutral, observational language, they are subject to empirical testing. The development of theory and the use of a theoretical language are also important to this goal of valid explanation. By definition, a theory is a well-developed or systematic set of statements, including laws, that will allow one to explain laws and to give an account of how diverse laws and events are related. Thus, social inquiry succeeds when it discovers laws and then is able to connect abstract theory to laws, with their empirical import, to explain and predict events.

For the interpretive approach, this goal is considered not only inappropriate, but also impossible to achieve, for social and educational inquiry. Social investigation is a matter of attempting to understand the intentional and meaningful behavior of people. Although various reasons have been given for the rejection of the empiricist goal of explanation, one of the most important centers around the idea that the meanings, intentions, and motives of human beings cannot be "treated in the manner of brute data" (Rubinstein, 1981, p. 15). For the human studies, all inquirers can offer are interpretations of the meanings people give to their own behavior and their interactions with others. Moreover, because such meanings can only be read or understood within a context, the process of interpretation/understanding is inevitably hermeneutical. Thus, social and educational inquiry succeeds when it clarifies, through a never-ending process of interpretation, the interpretations of others that were previously unclear.

SCIENTIFIC EXPLANATION

This discussion of scientific explanation must begin by considering the possible meanings given to the term *explanation* in everyday discourse. At this level, explaining something generally involves either making something clear or giving reasons for something. In the first instance, the focus is on the *how* of a situation, and the request is to say something in such a way that it can be understood by others. A child, by saying to his or her parents, "Tell me about tying shoes," is asking about the *how* of that event. In the second instance, the focus is on the *why* of the event: "Why should I tie my shoes?"

Although the meaning of explanation in the scientific sense is very much related to its daily-life meanings, the term does have "special-case" connotations at the scientific level. In other words, scientific explanation has its own special logic beyond the everyday, commonsense level; at the scientific level the principal interest is in the *why* of an event. According to the widely accepted model under consideration here, explanation is a matter of bringing the event to be explained under a general concept or law-like generalization. As Wartofsky (1968) puts it, "An event is explained if it can be subsumed or can be shown to follow inferentially as the consequence of a universal or law-like statement" (p. 248). This point can be clarified by going back to the difference between how and why. To explain how (learn how) is basically a matter of detailing the procedures to be followed. The *how* of tying shoes involves details about making loops and so on. To explain why (learn why) involves the reasons for proceeding one way as opposed to another or the reasons why something is one way as opposed to the many other ways it might be.

The focus on reasons is apparent in the special-case meaning of explanation in the scientific sense: A child, if asked by a friend, "Why did you tie your shoes?" might respond with "My parents told me to." Although this response gives a reason (very likely sufficient to the conversation at hand), it may not be a good reason in the scientific sense. To have force as an explanation in this sense, a reason must be seen within the context of a general premise, such as "children should obey their parents." Whether one agrees with this premise or not, the point is that it allows the event to be explained. Thus, the *why* of tying shoes has been explained to the extent that it is an instance of the generalization, or "moral law," that children should follow the directives of their parents.

Although this example contains a value premise (*should*), the same points can be made with an example in the *is* form. (Laws are generally held to exist only at the *is* level and not at the *should be*, or moral, level.) The event to be explained in this example, why a puddle is frozen, requires the law-like statement that, other things being equal, water freezes at 32°F. Given this law and the fact that the temperature fell below 32°F during the night, one has explained why the puddle is frozen in the morning. Of course, one can inquire, at the level of theory, why water freezes at that temperature, but clearly at the level of law, the event has been explained.

These examples indicate that explanation is a matter of subsuming an event under a law. This is the basic structure of the covering-law model, which, even though it has been seriously criticized over the last few years in the philosophy of science, has dominated and still dominates thinking about the purpose of empiricist social and educational inquiry.

Laws

Because the empiricist version of social and educational inquiry has been based on developments in the natural sciences, the discovery of laws is as crucial to social explanation and prediction as it is to the explanation and prediction of natural events. As noted, a law states a universal, invariant relationship between or among events. Laws indicate how things really are out there at all times and in all places; they are not evaluations or expressions of how one might wish things to be. Thus, laws can be empirically assessed as to the extent they correspond to or accurately reflect an independently existing reality. In other words, laws must be tested against independently existing or "extralinguistic" facts, and judgments about them require the properly conducted observation and analysis of such facts (empirical methods). Statements that cannot be observationally or empirically grounded, such as theological, value, or metaphysical statements and tautologies or statements that are true by definition, cannot have the status of laws.

To qualify as a law, a statement must possess various characteristics. First, given the claim of universality, the form of a law must be as follows: "All As are Bs" or "Whenever A is the case, B is the case." This form poses the conditional situation that if something has the characteristic or property A, it also has the characteristic or property B. Placed in more tangible terms, the form can be expressed in statements such as "All water below a temperature of 32°F (A) is frozen (B)" or "Whenever water is cooled to below 32°F (A), it freezes (B)." In an educational situation a hypothetical example might be that "All students who have been taught mathematics with the XYZ program (A) are masters of basic addition (B)" or "Whenever students are taught mathematics with the XYZ program (A), they will master basic addition (B)."

Second, a law must contain specific modifiers concerning scope and applicability. These modifiers, such as those that delimit the gas laws in regard to conditions of very high pressure and very low temperature, must be precisely stated if one is to establish the conditions under which a law holds or does not hold. Moreover, the terms employed in a law must be clear and unambiguous. One must be able to determine exactly how a law relates to reality or, put differently, when the facts support a law and when they do not. A law should also be general in scope or, if not, subsumable under more general law-like statements—including theoretical laws. This aspect is important because one of the major goals of scientific inquiry is to establish a system of deductively related laws.

These characteristics, such as precision and clarity of the terms employed, are integral to that most important condition mentioned above—that laws must be subject to empirical testing. As noted in Chapter II, one particular type of statement that appears with some frequency in social and educational inquiry does not meet this important condition. This type of statement is analytical in nature, or true by definition. In other words, its truth is apparent based solely on an analysis of the terms it employs. For example, if we say, "All triangles have three sides," it is obvious that all three-sided objects are triangles, and vice versa. Or if we say, "Bright children can learn more than dull children," it is difficult to conceive of *bright* as being anything other than learning more, and learning more as anything other than being bright (see Louch, 1966, pp. 36–38, for a discussion of this example and others from the area of learning theory). The point is that one cannot deny the truth of such statements, which are virtually tautologies in many cases.

Laws must therefore be stated in what is called synthetic form. These are statements in an observational language, on the order of "Metals expand when heated" or "Positive reinforcement results in greater learning," in which the terms *expand* and *learning* contain more than the antecedents *metal* and *reinforcement*. To deny the truth of a synthetic statement does not involve a contradiction, as it does with analytic statements and tautologies. True and false in this case depend on observation and measurement. The previous example of water freezing at 32°F fulfills this condition because judgments about it require a systematic observation of reality. Of course, *systematic* in this sense means that science sponsors a particular method for undertaking and analyzing observations and specific criteria for judgment.

Although there can be different types of laws (Kaplan, 1964, pp. 104–113), two of the most important types are laws of causal relationships and—especially for empiricist social and educational research—probabilistic laws, or laws of association or functional dependence. In the case of cause, a law describes the kind of relationship noted above—that of a regular, invariant succession of events. For example, the statement "Whenever ice is heated to above 32°F, it melts" implies cause because every time ice is heated above 32°F, other things being equal, it will melt. Or the example "Whenever a student is taught mathematics in the XYZ program, he or she will master basic addition" implies cause because every time a student completes the program, other things being equal, he or she will then master basic addition.

The concept of cause, however, is a very difficult one to disentangle philosophically because it involves complex considerations of whether an event, to be a cause, is a necessary and/or sufficient condition of another event. For our purposes in this chapter, we need only note that the empiricist approach to inquiry accepts the idea, one that is reflected in introductory social and educational research textbooks, that the cause of an event is another event that always and unconditionally precedes or accompanies that event.

Probabilistic laws describe a degree of relationship between or among the magnitude of variables. Such laws do not pose an invariant succession of events; the focus is instead on a form of relationship. In the physical sciences some of the more prominent examples of probabilistic laws can be found in quantum mechanics and in medicine. In the latter case, such laws might describe the percentage of people exposed to a disease who actually contract that disease or the likelihood of dying within a certain time if one has a particular illness. In the social and educational areas one might posit any number of possible statements that take this form—the relationship of grades and self-concept, the percentage of students receiving remedial reading instruction who improve their reading by a certain amount, and so on. Thus, probabilistic laws focus on the measurement of the magnitude of variables and then on assessing the strength and direction of relationships between or among variables.

Probabilistic laws, then, do not take the form of a universal, invariant succession of events, but rather that of a probabilistic relationship between or among events. Instead of "All As are Bs," the form is "X% of As are Bs." In the previous hypothetical example involving remedial help and student performance, the form would not be "All students receiving remedial help (A) will achieve at a certain level (B)," but that a specified percentage of the students receiving help (A) will achieve at a specified level (B). In these examples the referent point for such laws is the group as opposed to the individual per se. Thus, the focus is not on every A is B, but on the proportion of all events with one characteristic that also have the other characteristic.

The question that immediately comes to mind is whether or not probabilistic laws can also be causal in their import. If cause is defined strictly in terms of an event being a necessary and sufficient condition for a succeeding event, then cause cannot be inferred from probabilistic laws. A probabilistic law stating that remedial help is highly likely to result in better grades describes a relationship that is not an automatic, inevitable succession of events. In other words, A (remedial help) may not be a sufficient condition for B (better grades) and possibly may not even be a necessary condition (one could get better grades for other reasons).

Our commonsense notion of explanation and causation are not often troubled by this situation. As Lessnoff (1974) notes, "common usage . . . admits the idea that a particular sort of event may sometimes cause a given effect and sometimes not" (p. 25). In other words, at a day-to-day level we easily accept the explanation that most of the time better grades are the result of particular other events but that sometimes, even though these events are present, better grades do not result. Although this seems quite satisfactory at the commonsense level, it poses a problem for scientific explanation: Such a formulation does not allow probabilistic laws to be tested and then modified or eliminated in the same way as is possible for universal laws.

This point requires a background comment about the inductivist nature of empiricist inquiry. Since an acceptance of laws of both types is based on inductive reasoning as applied to experience, it is not possible to directly confirm laws. The much referred-to example of the "law" that "All crows are black" can be used to illustrate this point. Because the acceptance of a law requires observation and empirical testing to see if that law accurately corresponds to or describes reality, one must observe all crows past, present, and future. This prospect is clearly impossible and even nonsensical given the "future" aspect. The best one can do is assert that "All crows so far observed have been black" and hold that in the absence of a negative instance (a nonblack crow) the law will be accepted as rational or warranted. Even though it is highly likely that the next crow observed will be black, there is no logical way to move from the restricted statement to an unrestricted statement (one that holds for all times and for all places).

The point is that laws—both universal and probabilistic—are not directly confirmable; they can only be falsified. For universal laws, one negative case is sufficient to require the modification of or abandonment of the law. Probabilistic laws, however, are not fasifiable, in any strict sense of the term, by the single negative case. Whereas in the case of a universal law the discovery of a negative instance will serve (in theory if not in practice) to falsify a law, in the case of a probabilistic law an individual negative instance might simply be one of those not "covered" by the law-like generalization. In other words, probabilistic statements allow that there will be such negative instances. For a law that states that 85% of something is something else (85% of remedial students get better grades), the singular negative case could be one of the 15%. Only if one can observe all cases covered by the generalization, or if the relationship is a perfect one (1.00), or if one can exactly specify the percentage in "X% of As are Bs" can probabilistic laws be subject to falsification in the same way as are universal laws. Since none of these conditions obtains for the social and educational area, certainly in practice if not in principle, probabilistic laws present various difficulties for empiricist inquiry.

Finally, one must ask why the discovery of laws is so important to the empiricist perspective on inquiry. There are two reasons. First, laws are the essential ingredient in the covering-law model of scientific explanation, which defines the explanation of an event in terms of its being subsumed under a law. Unless inquiry discovers enduring generalizations that have "stood up" to repeated empirical testing, we are left with commonsensical explanations of events. Second, social and educational inquiry have long had a strong utilitarian thrust, as was noted in the discussion of Comte and others. Because they enable us to predict the consequences of our actions, laws are crucial to this desire to employ inquiry to shape and mold our social and educational lives. In the absence of strong prediction, we would be missing the "connecting link between theory and practice" (Giddens, 1977, p. 25) and the essential condition for "rational human intervention" (p. 25) in the social and educational domain.

Two very simple examples—one from the natural world and the other from the educational world—will demonstrate the force of this point. If a metal bar, when heated under the same conditions, sometimes expanded and sometimes contracted, immense problems of a practical and technical nature would result. Clearly, the lives of engineers and architects would be immeasurably more complicated. Similarly, if a particular teaching strategy, under the same conditions, sometimes led to greater learning and sometimes did not, we would be missing that essential connecting link between a scientifically based conceptualization of the instructional process and the practice of instruction. As long as the empiricist approach to social and educational inquiry harbors a desire to serve practical purposes, the discovery of laws is essential.

To sum up, laws are not a representation of the world as shaped by our knowledge; they represent what our knowledge must conform to (see Wartofsky, 1968, for an extended discussion of this point). The fact that a law must be subject to testing and to the possibility of falsification is a "check" on the character of that law. A law that cannot be falsified is of little use to empiricist research. Laws must be stated in observable terms, must not be tautological, and must not be so general or imprecise as to prevent the possibility of empirical analysis.

Covering-Law Model

The most widely accepted account of scientific explanation is the covering-law model, or explanation by deduction based on laws, as elaborated by Hempel (1965, 1966). This model of explanation is structured around statements of laws and statements of factual conditions from which the event can be deduced—meaning that given a law and the appropriate conditions, the event had to or will have to occur. In the case of the example used in the last section, the reasoning is as follows:

1. Water always freezes at 32°F and below.   (Law)
2. The liquid in the puddle is water.   (Condition)
3. The temperature is below 32°F.   (Condition)
4. As a result, the puddle is frozen over.   (Event)

Or, in more formal terms,

L1, L2 . . . Ln   (universal statements)   Explanans
C1, C2 . . . Cn   (individual conditions)

E   (statement of the event) Explanandum

At the level of practice, however, explanations are not necessarily placed within such a detailed, formalized schema. Very often an explanation is based on certain generalizations and certain conditions that are simply taken for granted as common knowledge and are not specifically mentioned. Hempel (1966) gives the following example: "The slush on the sidewalk remained liquid during the frost because it had been sprinkled with salt." As he notes, for this explanation at least one law is assumed—that salt lowers the freezing point of water—and certain conditions are also assumed—that the temperature did not drop to a very low point (pp. 52–53). The same situation applies to explanations resulting from social and educational inquiry. Very often, the phrase *other things being equal* is used to express that certain things are being taken for granted.

One of the most important things about this deductive-nomological approach is that in regard to logical structure, scientific explanation and scientific prediction are identical. The major difference is the element of time—whether the event has already occurred or has yet to occur. On the one hand, scientific explanation is concerned with subsuming an event that has already occurred under certain laws and conditions. Scientific prediction, on the other hand, begins with the laws and conditions and predicts that an event will occur. Rudner (1966) expressed this idea of symmetry when he said, *"we have an explanation for an event if, and only if* (from a different temporal vantage point), *we could have predicted it"* (p. 60).

One important point about laws, which must be restated in regard to explanation and prediction, is that laws cannot be directly confirmed—they can only be falsified. That is, "the criterion for valid inference is that true premises may not yield a false conclusion, but falsehoods may yield truths by such inference" (Wartofsky, 1968, p. 267). A simple example will clarify how, on logical grounds, the occurrence of an event cannot be used to confirm a law, whereas the nonoccurrence or negative instance will serve to falsify a law. Suppose one has stated the law that "Every time the squirrels feed in the oak tree, they scatter acorns on the ground." From a predictive point of view, if the explanans are true, then the event must follow. If the prediction is not realized, then logically the major premise (the law of scattered acorns) cannot be true because it does not state a universal, invariant relationship. The premise has been falsified. From the other direction, however, the presence of acorns does not allow one to confirm the conditional statement "If the squirrels are feeding in the oak tree, they will scatter acorns on the ground"—the acorns could be there for other reasons, such as high winds. If the event is used for such inference—that the premise is true—this can result in the logical fallacy of "affirming the consequent."

Thus, the covering-law model allows for predictions that, if not realized, lead to the falsification of the major premise. At least in theory, if a law is accepted as true, it cannot yield negative instances.

One further point must be clarified. Since one can never directly confirm a law as true but can only hold that it has not yet been falsified, does this mean the covering-law model is really inductive rather than deductive? In other words, is the model really based on a listing of instances (all crows so far are black), thereby violating the idea of deductive explanation? Not really, because empiricists generally assume that a statement that has "held up" against attempts to falsify it can be thought of as a law of nature and used as the basis for deductive inference. It is a matter of separating the grounds of the event from the grounds of our acceptance of, or belief in, the event. If we accept something, based on a thorough review of the existing evidence, as a universal statement, then it can be employed along with statements of conditions to explain and predict events deductively. In the end, it is a matter of logical form and not one of the strength of evidence.

There is a second major form of explanation for statistical, or probabilistic, laws. In outline this probabilistic form very much resembles that of the deductive-nomological form.

1. The probability is high that students who receive remedial help will improve their grades.
2. Student "X" received remedial help.
3. It is highly likely that student "X" improved his or her grades.

The symbolic form of the model is as follows:

$$p \ (A, \ B) \text{ is high}$$
$$X \text{ is a case of } B$$

$$X \text{ is a case of } A$$

In this instance the form may be read as the probability of A (improvement), given B (remedial help), is high; X is a case of B (student who received help), which makes it highly likely that X is a case of A (student with improved grades).

The crucial difference between these two approaches to explanation is that whereas the deductive-nomological form is deductive, the probabilistic approach is inductive. In the former case, the event follows from the premise with deductive certainty; thus, this approach provides for the strongest form of explanation. In the case of probabilistic explanation, since the event is only more or less likely to occur, certainty is not possible; the premises provide only greater or lesser degrees of inductive support. Even so, it is still reasonable to hold that the probabilistic form allows for the explanation of events.

Theory

The discovery of laws of either a universal or probabilistic type and their employment to explain events does not provide for a total account of the process of scientific explanation. Something more is needed to explain why the relationships specified in the laws are the way they are or operate the way they do. In other words, to know that a relationship exists does not necessarily tell us why it exists. This is why theory is not only important, but essential, to our understanding of both the physical and social worlds.

In a basic definition, a theory is *"a systematically related set of statements, including some lawlike generalizations, that is empirically testable"* (Rudner, 1966, p. 10). The role of these sets of systematically related statements is to explain or provide a deeper understanding of the regularities that are expressed in laws. Theory tells us why a relationship works the way it does. For example, theory is necessary to answer questions like the following: Why does ice melt at 32°F and above? Why is there a relationship between remedial help and the improvement of grades? Theory also increases our understanding by demonstrating the relationship among seemingly diverse phenomena. One of the most well-known examples in this case is Newton's theory of gravity, which brought together the tidal movements, the swinging of pendulums, the motions of planets, and so on.

From an externalist perspective, the distinction between law and theory is discernible in the distinction between properties in and of themselves and properties as properties of things. Laws express properties in and of themselves in observational terms, such as pointer readings in the physical sciences and test scores in the educational area. Theory tells us that these properties are properties of things such as pressure and intelligence. As Wartofsky (1968) puts it, theories are distinct from laws in that "a theory explicitly asserts that something exists of such and such a sort, whose operations and whose relations are described in laws" (p. 279). In other words, our observational terms actually denote entities, and what is observed are not simply pointer readings and test scores, "but things or relations of which these are the marks" (p. 279).

Finally, theories can be assessed at two levels. They can be judged "externally" to the extent that they can be supported or refuted based on empirical testing. This, of course, means that the theoretical terms must be translatable at some point in the process into observational terms. Only if this is possible can it be held that a theory will assist in explaining reality. Thus, terms such as *electron* and *intelligence* must eventually be given operational or measurement status. Theory also can be judged "internally." The key element here is how systematic the set of statements is—meaning that the statements have been arranged in an orderly, coherent fashion.

INTERPRETIVE UNDERSTANDING

In contrast to the empiricist approach, which will supposedly result in the explanation and prediction of events, is an approach that focuses on the interpretive understanding of meaningful human action within a social context. The contrast in goals between the two approaches is striking: The search for law-like generalizations and accurate predictions is not the goal of the human studies. Rather, the focus is on the interpretation of people's motives, meanings, and intentions—that is, the interpretation of the interpretations people give to their own subjective experiences.

The bottom line for this perspective is that people—including investigators, of course—act purposefully and intentionally; they ascribe meaning to (interpret) their own actions and those of others and react to the meanings others ascribe to their actions. These interpretations are constitutive of social reality as opposed to being merely neutral descriptions of an independently existing social reality. Thus, the human studies engage in what Giddens (1976) calls the "double hermeneutic"—the second-order interpretations of people's first-order interpretations in an attempt to make clear what seems confused, unclear, and so on. Moreover, since meaning can only be realized within a context, interpretation requires a movement back and forth between event and context. In this sense the process of social and educational inquiry is inevitably hermeneutical.

The Rejection of the Empiricist Goals

There are various reasons why some researchers have rejected empiricist goals in favor of an interpretive perspective. First, these inquirers reject the possibility that laws governing social and educational life can ever be discovered. At a practical level, their claim is that no one has ever discovered laws that will make it possible to explain and predict. They believe that those statements put forward as candidates for laws contain vague and imprecise terms, are unclear as to scope and applicability, and defy testing and falsification. Interpretive inquirers cannot make much of terms such as *participatory management, engaged time, teacher praise, ruling class, pressure groups,* and *means of production* (see Lessnoff, 1974, pp. 53–58, for a discussion of this point). In fact, for many critics, the laws discovered by empiricist inquiry are actually little more than "truisms," "aphorisms," and "tautologies" (Holmes, 1986, p. 9).

At a more conceptual level, various arguments have been advanced in regard to why it is impossible to discover laws. Chief among these is the one that claims that what are passed off as "laws" in the social and educational areas always turn out to be highly mutable—a problem that is often referred to as self-fulfilling or self-negating prophecies. As Giddens (1977) puts it:

> Laws in the social sciences are inherently unstable in respect of the 'environment' to which they refer, i.e., human social conduct and its institutional forms. The circumstances of application of laws in natural science can be altered by the manipulation of their limiting conditions. Except in the case of laws that influence social life from the 'outside', e.g., the laws of genetics, laws in the social sciences do not have this form; they are in principle mutable in the very conditions of their application. They are unstable in respect of new knowledge that comes to be embodied in the rationalization of action of those to whose conduct they refer, including knowledge of such laws themselves. (pp. 27–28)

This rejection of the possibility of discovering laws is, of course, directly related to the rejection of an externalist ontology and epistemology (see Chapter IV). The empiricist perspective has depended on the possibility of "brute data," or "extralinguistic facts"—data that stand free from any further readings. The idealist approach, however, holds that there can be no such thing as data "whose credibility cannot be founded or undermined by further reasoning" (Taylor, 1971, p. 8). The claim is that the existent reality of the empiricist position is actually the

> creation of the practices individual people use to render their world an accountable and meaningful thing. It is their versions, admittedly through many negotiations and processes, which find their way into figures, a record which cannot stand for an objective reality, or be 'brute data', in the way proposed by social scientists of a positivist persuasion. (J. Hughes, 1980, p. 99)

Second, advocates of an interpretive approach argue that their position is more cognizant of and responsive to our basic human condition. Because we are self-interpreting animals, there can be no such thing as a structure of meaning apart from our everyday interpretations of actions and events, from others' interpretations of our interpretations, from our interpretations of others' interpretations of our interpretations, and so on. Any attempt to avoid this never-ending circle of interpretations of meaning by, for example, attempting to describe ourselves in a foundational or neutral scientific language as opposed to an everyday language, does not take account of this human condition.

To take these first-order constructs out of the context of everyday life is to trivialize, if not distort, the reality of which they are designed to make sense. As Outhwaite (1975) puts it, "where social scientists have strayed too far from 'common sense' constructs, the result has been not greater sophistication, but trivialization" (p. 111). That is, such a tactic, because it imposes by fiat the idea that there is an independently existing social reality that can be objectively described, is insensitive to how the social world is meaningfully constructed and constantly reconstructed by those who live in and through it (see J. Hughes, 1980, p. 100, for a further discussion of this point). Thus, one of the major claims of the interpretive approach, which focuses on the interpretation of meaning at the level of everyday life, is that it avoids the trivialization and distortion that come with the attempt to develop a science of society.

The Focus on Meaning and Action

Any attempt to discuss the goals of the interpretive approach must begin by addressing the concepts of meaning and action. It must be noted at the outset, however, that these topics, as well as those of *verstehen* and hermeneutics, which follow, are not easy to discuss clearly and precisely. Unlike the seemingly obvious definitions and clarity of the various elements of the empiricist perspective, much debate and disagreement still exist concerning crucial aspects of the interpretive perspective. This situation results in part from the fact that this approach has been built on various strands of thought in our recent intellectual history (phenomenology, existentialism, idealism, and so on) and in part because the concepts themselves are often difficult to grasp— especially for those of us raised in a predominantly empiricist tradition.

Taylor (1971), in his discussion of the characteristics of meaning, noted three elements that define this concept. Even though the following discussion differs from Taylor's (and includes comments with which he might not agree), his three points provide an excellent framework for a discussion of the concept of meaning. First, meaning is of something, and the meaning of an event or action can be separated from the event or action itself. This point leads to the classic distinction between behavior as physical movement in time and space and human action. Second, the meaning of a specific act or event can only be understood within a context, or a field of meaning. Not surprisingly, this premise means that a change in the field of meaning will lead to a change in the meaning of an event. The ideas of action as social and of hermeneutics are important in this regard. Finally, although meaning is for an individual, it can be shared by a group or community of people. Based on this point, the ideas of reflexivity and of self-definitions made in value terms, or in terms of what Taylor (1980) calls "desirability-characterizations" (pp. 31–38), become crucial to interpretive inquiry.

The most appropriate way to pursue the point that the meaning of an event can stand separate from the event itself is to focus on the term *action*. Action, when undertaken with the qualifier *human*, is a crucial concept for the interpretive approach to inquiry. As defined by Weber (1947), action includes

> all human behavior when and insofar as the acting individual attaches a subjective meaning to it. . . . action is social insofar as, by virtue of the subjective meaning attached to it by the acting individual (or individuals), it takes account of the behavior of others. (p. 88)

To see the importance of this concept, we must backtrack for a minute. At one level, action can be thought of as behavior or physical movement. Both perspectives on inquiry recognize that people move in time and space—they raise their arms, issue verbal utterances, walk across rooms, and so on. Where the two perspectives distinctly part company is over the relationship of this behavior to the mental categories employed to interpret that movement.

For the empiricist perspective, the emphasis necessarily falls on the side of the objective description of overt behavior. The mental becomes almost a "residual" to be dealt with in one of two general ways. In the more extreme forms of behaviorism, this aspect is virtually ignored, since intentions and purposes are not observable. As Polkinghorne (1983) notes, "In these systems of inquiry about human action, such mentalistic terms as *purpose* and *thought* are left out by the definition of what is admissible as data" (p. 175). A science of society can only be based on the systematic description, in a neutral scientific language, of overt behavior.

"Mainstream" empiricist approaches take the view that mental phenomena can be studied, at least from one step removed, because these phenomena are directly reflected by or directly correspond to overt behavior. In other words, "Mental concepts are translated into observational terms by means of operational definitions that specify which observable behaviors represent a particular mental concept" (Polkinghorne, 1983, p. 175). Thus, to mark a test in a certain way (overt behavior) is seen as a direct reflection of a mental phenomenon (for example, the "amount" of an attribute, such as intelligence, that one possesses).

Given the basic assumptions supporting the empiricist approach to inquiry, the mental must be dealt with in these ways. As previously noted, this perspective measures the truthfulness of its descriptions on the basis of whether they correspond to how things really are out there, and correspondence can only be realized through the objective observation of the facts or of that independently existing reality. If the mental cannot be so observed, then it cannot enter (at least unambiguously) into the empiricist study of social life. Moreover, this problem cannot be solved by the idea that an individual has direct access to his or her own mental life. Science is about publicly verifiable knowledge. The singular report of an individual has no scientific standing and cannot be the basis for scientific knowledge. Thus, the empiricist approach must focus on behavior and can treat the mental only indirectly, by presuming it is reflected in that behavior.

For the interpretive approach, this treatment of intentions and purposes is insufficient. The main point about action as human, which separates it from action as purely physical movement, is that it involves interpretations or is undertaken in terms of meaning. Lessnoff (1974) notes:

> When people perform actions their bodies can be seen to move relative to other objects, parts of the body change their spatial orientation and relations, sounds can be heard coming from them and so on. But this description of the physical aspects of behavior is clearly not a description of *actions*, of people doing things. (p. 37)

In other words, people doing things are social and moral beings who have intentions and purposes and who interpret their own behavior and that of others in social and moral terms. The task of interpretive inquiry is the interpretation of these interpretations—the attempt to make sense of the meanings people give to their actions by engaging people at the level of the meanings they give to their actions.

An example, much simplified from the treatment given it by Melden (1961), will help illustrate this important difference between behavior and human action. Suppose a person driving a car puts his or her arm out of the window in a certain way. This action can be described at two levels. First, assuming one has a concept of the physical objects involved, such as arms and cars, there can be a description of the physical movement—body parts moving in time and space relative to other objects. Second, the same event can be described as human action to the extent that it is interpreted in categories of meaning and intention. In this sense the description may well involve the notion of signaling, as in signaling for a turn. However, because the physical movement itself can be distinguished from the meaning of that movement, it is possible that the same event can be given different meanings and that the same meaning may be given to different events.

Both the movement and the human action are in one sense the same thing. In another sense, however, because they are alternative descriptions, the two can be held separate, but the relationship between movement and human action is actually, in Taylor's term, a "nonsymmetrical" one. Clearly, there must be a description of overt behavior if there is to be a description of meaning; yet, the meaning of an event is not determined by and cannot be read directly or solely from the event itself. As Taylor (1971) puts it:

> The description in terms of meaning cannot be unless descriptions of the other kind apply as well; or put differently, there can be no meaning without a substrate. But on the other hand, it may be that the same meaning may be borne by another substrate—e.g., a situation with the same meaning may be realized in different physical conditions. (p. 11)

Meaning can be distinguished from the action or event—which, accordingly, leads to the prospect that any particular event or bit of overt behavior can be given different descriptions.

Let us consider an example that will illustrate this point and will lead to a discussion of the second characteristic of meaning. One day a friend of mine was riding his bicycle home from work. As he approached a corner, a car drove past him. The driver made a "wagging" motion with his right hand, with his finger pointing to the right. As the car and the bicycle reached the corner at approximately the same time, the car turned to the right in front of my friend, who immediately applied the brakes and went flying over the handlebars of his bike. The car stopped, the driver got out, and a discussion ensued. My friend thought the gesture was a greeting from an acquaintance whom he did not recognize. The driver of the car insisted the gesture was an expression of his intention to turn right at the corner: The hand movement was to advise my friend of what was going to happen. Although the physical gesture was clear enough, there was a problem at the level of meaning-description. The same physical movement obviously had a very different description at the level of meaning.

Why was this the case? The reason is that meaning must be undertaken within a context, and not surprisingly, different fields of meaning result in different meanings given to an event. As it happened here, the driver of the car was from a foreign country where, he insisted, such a gesture would be interpreted as he intended. Of course, given the traffic rules and social conventions of road use in this country, such a physical movement would not be interpreted in this way. (My friend, however, has changed the field within which he will interpret similar gestures, and a change of field will, in the future, lead to a change of interpretation for him.) Melden (1961), with reference to his example, has put the issue in more formal terms:

> One could not have a conception of a human action unless one had the conception of traffic rules, or of those particular rules, laws, or conventions governing the social intercourse of persons which happen to obtain in our society at this or that particular time . . . we need to recognize, in other words, the relevance and applicability of reasons that operate, not only in the privacy of one's study, but also in the social arena where persons take account of each other in doing what they do and are guided in their thought and actions by an intricate network of social and moral considerations. (pp. 179–180)

The dependence of the meaning of an action or event on context leads to a series of questions for which no general agreement exists within the interpretive camp. If we maintain that meaning can only be realized within a field of meaning, we are saying in effect that human action is social action because interpretation must be undertaken within a social context. The basic point is that humans are social animals: We possess intentions and purposes and can interpret the intentions and purposes of others only as a result of our experiences in social interaction with others. To grant that the behavior of another is purposeful is to invoke the concept of reciprocal social awareness or the sense that one's actions can be interpreted only on the basis of an awareness of the interpretations others give to one's actions.

One of the thorniest issues raised by invoking the idea of the social context of meaningful action was foreshadowed by the bicycle example. If the meaning of an event can only be understood within a field of meaning, what happens when the same physical movement is interpreted by people with different fields of meaning—actor versus inquirer, one inquirer versus another, and so on? At the root of this issue lies the Dilthian problem of whether or not there can be any such thing as a correct interpretation. For interpretive inquirers who claim there are no brute data the answer is no. Any agreement over the interpretation of an action or event is not a matter of an appeal to the neutral facts, but is the result of the interpreters coming to share a similar field of meaning. To resolve differences of interpretation all we can do is attempt to show another

> through the reading of other expressions why this expression must be read in the way we propose. But success here requires that he follow us in these other readings, and so on, it would seem, potentially forever. We cannot escape an ultimate appeal to a common understanding of the expressions, of the "language" involved. (Taylor, 1971, p. 6)

In the end, the problem of relativism (a major topic of the next chapter) is one that must be addressed by interpretive inquiry.

Two points concerning language must be appended to this discussion. As with empiricist inquiry, language is crucial for interpretive inquiry. Even though the previous examples dealt with physical behavior, language must also be included when they are analyzed. Language is probably the ultimate social phenomenon, and social life, including social inquiry, would be impossible without it. In fact, a case can easily be made that for social inquiry the interpretation of action is less important than the interpretation of linguistic accounts of human action. The crucial aspect of language in this sense is similar to the point made about overt behavior: The fact that people utter sounds poses no problem; it is the meaning of these sounds that is problematic. That is, for one to recognize sounds as words and to understand what is meant by certain words can only be undertaken within a context of meaning. The meaning of a word depends on the meaning of other words or on a series of statements of which they are a part. And the meaning of that series of statements requires an interpretation of the individual words. Ultimately, people do not communicate unless they intend to convey meaning, and if meaning is conveyed, it is the result of such an interpretive process.

Given that the meaning of words can only be understood within a context of meaning, it is clear why interpretive inquirers object to the attempt to employ a neutral scientific language as opposed to the language of everyday discourse. "Translating" the everyday language of people into neutral scientific terms or imposing such a context on everyday language not only changes the meaning of what people say but actually "strips" their utterances from their original meaning context. Under these conditions it is particularly difficult for social scientists and laypersons to understand one another or negotiate meaning. Rorty

(1982) speculates on what happens when empiricist social inquirers hand over recommendations to policymakers in language barely intelligible to the latter:

> When they [the policymakers] get predictions phrased in the sterile jargon of "quantified" social sciences ("maximizes satisfaction," "increases conflict," etc.), they either tune out, or, more dangerously, begin to use the jargon in moral deliberation. The desire for a new, "interpretive" social science seems to me best understood as a reaction against the temptation to formulate social policies in terms so thin as barely to count as "moral" at all. (p. 196)

The introduction of the term *moral* brings us to the last characteristic of meaning—that meaning is *for* an individual or for individuals as members of a community. The two most important points in this regard are reflexivity and the fact that self-meaning must invoke the image of human beings as moral beings. The implication of this latter point is that social inquiry must focus on understanding in terms of "desirability-characterizations" (Taylor, 1980, p. 30).

Possibly the most important characteristic of human beings is that we are self-defining. People ascribe meaning to their actions based on their ability to monitor their conduct in relation to the conduct of others. That is, people can understand or make sense of what they do by meaningfully describing or making sense of what others do in reference to their conduct, and vice versa. The important point is that throughout this process of reflexive monitoring, meanings are for people. Feelings such as joy, shame, and so on are for individuals with situations. These feelings or the characterizations people give of their feelings cannot be taken in terms of their supposedly phenomenal qualities or placed in a "thing" language. Such an attempt simply impoverishes our descriptions of social and human life (recall the example in the last chapter of the possible descriptions of what happened in Nazi Germany). The emotions of people must be described in "subject-related" terms. This is what Taylor (1980) calls "understanding people in terms of the value or significance of the things in their world" (p. 33). Interpretive inquiry is concerned with how people feel and not, as for empiricist inquiry, with feelings as "self-subsistent entities" (Rorty, 1979, p. 30) that float free from the people who feel.

The second point is that meaning-descriptions are essentially evaluative or moral. People are moral and evaluative beings, and they must be understood in this sense. As Taylor (1980) puts it:

> To understand someone is to understand his emotions, his aspirations, what he finds admirable and contemptible, what he loathes, what he

yearns for and so on. Understanding doesn't mean sharing these emotions, aspirations, loathings, etc., but it does mean seeing the point of them, seeing what is here which could be aspired to, loathed, etc. Seeing the point means grasping the objects concerned under their desirability-characterizations. (p. 32)

The language of daily discourse is so heavily laden with evaluative terms or terms used evaluatively that one might even claim that all of the crucial terms in our daily lives are in essence value terms. From the qualitative perspective, a failure to take this situation into account means a failure to understand the meanings people assign to their actions and activities.

Understanding and Hermeneutics

In Chapter III it was noted that the contemporary interest in an alternative to empiricism began with the elaboration by Dilthey and others of the ideas of understanding and hermeneutics. Since that time, various changes have occurred in the general thinking about these fundamental concepts and in their formulation. An understanding of these changes is essential to an understanding of the goals of interpretive inquiry. Moreover, as this discussion proceeds, it will become apparent that one of the major differences between the two perspectives resides in the related areas of objectivism versus relativism and of how we are to define rationality.

What does it mean to understand? For our purposes there seems little reason to go beyond the everyday meaning of the term. One can agree with Outhwaite's (1975) point that "despite the mystique with which the concept of *Verstehen* (understanding) has been invested, there seems no reason to suppose that historical or sociological understanding is essentially different from everyday understanding" (p. 13). In this sense, then, to understand is to grasp the meaning of an expression, utterance, or action. This condition responds to questions such as, "Why did you do that?" or "What did you mean by that expression?" Thus, from the point of view of interpretive inquiry, to understand is to clarify or make sense of something that was in some way "confused, incomplete, cloudy, seemingly contradictory—in one way or another, unclear" (Taylor, 1971, p. 3).

The most significant thing about any attempt to clarify is that it must take place within a context. Since the meaning of an action or utterance cannot take place apart from an understanding of the context within which the action or utterance occurred, all understanding is hermeneutical. Hermeneutics, even though not a common term in the area of social inquiry or even, until recently, in the philosophy of science, has had a long history. The root of the word goes back to the Greek words *hermeneuein* (verb) and *hermenein* (noun), which mean respectively to *interpret* and *interpretation* (see Palmer, 1969, pp. 12–32, for a concise discussion of the origin of hermeneutics). The oldest use of the term (and the origin of its modern use) has been to describe the area of biblical exegesis and the methodology of philological analysis in general.

Even though the treatment is much simplified here, the basic conceptualization of the process as employed for biblical interpretation and text interpretation in general can serve to illustrate the intent of hermeneutics: To understand the meaning of a text, one must grasp the meaning of its various individual parts; and to understand the individual parts, one must understand the text. That is, to understand the meaning of individual words, one must understand the context of sentences, paragraphs, and so on within which the words are embedded, and vice versa. In other words, the whole can be defined only in terms of the individual parts, and reciprocally, the individual parts can be understood only in terms of the whole. Interpretation requires a constant movement back and forth between parts and whole in the attempt to make sense of a text.

This approach can be extended to the interpretation of events, actions, and utterances in the social and educational world. In this case, to grasp the meaning of a human action or utterance, one must interpret it within a context of meaning. Just as with text interpretation, the context may well include the intentions, purposes, and motives of the actor. To revive Melden's (1961) point, to understand a hand movement as a signal to turn requires that one understand not only the laws and conventions of driving, but also the immediate situation within which the movement occurred and the intentions of the person making the movement. And, of course, to understand the context requires that one understand the individual parts. This circularity of interpretation, be it of texts or of human action, has some very important implications: A hermeneutic circle has no definitive beginning or ending points, and there can be no such thing as presuppositionless interpretation. These basic points can now be applied more directly to our discussion of the study of social and educational life and to the current conceptualization of hermeneutics.

Over the course of this century some changes in the conceptualization of hermeneutics have taken place that are of major consequence for the interpretive approach to inquiry. Dilthey, because he held that the *Geisteswissenschaften* (more or less what we think of as the social sciences and humanities) dealt with a subject matter distinct from that of the natural sciences, believed that a distinct methodology was necessary. Especially in his early writings, he saw hermeneutics as that method, one that would allow for objective, valid knowledge of the expressions of our inner lives just as the positivist methodology allowed for objective knowledge of the natural world. As Bernstein (1983) notes, Dilthey attempted to show that "there is a distinctive subject matter and method appropriate to the *Geisteswissenschaften* that can equal and even rival the claim of the natural sciences to achieve 'objective knowledge' " (p. 37). Hermeneutics would provide for the human studies the "objective" understanding of human expressions just as the "objective" explanation of natural phenomena was available to the natural sciences.

The second characteristic of Dilthey's hermeneutics, again most evident in his early work, was its psychological overtones. He conceived of understanding in terms of reenactment, or imaginative reconstruction. If one's focus was on the "inner experiences" of another, either a historical or contemporary being, the task was to reexperience, or recreate, the other's inner world of experience. Understanding thus became a matter of one mind grasping the mind of another—in other words, an identity of minds. This was not purely an operation of one's cognitive processes, but rather it was a movement toward that particular moment when life achieves an understanding of life itself. Thus, hermeneutics in this early phase was seen as a method particularly for the study of the meaning of human expressions.

In his later years Dilthey sought to overcome many of the problems associated with his focus on imaginative reconstruction and with making hermeneutics a method for obtaining objective knowledge in the cultural sciences. In particular, as previously noted, he was troubled by the inevitable circularity of interpretation—a process with no definitive beginning or ending—which made it impossible to distinguish a correct interpretation from an incorrect one. Even though he was not successful in solving these problems, his later work clearly is important to what is now the most important characterization of hermeneutics—philosophical hermeneutics.

Gadamer (1975), in addition to drawing on Heidegger's (1962) phenomenological definition of hermeneutics, developed philosophical hermeneutics in reaction to Dilthey's conceptualization in two areas. First, hermeneutics, according to his view, is no longer seen as a method of the human studies that can be employed to obtain objective knowledge of meanings. The basic idea is that hermeneutics is not a set of procedures, privileged to social inquirers, but is rather the ontological and universal condition of our existence as human beings in the world. Second, the psychologistic emphasis on understanding as reenactment or reexperience of the inner life of others is replaced by understanding as a dialogical encounter between different traditions or ways of life. These

changes in conceptualization and what they mean for the goal of interpretive inquiry, even though still somewhat unclear, are of major consequence.

With the advent of philosophical hermeneutics, interpretation has
come into direct conflict with various externalist-oriented tenets such as
subject-object dualism and inquiry as a means of gaining the objective
interpretation of an independently existing reality. This characterization
has also seriously challenged the attempts, most prominently by Betti
(1980) and Hirsch (1967), to realize Dilthey's goal of hermeneutics as a
method for objective interpretation. (These two versions of hermeneutics and the implications each has for the role of methods in the interpretive process are discussed in the next chapter.) For Gadamer, interpretation is not method—it is the essence of our being as human beings. In
Polkinghorne's (1983) terms, "interpretation, then, is not a tool for
knowledge; it is the way human beings are" (p. 225). As human beings,
we are "thrown" into a world that we then must seek to understand.
Hermeneutics is all-encompassing because it underlies all activity and is
not just one activity among many that we engage in; in principle, there
can be nothing beyond understanding.

The critique of method advanced by this version of hermeneutics can
best be understood with reference to the claims made for the empiricist
approach. For the latter, method is the way to avoid one's own historicality; we must be methodical if we wish to be objective and to seize the
God's eye point of view. For philosophical hermeneutics, none of this
makes sense. If we realize our historicality, thereby admitting to the
possibility of presuppositionless knowledge, we realize that a God's eye
view is unavailable to us. If our mode of being in the world is hermeneutical, then investigators, like everyone else, are a part of the circle of interpretation. Any attempt to be methodologically foundational is contradictory in the face of epistemologically nonfoundational assumptions.
For philosophical hermeneutics, method does not lead to apodictic truth
because no rules can be specified that will allow one to break out of the
circle of interpretation.

If hermeneutics is not a special procedure, but rather the ontological
and universal condition of human life, then the difference between what
investigators do and what people do in their day-to-day lives must be
markedly narrowed. Just as social actors generate meaning-descriptions
that come to constitute social life and social reality, so, too, do social inquirers. Both draw on the very same resources or skills—including
language—that are available to them as practicing members of a society.
As Giddens (1977) puts it, "Every social theorist is a member of society,
and draws upon the skills associated with such membership as a re-
source in his investigations; it is equally important that every member of

society is a 'practical social theorist' " (pp. 172–173). Investigators interpret the interpretations people give to their activities and those of others, and people likewise interpret the interpretations of investigators,
and so on. This never-ending circle of interpretation constitutes social
reality as it is for those involved in it, at any given historical time and
cultural place. The social world is not simply out there awaiting description via methodologically correct procedures; it is made to happen
through the processes of interpretation and meaning-description.

What, then, is the goal of inquiry? The analogy with text interpretation will help answer this question. From the perspective of philosophical hermeneutics, the interpreter of a text can never claim to know exactly what is meant by the text or exactly what the author intended.
Hermeneutics is not a matter of seizing the objective meaning of something because method has freed us from values, interests, preunder-
standings, and so on. Rather, our hermeneutical situation means that
we must be open to the text in the sense of a dialogical encounter in
which we allow the text to question us equally as we question the text.
Understanding another entails opening up oneself to another and
risking one's own traditions in a free and open dialogue with another.
Thus, understanding is not a matter of manipulation and control, particularly via method, but rather it is a question of openness and dialogue;
the purpose of hermeneutics is not to lay out rules of procedure for objective understanding, but rather to conceptualize understanding as our
mode of being in the world as finite creatures.

SUMMARY

The goal of the empiricist approach to inquiry is clearly to produce empirically verified knowledge, knowledge that can be used to realize
strong prediction, thereby leading to the shaping and molding of social
and educational life. By definition, empirically verified knowledge accurately describes how things really are out there in the social and educational world. This knowledge of social objects and events is independent of, or can be held separate from, our prejudices toward, feelings
about, and normative evaluations of those objects and events. Obtaining such knowledge requires an objective assessment/description of
the facts and involves the discovery of laws and the development of
theory. Thus, empiricist social and educational inquiry succeeds when
the process is able to explain and predict events with reference to laws
and theory.

Interpretive inquiry focuses on the intentional, meaningful behavior
of people and the interpretations people give to their own behavior and

that of others. The goal is to make clear what was previously not fully understood. This process is inevitably hermeneutical because interpretive inquiry recognizes that meaning must be undertaken within a context. Such an interpretive process has no definite beginning or ending points, and no specific procedures or established criteria can be applied to sort out correct interpretations from incorrect interpretations. In the end, interpretive inquiry succeeds when it produces interpretations that not only sustain but deepen and enlarge our sense of community as social and moral beings.

CHAPTER VII
The Role of Procedures
in the Inquiry Process

The French fathers of modern social science took little notice of the peculiarity of social reality as conditioned by the subjective character of social action, and were largely unconcerned with the resulting complexity of research strategy. Neither Comte nor Durkheim, nor the most eminent among their heirs, were seriously worried by the danger of relativity in the study of the social. . . . Believing that social facts are 'things' like all others, i.e. that they exist in their own right as real entities 'out there', outside the realm of individual experience, they naturally concluded, first, that one can study social realities without necessarily looking at the process of their social production and, second, that whoever does this study with proper method and diligence will certainly arrive at the same results. Faithful to the unbroken French rationalist tradition, they regarded true knowledge as, above all (if not solely), the question of method and of its systematic application.

That was, exactly, the assumption challenged by the German intellectual tradition. . . . There, the interpretation of social reality came to be revealed as a conversation between one historical era and another; or between one communally founded tradition and another. . . . To anyone concerned with reaching an objectively valid knowledge of the social, relativism was a real danger, which could not be staved off simply by discarding wrong methods, or by being sceptical towards uncontrolled assumptions and 'evidencies'. (Bauman, 1978, pp. 15-16)

Chapter II ended with a brief discussion of the importance of method for conducting empiricist inquiry. From this perspective on inquiry, what counts as genuine knowledge is "above all (if not solely), the question of method and of its systematic application" (Bauman, 1978, pp. 15-16). Although the actual terms may vary, this same point is made in many introductory social and educational research textbooks, which very often express the idea as follows: The proper application of the proper procedures (usually labeled scientific) is essential because it allows one to have confidence in the research findings, allows researchers to achieve valid findings, and so on.

Exactly how terms like *confidence* and *valid* are defined is not usually discussed at length in these textbooks. However, given the externalist assumptions of empiricism, one can conclude that these terms refer to results that have made "contact with reality." These are findings that accurately reflect how things actually are "out there," findings that have not been biased by the researcher's particular interests, purposes, and values. Thus, the proper application of the proper procedures will certainly minimize, if not eliminate, the possible "distorting effect" of the researcher's personal dispositions upon the logic of evidence and will ensure that both the research process and the results are objective as opposed to subjective. Various procedures are therefore considered what might be called epistemologically privileged.

The interpretive/hermeneutical perspective on social and educational inquiry cannot subscribe to the idea that special procedures—ones that constrain the researcher's subjectivity—can be inserted between the researcher and the subject matter. Ever since Dilthey had to abandon his quest for a methodology for the *Geisteswissenschaften*—a methodology that would lead to true understandings—the whole idea that certain procedures are essential for valid interpretations, or interpretations in which one can have confidence, has been very problematic.

Notwithstanding Dilthey's problems, over the years various attempts have been made to ground interpretive inquiry methodologically. At a more conceptual level, Hirsch (1967) and Betti (1980) have similarly argued, although with different terminologies, that hermeneutics can be a disciplined form of interpretation—one that can lead to valid or objective interpretations of an author's intention or of a historical phenomenon, respectively. At a more practical level, various educational inquirers have attempted to develop "how-to-do-it" lists of activities, the idea being that if interpretive inquirers employ certain techniques, they are much more likely to obtain valid results. If these techniques are not applied, then the confidence placed in the findings must certainly be assessed very carefully, if not withheld. A good argument can be made that success has not attended any of these efforts at either level.

The most basic reason for this lack of success is that interpretive inquiry is epistemologically nonfoundational. Given this fact, how can one claim that interpretations can be grounded via a prescribed set of procedures? Although there can be norms for negotiating agreement between inquirers and between inquirers and their subject matter—norms very much like those that guide negotiations over meanings and intentions at the day-to-day level—there can be no procedures to govern inquiry itself. As Bauman (1978) puts it, there can be no privileged or special "method of interpretation which can be seen as leading to objective, i.e. universally acceptable, results" (p. 231). Just as the particular interpretation one arrives at depends on the context within which that interpretation is undertaken, so, too, the particular procedures one employs in arriving at that interpretation depend on the context. And, of course, *context* in this sense very much includes the background of significance—the interests, purposes, and values—that the interpreter brings to the interpretation.

Therefore, the issue of the role of methods or procedures in the inquiry process must be conceptualized in light of what is often called the challenge of hermeneutics to social and educational inquiry. In other words, how can one "render accounts of subjectively intended meaning objective in the face of the fact that they are mediated by the interpreter's own subjectivity" (Bleicher, 1980, p. 1)? For empiricism, the proper methods properly applied are thought sufficient to meet this challenge—although serious criticism of this position has recently been raised. For interpretive inquirers, the positions adopted range from a belief that certain prescribed methods can, if not absolutely guarantee, very much enhance the possibility of valid/objective interpretations to a rejection of this idea and of the empiricist claim for method. A number of interpretive-oriented inquirers, finding both of these positions unsatisfactory, have attempted to find a "middle ground."

WHAT IT MEANS TO BE A PERSON

Why do the two approaches to social and educational inquiry take such different positions on the role of methods in the research process? One reason is that the positions taken by each side are based on very different, deeply held, underlying images of what it means to be a person (see J. Smith, 1988, for a further discussion of this issue and its implications for inquiry). As Reason and Rowan (1981a) note, "the theory we hold about persons, and about persons as inquirers, must have extended implications for the research method we choose, and also for how we carry it out in practice" (p. xix). The idea that researchers can, via the appropriate methods, detach themselves from what they study and thereby offer objective depictions of people's intentions, motivations, and so on is very much associated with a representation view of the person. The interpretive position, which finds the idea of detachment, especially via method, highly implausible, is based on a significance view of the person.

Taylor (1985) has clearly and coherently discussed these two different concepts of what it means to be a person. Although the differences in these conceptions can be clearly drawn at a theoretical level, the daily lives of most people, including researchers, reflect various combinations of the two without any conscious thought on the part of the actors. This does not mean, however, that these theoretical considerations are insignificant. As Taylor notes, "Theoretical models with their inner coherence have a great impact on our thinking even where—perhaps especially where—they are not fully conscious or explicit" (p. 114). In any event, since these theoretical models of what it means to be a person are fundamental to "rival pictures of morality and human life" (p. 97), they are clearly of consequence to a wide array of issues concerning social and educational life—including this discussion of the different perspectives on inquiry.

Both conceptions begin with a standard, commonsense notion of what it means to be a person. A person is defined as one who possesses certain capacities such as the ability to plan, evaluate, choose from among alternative courses of action, and act to achieve certain desired ends. Beyond this, the two conceptions differ distinctly in terms of what is ultimately associated with these capacities and how one can distinguish a person from other agents (such as certain animals and even certain machines) that also act to achieve ends and can generally engage in adaptive behavior.

The Representation View

From the representation view, the nature of agency is considered relatively unproblematic. Since all agents, by definition, have at least some capacity to interact with their environments in an attempt to achieve various ends, human agents do not differ in principle from other agents. In this view persons are distinguished from other agents because they are able to "envisage a longer time scale, to understand more complex cause-effect relationships, and thus engage in calculations, and the like" (Taylor, 1985, p. 102). The difference is quantitative rather than qualitative: The superiority we grant to persons over other agents relates to their greater capacity to "conceive different possibilities, to calculate how to get them, to choose between them, and thus to plan their lives" (Taylor, 1985, p. 104).

According to the representation view, the central factor of greater strategic power is consciousness, which is seen as the "power to frame representations of things" (Taylor, 1985, p. 98). People possess consciousness in a more developed way than do other agents. This means that people have the capacity to take a detached or objective stance in regard to what confronts them in any given situation—the capacity to give an account of things as they really are—apart from the feelings or dispositions they may have about them. This view assumes that persons have the ability to understand the world in abstraction from their particular place in it. The ability to describe clearly and accurately the objects surrounding them—objects that are assumed to exist independent of the description and that thereby constitute the standard for the accuracy of the description—is precisely what gives persons the greater capacity to plan, evaluate, and choose the most effective means to achieve certain ends.

From this perspective, the issue of the particular goals or ends one pursues is seen as relatively unproblematic. Because goals, unlike the means employed to reach goals, are not subject to calculation and a detached stance, they are generally consigned to the category of givens or "as given for one part, and for the rest as arbitrarily chosen" (Taylor, 1985, p. 104). The emphasis on means as opposed to ends permits most judgments to be taken with reference to a performance criterion or an effectiveness criterion—which in turn requires that one be able to give an accurate account of the situation. In other words, persons are assumed to be already aware of and understand their ends; their world is dominated by a concern over potential means, which are understood "with a view to control" (Taylor, 1985, p. 112).

Finally, the representation concept sponsors a certain approach to moral deliberation and moral choice. Since the ends are more or less given and the emphasis is on the choice of means, there is a tendency to separate the moral from the instrumental (analogous to the separation of values from facts) in our thinking. The desire for a detached stance is, in effect, the attempt to compartmentalize the particular significance things have for us as human beings. Taylor (1985) argues that this desire may represent a wish for freedom from the ambiguities of moral deliberation, the hope that the merely human about us can be set aside and that the influence of our dispositions and emotions can be controlled.

The Significance View

In contrast to the representation perspective, the significance concept of the person views the distinction between persons and other agents as not simply a matter of degree but as one of kind. Crucial to the notion of personal agency within this perspective is that things matter to people (including researchers) in a very strong, original way. In other words, we define ourselves, our interactions with others, and so on in terms of our values or in terms of judgments of worth. This is expressed by the fact that we attribute to human beings a reflexive, evaluative awareness of such things as purposes, intentions, likes, and dislikes. If we understand "an agent essentially as a subject of significance, then what will appear evident is that there are matters of significance for human beings which are peculiarly human, and have no analogue with animals" (Taylor, 1985, p. 102).

If we accept that an evaluative stance toward intentions, purposes, motivations, and emotions is integral to the sense we have of ourselves as persons, then we must also accept that there is much more to consciousness than the capacity to frame representations. For the significance view, "objects" such as intentions and emotions do not stand independent of the act of depicting those intentions and emotions. This is so because an interpretation of an emotion or intention cannot be undertaken apart from an interpretation of the context—including the values and purposes the interpreter brings to the situation—within which that emotion or intention was expressed. In other words, if the interpretation of a situation is somehow altered because one brings, for example, a different sense of significance to it (which is easily possible, since any particular situation can be interpreted in countless ways), the emotion or intention is thereby altered. The interpretation of an emotion or intention is not simply a matter of depicting independently existing objects; the interpretation is actually constitutive of the emotion or intention (reality as mind-dependent). Certain things about persons cannot be grasped fully with the representation concept and the traditional idea of consciousness; the issue of greater strategic power is not sufficient to differentiate people from other agents.

In light of these points, any interpretation of an emotion or intention in terms of a particular situation requires that the situation be of significance (undertaken in value terms or characterized in desirability terms) to the person making the interpretation. An intention can only be made intelligible if one brings a background of significance to it and to the context of its expression. For example, if A conceals something and B attributes this to a desire to avoid embarrassment, B's interpretation makes no sense if A is insensitive to what it means to be embarrassed. Undoubtedly, different persons can and will attribute various "senses of significance" to a situation and hence give various meanings to it. Intentions and emotions cannot be described in absolute, objective terms—accounts that are free from personal discernment, or that are interpretation-free. For the significance view, the idea of a person as "accurate representer," who can plan, evaluate, and choose in a detached, calculative manner, yields an incomplete view of what it means to be a person.

The fact that we cannot think in terms of absolute accounts has important implications for moral deliberation. Engaging in moral deliberation requires that one be sensitive to certain standards. *Sensitive* in this context means that one is reflexively aware of the standards one is attempting to live by. Moral agency requires a reflexive awareness of the demands placed on us that go beyond the utilitarian desire to match means to ends. However, these standards cannot be given in absolute terms; because they can no longer be seen as given or as more or less arbitrarily chosen, "ends" become of crucial concern. The significance view of a person requires that one be open to one's goals or ends. Moral deliberation is therefore a never-ending process of attempting to construct the meaning of intentions and emotions—one's own and those of others.

In short, the significance concept and the representation concept present very different perspectives of what it means to be a person. These two views of the person can also be directly associated with the issue of the separation of facts and values. The representation view both supports and reflects the claim that facts can be held separate from values. The idea that human beings can frame accurate representations of things, calculate possibilities, use this knowledge for utilitarian purposes, and so on requires that there can be a separation between a description of how one desires things to be and a description of how things really are. In other words, on the one side we are able to describe the world cognitively in a value-neutral language; on the other side we can use an evaluative language to address how we think the world should be. This division is, of course, reflected in the previously discussed example of construct validity. The process of establishing the validity of a measuring device is thought to have a cognitive, or statistical/technical, side that can be held apart from a normative, or evaluative, side. From an empiricist point of view, the former can be pursued independently of the latter.

The significance view is very much associated with the position that facts and values are intimately related. According to this view, even what counts as a fact presupposes values. The interpretation that researchers give to motives, intentions, and actions, both their own and those of others, is not merely a more or less accurate depiction of independently existing objects. These interpretations must be made against a background of significance, or in terms of the interpreters' interests, purposes, and values. In other words, an interpretation is not merely an accurate reflection of independently existing objects, but rather constitutes the reality of these objects. As such, evaluative language cannot be decisively separated from neutral, descriptive language. The significance perspective of the person leads to the conclusion that inquiry is not a matter of detachment and objectivity, but is a process that is irrevocably influenced by the interests, purposes, and values of the inquirer.

EMPIRICISM AND METHODS

The empiricist perspective, especially as it is elaborated in introductory textbooks on social and educational research procedures, has adopted a generally agreed-upon role for methods: Methods are a constraint on researcher subjectivity, and if the proper procedures are properly followed, valid results, or results in which one can have confidence, are available to us. Thus, methods are the major referent point for sorting out the correct from the incorrect and for adjudicating differences over results.

Philosophical Background

The representation view of the person underlies, and is in turn strengthened by, the empiricist perspective on social and educational inquiry. One of the fundamental points that makes the empiricist position on methods intelligible is that we think ourselves able to take a detached stance toward not only the physical world, but also the social and educational world. To the extent that such detachment is achieved, researchers are then able to describe social and educational objects not merely as these objects seem to them, given their particular historical time and cultural place, but in terms of how they really are.

Very much associated with this idea of a detached stance toward the world is the desire for a greater control or practical mastery of our social and educational lives (that utilitarian thrust that was early on given to social inquiry by Comte and others). This detachment is the foundation upon which empiricists build their attempts to discover law-like and predictive generalizations. Such generalizations provide the connecting link between an intellectual mastery of the subject matter and its practical mastery. As Giddens (1977) puts it, in the absence of strong and accurate predictions, we would be missing the "connecting link between theory and practice" (p. 25) and thus missing the essential condition for "rational human intervention" (p. 25) in human affairs.

Obviously, the most tangible referent point that has inspired this motivation for greater practical mastery of the social and educational world is the outstanding success of the physical sciences. One of the crucial features in this success story is the presumed ability of physical scientists to describe things as they really are in and of themselves and not merely as they might seem to us as human beings located at a particular time and place. Thus, the lesson that has been extracted from the story of the physical sciences is that one gets better predictions and a greater practical mastery if one thinks of things in terms of, for example, wavelengths and molecular motions (primary, "objective," or observer-independent qualities) as opposed to colors and felt heat (secondary, "subjective," or observer-dependent qualities). As Taylor (1985) puts it:

> [The] eschewal of anthropocentric properties was undoubtedly one of the bases for the spectacular progress of natural science in the last three centuries. And ever since, therefore, the idea has seemed attractive of somehow adapting this move to the sciences of man. (p. 106)

Given this situation, the dominant concern within the empiricist approach to social and educational inquiry has been to find a way to ensure that the descriptions of inquirers go beyond how things seem to us as time- and place-constrained beings—the kind of descriptions, in other words, we generally attribute to laypeople. The fact that this same point has been expressed in a variety of ways at both the philosophical and research levels illustrates how very critical it is to the empiricist perspective.

For example, the issue is often stated as follows: All of us, including researchers, obviously have a particular place in the world—but, at the same time, if we are to render objective accounts of that world, we must be able to abstract ourselves from our particular places and adopt a "view from nowhere" (T. Nagel, 1986). The problem, then, is to find a way to accomplish this "abstracting" so that a view from nowhere in particular is possible. Or, if framed in terms of facts and values, the idea is that we must think of ourselves as similarly divided into two parts—cognitive and normative—a separation that reflects the division between facts and values. In this case the problem can be expressed as how our cognitive side, the side with which we objectively describe reality, can be protected from the distorting influence of our normative side. Finally, as the issue has been most commonly expressed at the research level, the concern is to find a means to "control" the subjectivity of researchers so that the accounts they give of the world are objective, unbiased, and valid.

The Practice of Inquiry

Empiricism has offered basically two solutions to this problem of detachment/objectivity. The first, which is almost always discussed in conjunction with the second solution, is that researchers can, through self-reflection, control their particular interests, values, and biases. The second solution, by far the more important and well established, involves procedures or methods.

The injunction of self-reflection and self-restraint consists of a number of interrelated ideas. First, there is the idea that if researchers are aware of their own values and biases, they can exercise the necessary self-restraint, which will hold their personal dispositions in check and thereby enable them to pursue inquiry in an objective manner. Second, researchers must discipline themselves to adhere to certain other values crucial to the inquiry process—namely, the values of honesty, open-mindedness, and so on. These two points are generally coupled with the idea that researchers should make directly known their particular interests, purposes, and values to those who read the results of their research. To the extent that this is done, there is a communal check (by other researchers) on possible bias on the part of any individual researcher.

There are, however, a number of problems with the solution of self-reflection and self-restraint, the first of which is that these injunctions have continued to resist specification. That is, no one has been able to specify either how researchers can go about the process of self-reflection or what criteria can be used to determine whether someone has actually been self-reflective and has exercised the proper self-control. Moreover, the assumption that it is possible for one to truly know one's own values, dispositions, interests, and biases is highly questionable. The problematic nature of this assumption is reflected in the fact that at the level of daily discourse we often think of people who claim to truly know themselves as shallow. Even though some very interesting philosophical arguments have been made in favor of self-reflection and self-restraint (see, for example, Kaplan, 1964; Myrdal, 1958; and, especially, T. Nagel, 1986), the point is that these injunctions have not been translated into a specific, publicly verifiable way to detect researcher subjectivity or to judge when it has distorted any particular piece of research.

The idea that procedures or methods can solve the problem is by far the solution of choice for empiricism. The importance empiricism assigns to methods is amply reflected in the fact that inquirers spend a great deal of time discussing methods, teaching them to students, and deciding whether students, in dissertation settings, for example, have correctly or incorrectly pursued their research. These procedures must be correctly applied, in various combinations depending on the nature of the research, because they constrain the researcher and thus protect the process and results from bias and subjectivity. Such methods include the well-known ones of sampling, experimental and quasi-experimental design, statistics, and so on.

The underlying belief is that if researchers follow the rules, they will be able to assess things as they really are, without the distorting effect of their personal interests, values, or dispositions. Random sampling and assignment, for example, are essential because they prevent the researcher from biasing, even if only unconsciously, the selection of the sample or the groups. The design of studies is important because it ensures that the results are a function of the treatment and not of some other uncontrolled factor—one of which may be, of course, the researcher's conscious or even unconscious desire for a particular result. Or, in a further example, statistical techniques of both descriptive and inferential types are important because they allow researchers to go beyond the level of how things seem to the level of how they really are. That is, in the first instance, even though some variables may appear to be related, correlational statistics allow us to determine if they are in fact related. In the second case, even though a particular treatment may appear to produce a result, the statistical testing of the null hypothesis tells us whether we can continue to accept a result pending further research.

These procedures are therefore thought of as much more than a series of guidelines for negotiating disagreements among researchers. First, they are considered rules for preserving objectivity, rules that must be followed, and followed correctly, if one wants to make "contact with reality." Because they are independent of anyone's particular interests and purposes, these procedures are considered neutral ones that can and must be applied universally. Second, because the proper methods, properly applied, lead to an accurate description of reality, which is the ultimate referent point for adjudicating competing knowledge claims, they protect researchers from the possibility of a never-ending clash of interpretations based on different interests, purposes, and values. Once a situation has been objectively depicted, the findings, until they are superseded by the results of other methodologically sound studies, must be thought compelling and sufficient to resolve disagreements; others must accept the results regardless of their normative dispositions about that situation. Finally, the application of these methods separates the descriptions of social and educational inquirers from those of laypeople at the day-to-day level. Laypeople describe the world as it seems to them at any given time and place, whereas the use of methods enables researchers "to penetrate beneath the appearances and see nature 'in its own terms' " (Rorty, 1982, p. 192).

INTERPRETATION AND METHODS

Because empiricism is based on a representation view of the person and on the externalist assumptions of subject-object dualism, facts separate from values, and so on, empiricists have had no impediment to conceptualizing methods as the crucial element for preserving objectivity.

However, it has been much more difficult for the interpretive perspective to work out an agreed-upon position on this issue. The problem is that the significance view of the person and internalist assumptions such as reality as mind-dependent and the inseparability of facts and values leave unclear the exact role of methods in the research process. In fact, this is probably the most confusing issue facing interpretive inquiry.

At present, then, there is no generally accepted position among hermeneutical philosophers and/or interpretive inquirers on the role of methods. At the philosophical level, there is the position that an objective or valid interpretation of meaning, given the application of certain canons or procedures, is quite possible. This idea has been countered with the argument that not only does method not lead to objective understanding, but the adherence to method *prevents* true understanding—for both empiricist and interpretive inquiry. At the research level, some people have argued that certain specific procedures, if properly followed, will constrain researcher subjectivity and thus allow "more objective" descriptions of social and educational reality. Other interpretive inquirers, however, have argued that the assumptions of interpretive inquiry make the whole idea of detachment, objectivity, methodological constraints, and so on inherently insupportable. The types of arguments made at both levels and on both sides are briefly described in the next sections.

Philosophical Positions

Betti (1980) and Hirsch (1967) are the foremost advocates of hermeneutics as a method for the validation of meaning, or of what might be called, with reference to the two views of the person, a hermeneutics of the representation of meaning. Even though the former is primarily interested in the interpretation of historical phenomena and the latter in the interpretation of literary texts, both have argued that an objective interpretation of meaning is possible and that norms can be applied to sort out a correct interpretation from an incorrect one. Thus, both have attempted to revive Dilthey's idea—avoiding in the process his psychologistic emphasis on interpretation as the reexperiencing or reliving of the life of another—of hermeneutics as a methodology for the cultural or human sciences.

However, before discussing the general thrust of Betti's (1980) and Hirsch's (1967) more or less commonly held position, we must clarify one major point. By the term *method*, Betti and Hirsch do not mean specific procedures, or a series of definitive how-to-do-it activities. Hirsch notes that

it may be set down as a general rule of interpretation that there are no interpretive rules which are at once general and practical. . . . Every practical rule of interpretation has an implicit "unless" after it, which means, of
course, that it is really not a rule. What then is the status of the many traditional canons and maxims of interpretation, and what is their purpose?
Clearly, they are provisional guides, or rules of thumb. (pp. 202-203)

The principal focus for both authors is on the theoretical aspects of
valid interpretation, and accordingly, the term *method* is defined as logic
of justification rather than in terms of neutral, universally applicable
procedures. Thus, Betti (1980) discusses a number of philosophical considerations in support of various principles or canons of objective interpretation, and Hirsch (1967) elaborates what he calls a "logic of the validation" (p. 207) for objective interpretation.

The foundation upon which their claim to objective interpretations is
built involves a separation between meaning and significance. For both
Betti (1980) and Hirsch (1967) a distinct difference can and must be made
between the actual meaning that the author gives to a statement or text
and the meaning or significance that the statement or text has for the
interpreter. For Hirsch, given his focus on text interpretation, it is a matter of the difference "between the meaning of a text (which does not
change) and the meaning of a text to us today (which changes)" (p. 255).
For Betti, given his historical interests, this same point is expressed as
follows: There is a need to distinguish between the "meaning of historical phenomena on the one hand, and [on the other hand] the significance of the phenomena for the present" (p. 69).

The meaning of a passage or a text, then, can and must be interpreted
in terms of the author's intended meaning. This intended meaning is
thought of as fixed, determinate, changeless, and susceptible to accurate
depiction. The author's intention is thereby the norm, and the only
compelling norm, against which the validity or objectivity of any particular interpretation can and must be judged. Thus, for Hirsch (1967), an
author's intention is a fixed entity that is susceptible to objective evidence gathering—an intention about which a valid determination can be
made.

In contrast to the author's intended meaning or the meaning of a historical phenomenon stands the significance of that text or phenomenon
for the interpreter. (Of course, the original author may later decide the
work means something different for him or her from what it did at the
time it was written.) Since the significance of a text depends on the interpreter's interests, purposes, values, and so on, it can change if the interpreter changes his or her interests and purposes. Furthermore, because
the interpretation depends on what the interpreter brings to the situation, different interpreters with different senses of significance will very

likely give different interpretations to a passage. However, although each of us has the right to interpret a passage according to our own sense of significance, this does not relieve the interpreter of the need for a valid interpretation in terms of the author's original intent or meaning. The latter is the task of Betti's and Hirsch's version of hermeneutics. It is based on the idea that an objective interpretation—one that corresponds to the "meaning which is represented by the text" (Hirsch, 1967, p. 10)—is both possible and necessary.

The primary problem for both Hirsch (1967) and Betti (1980) is how to maintain this separation of meaning and significance. This problem is particularly acute because the person who interprets the text in terms of its significance is the same person who attempts to describe objectively what the author originally meant. For Betti, this problem is addressed, theoretically, in terms of a number of canons of interpretation, among which are the autonomy of the object of interpretation, the coherence of meaning, and meaning adequacy (for a more complete discussion of Betti's canons, see pp. 58–86).

The first of these refers to the idea that the interpretation must be undertaken in terms of the "point of view of the author" (Betti, 1980, p. 58) and not with reference to "any other external purpose that may seem relevant to the interpreter" (p. 58). The second canon requires that the "meaning of the whole has to be derived from its individual elements, and an individual element has to be understood by reference to the comprehensive, penetrating whole of which it is a part" (p. 59). The third canon invokes the idea that the interpreter must move into "harmony with the stimulation he receives from the object in such a way that the one and the other resonate in a harmonious way" (p. 85).

In Hirsch's (1967) logic of validation, the essential point is that "an interpretive hypothesis is ultimately a probability judgment that is supported by evidence" (p. 180). In other words, even though there are no set rules or definitive procedures for developing an interpretive hypothesis, "an objectively grounded choice [can be made] between two disparate probability judgments on the basis of the common evidence which supports them" (p. 180). Hirsch thus holds out the possibility that our "imaginative guesses" about an author's meaning can be methodically tested by constantly asking about the most likely meaning of a text or statement. This is not a process of assembling directly confirming evidence, but rather one of falsification. As Hirsch puts it, "since we can never prove a theory to be true simply by accumulating favorable evidence, the only certain method of choosing between two hypotheses is to prove that one of them is false" (p. 180). Thus, Hirsch believes that it is possible to move from "imaginative guesses" about an author's meaning to an evidence-based conclusion about original meaning (see Hirsch, particularly pp. 165–207, for a discussion of these points).

In contrast to the validation, or objectivist, hermeneutics of Betti (1980) and Hirsch (1967) stands the philosophical hermeneutics of Gadamer (1975). Wher?as the former have attempted to elaborate a hermeneutics for the objective representation of meaning apart from significance, the latter has attempted to develop a hermeneutics of significance—one that collapses interpretation (meaning) and understanding (significance). Whereas Betti and Hirsch have attempted to develop hermeneutics as a method for objective interpretation in the cultural sciences, Gadamer has attempted to elaborate a hermeneutics that is not "a methodology of the human sciences, but an attempt to understand what the human sciences truly are, beyond their methodological self-consciousness" (Gadamer, 1975, p. xiii). Gadamer thus represents a hermeneutics that moves well away from the constraints of a "narrow striving for methodically secured objectivity" (Bleicher, 1980, p. 127).

From Gadamer's (1975) perspective, all of those who have cast hermeneutics in terms of method have made a very fundamental mistake. When they think in terms of objective understanding, they are led to perpetuate at least two unacceptable ideas—ones that are also common to the empiricist perspective. The first is that they accept, either implicitly or explicitly, a subject-object dualism, or a separation of interpreter from what is interpreted. The second is that they limit genuine knowledge (i.e., valid knowledge, or knowledge in which we can have confidence) to methodologically self-conscious knowledge. Put in other terms, the objectivist stance is based on the idea that we can stand outside our historical time and cultural place and then look back to describe objectively what has been or is happening. This is an illusion because, in Palmer's (1969) words, "finite, historical man always sees and understands from his standpoint in time and place; he cannot, says Gadamer, stand above the relativity of history and procure 'objectively valid knowledge' " (p. 178).

From Gadamer's (1975) very complex discussion of philosophical hermeneutics, we will extract only a limited number of elements that are of the greatest consequence to the issue of methods and objectivity in inquiry. One of Gadamer's first points is that the idea of a subject-object dualism, commonly espoused by empiricists and by those who see hermeneutics as a method of objective interpretation, is inappropriate to the goal of true understanding. He makes his case somewhat indirectly by linking our experience of art to our experience of play or games. His discussion of art begins by noting the modern tendency to separate the aesthetic from the nonaesthetic in our lives. This separation is associated with the commonly held idea that truth and knowledge are the province of the nonaesthetic and that sensual or emotive reactions are the province of the aesthetic. Thus, Gadamer begins his work on philosophical hermeneutics with a critique of the idea "that the appreciation of art and beauty has nothing to do with knowledge and truth" (Bernstein, 1983, p. 118).

Gadamer (1975) says this attempt to differentiate and isolate the aesthetic from the nonaesthetic runs counter to what our experiences are, or at least should be, with art. Our encounter with a work of art can and should go far beyond whether or not we are "taken with it." If we think of our relationship to art in only subject-object terms (as spectators of art), then art has no particular place or function in the world. Under these conditions, art illuminates nothing of consequence about the world because it has been reduced to simply an expression of aesthetic pleasure. For Gadamer, we only understand a work of art when "we bring what we have experienced and who we are into play. The experience of a work of art is encompassed and takes place in the unity and continuity of our own self-understanding" (Palmer, 1969, p. 168). There is an interaction between a work of art and the person who attempts to share in that work of art in the sense that a painting or a poem puts questions to the person just as the person puts questions to it. The interpreter of a work of art

> is not someone who is detached from the work of art but is someone upon whom the work of art makes a claim. The spectator, then, is present to the work of art in the sense that he or she participates in it. (Bernstein, 1983, p. 123)

Gadamer's (1975) critique of conceptualizing art as an object separate from the interpreter is reinforced by his use of the analogy of the game or of play. If a game is to fulfill its purpose, the participants must be totally absorbed in the activity. If someone "stands back" from the game and resists such absorption, then the activity is ruined for both that person and the others. The game has its own driving forces, and in a sense, it is no longer people playing a game, but a game being played out through people. In other words, the structure is such that it totally involves the players and play can only be presented through the players.

So it is for art: Art can only be played out through people who share in that art because the work has made a claim on them or "questions" them. A work of art reaches its presentation through the interpreters. The subject-object dichotomy of the spectator, on one side, ridding himself or herself of preconceptions so as to apprehend the meaning (artist's intention) of the object, on the other side, is for Gadamer an insufficient view of understanding. But does such understanding extend beyond art? For Gadamer (1975), clearly this is the case:

> Understanding must be conceived as a part of the process of the coming into being of meaning, in which the significance of all statements—those of art and those of everything else that has been transmitted—is formed and made complete. (p. 146)

To understand a work of art, a statement, a text, or a historical phenomenon requires a preunderstanding or preconception. There can be no such thing as presuppositionless understanding because if we could rid ourselves of presuppositions—of our sense of significance, in Taylor's (1985) terms—by methods or by self-reflection and self-restraint, there would not be understanding at all. These presuppositions come from the tradition of which we are a part, a tradition that does

> not stand over against our thinking as an object of thought but is the fabric of relations, the horizon, within which we do our thinking. Because it is not object and never fully objectifiable, the methods of an objectifying type of thought do not apply to it. (Palmer, 1969, pp. 182–183)

Understanding is not a matter of the subject appropriating the meaning of an object through the proper application of the proper methods, but is a dialogical process between the self-understanding person and what is encountered—be it a text, work of art, or the meaningful behavior of another person. To interpret, then, is to "use one's own preconceptions so that the meaning of the text can really be made to speak for us" (Gadamer, 1975, p. 358).

A most important implication of Gadamer's (1975) position on hermeneutics/interpretation—especially the idea of no presuppositionless knowledge—is that there can be no such thing as a "right" interpretation. Every interpretation must be undertaken with reference to the interpreter in the sense that it involves a dialogue of questions—those the interpreter asks of the text and those the text asks of the interpreter. Since the tradition one brings to a text is constantly evolving, "an interpretation that was correct 'in itself' would be a foolish ideal that failed to take account of the nature of tradition. Every interpretation has to adapt itself to the hermeneutical situation to which it belongs" (p. 358). Moreover, since method provides no certainty of a correct interpretation, one must constantly risk oneself—one's presuppositions or preconceptions—in dialogue with a text or with another.

Finally, for Gadamer (1975), truth (a term that unfortunately he does not clearly define) does not lie at the end of method but can only be understood dialectically. Within his version of philosophical hermeneutics, truth and method are antithetical. Palmer (1969) summarized Gadamer's position on this issue as follows:

> Truth is not reached methodically but dialectically; the dialectical approach to truth is seen as the antithesis of method, indeed as a means of overcoming the tendency of method to prestructure the individual's way of seeing. Strictly speaking, method is incapable of revealing new truth; it only renders explicit the kind of truth already implicit in the method. . . . In method the inquiring subject leads and controls and manipulates; in dialectic the matter encountered poses a question to which he [the questioning subject] responds. (p. 165)

Thus, Gadamer has elaborated a hermeneutics much different from the methodological/objective hermeneutics of Betti and Hirsch—one that very much calls into doubt method and the possibility of objective interpretation. For Gadamer, understanding is a historical, dialogical process, and hermeneutics is not method but is rather our mode of being as finite, historical creatures in the world. The keys to understanding in his version of hermeneutics are openness and dialogue as opposed to the control of method. Hermeneutics is not a set of procedures for achieving valid interpretation, but is rather the basic condition that underlies all understanding.

In the end, Gadamer severely criticizes various ideas common to empiricism and to the objective/methodological version of hermeneutics: the ideas that knowledge and truth can only be judged against the criterion of accurate depiction, that we can stand outside our place in the world and see the world from nowhere in particular, and that there is a neutral method to apply that grounds our knowledge claims and thus requires that they be universally accepted.

The Practice of Inquiry

Among those who accept a general interpretive perspective on inquiry, different positions have been adopted on the role of methods. The term *general* is used here because at this point I wish to include all of those who express an allegiance to qualitative approaches, or to what are now often called new paradigm approaches, to social and educational inquiry. The reason for the broad categorization is that the descriptors *qualitative* and *new paradigm* often mean different things to different people.

There seem to be three broad points of view in discussions of this issue. First, some argue that a series of methods particular to interpretive inquiry can and must be developed, that these procedures will fulfill essentially the same role for interpretive inquiry—allow for detachment and objectivity—as similar methods do for empiricist inquiry. Second, some hold that although the ideas of objectivity, detachment, and methodological constraints as defined by empiricists are a fiction, interpretive inquiry must be made more systematic and rigorous. The claim here is that these methods cannot eliminate researcher subjectivity but that they can certainly minimize it; they are thereby the criteria against which to judge that some results are more objective than others. Finally, others argue that there are no particular methods to be applied for interpretive inquiry: An interpretive researcher cannot come to a study with a preestablished set of neutral procedures but can only choose to do some things as opposed to others based on what seems reasonable, given his or her interests and purposes, the context of the situation, and so on. In other words, there are no privileged methods for interpretive inquiry.

Before discussing these three viewpoints, a major point must be clarified. Although the three positions are differentiated for the purposes of this discussion, in actuality, the lines separating the three are quite blurred. As noted, this issue is one of the more confusing ones facing interpretive inquiry, and that confusion is reflected in some of the terminology used in the area. For example, well-known terms such as *objectivity, validity,* and *bias* may be defined very much as they are by empiricists, or they may be qualified or left vague as to their meanings. It is not uncommon to see the word *minimize* precede *bias* and to see *objective* discussed in terms of *more* and *less.* Exactly what is meant by these qualifiers is generally unclear. Similarly, "new" terms such as *catalytic validity* (Reason & Rowan, 1981b, p. 240), *trustworthy* (Guba, 1981, p. 85), and *objective subjectivity* (Reason & Rowan, 1981a, p. xiii) have recently gained currency, but their meanings, too, are unclear. Given this situation, any categorization of different positions is very tentative at best.

Among educational inquirers, those who have adopted the strongest position in regard to methods are probably LeCompte and Goetz (1982) and Miles and Huberman (1984a, 1984b). For the most part they define crucial concepts such as *validity, reliability,* and *objectivity* very much as they are defined by empiricists. Their concern is to make interpretive inquiry, or new paradigm forms of inquiry, "scientific in the positivist sense of the word" (Miles & Huberman, 1984a, p. 21). Or, as LeCompte and Goetz express the same point, the intent is to apply

> the tenets of external and internal validity and reliability as they are used in positivistic research traditions to work done by enthnographers and other researchers using qualitative methods. In doing so, these tenets are translated and made relevant for researchers in the qualitative, ethnographic, or phenomenological traditions. (p. 31)

LeCompte and Goetz (1982) then go on to discuss various procedures that inquirers can employ to achieve the objectivity that they believe is the dominant goal of all forms of inquiry—interpretive inquiry not excepted. Thus, the question that prompts the work of the strong methodologists is, "How does one actually proceed, step by step, through analysis to produce and document findings that other qualitative analysts would regard as dependable and trustworthy?" (Miles & Huberman, 1984a, p. 22).

Because this group defines certain crucial concepts in the same manner as do empiricists, does this mean that it also accepts, to a great extent, externalist-oriented assumptions? In other words, is the principal difference between these strong methodologists of interpretive inquiry and empiricists one of different methods to achieve the same end? Such questions are difficult to answer directly because methodologists tend not to discuss underlying assumptions at length. In fact, Miles and Huberman (1984a) argue that inquirers should not be particularly interested in such assumptions. As they say, "the grand debate should be left to those who care most about it" (p. 20) and "epistemological purity doesn't get research done" (p. 21).

Indirectly, however, one can infer that for the most part, these strong methodologists have accepted externalist assumptions and that accordingly, they find that procedural differences are the ones of consequence between empiricists and interpretivists. For example, their discussion of both the major concepts and of the procedures necessary to achieve the goals of objectivity, validity, trustworthy findings, and so on distinctly parallels the discussions of these topics by empiricists. LeCompte and Goetz (1982) lend strong credence to this inference when they note that "reliability and validity are problems shared by ethnographers, experimenters, and other researchers" (p. 32) and that whatever distinctions might exist among these perspectives on inquiry, they are of interest primarily because they result in "variations in the ways the problems of reliability and validity are approached" (p. 33). (See J. Smith, 1984, and J. Smith & Heshusius, 1986, for further discussions of this perspective on methods and interpretive inquiry.)

Advocates of the second position fall somewhere between the empiricist and strong methodologists who desire methodological constraints and those who argue against privileged or special procedures for interpretive inquiry. Although there are numerous variations within this category, advocates of this "middle ground" reject certain negative characteristics they attribute to empiricism, such as the reification of people into things, an overreliance on quantitative measurement, a reduction of processes into variables (Reason & Rowan, 1981a, pp. xiv-xvi), and the ideas of interest-free knowledge and validity as traditionally defined (see Lather, 1986, pp. 63–64). At the same time, however, they hold that researchers must avoid the "subjectivity and error of naive inquiry" and build an "approach to inquiry which *is* a systematic, rigorous search for truth" (Reason & Rowan, 1981a, p. xiii). For Lather (1986), this same desire is expressed in various ways: Inquirers must be "more systematic about establishing the trustworthiness of data" (p. 65); they must employ techniques that will mean their work must be "accepted as data rather than as metaphor" (p. 77); and self-corrective techniques must be formulated that "will check the credibility of our data and minimize the distorting effect of personal bias upon the logic of evidence" (p. 65).

The views of Betti (1980) and Hirsch (1967) on the issue of objectivity and methods definitely parallel those of the members of this group. This parallelism is present even though the former define methods more as logic of justification and the latter define methods more in terms of practical activities. The principal commonality is that neither Betti and Hirsch nor researchers representing a middle ground claim that there are specific, prescribed procedures that *guarantee* one can minimize bias or definitively answer the hermeneutic challenge of how to give an objective account of subjective meaning. Thus, just as Betti and Hirsch talk in terms of canons and logic of validation, advocates of a middle ground discuss various activities such as triangulation, member checks, feedback loops, and audit trails in terms of heuristic guides or general guidelines. These procedures are not employed because they ensure validity, but because "if used skillfully, [they will] increase the validity of an inquiry" (Reason & Rowan, 1981b, p. 244).

There is a significant lack of precision in these discussions of a middle ground for methods in the inquiry process. This lack is directly traceable to the question of how subjective interpreters can achieve an objective account of subjectively intended meaning. Put in different terms, the problem is that the underlying assumptions of interpretive inquiry are epistemologically nonfoundational. A recognition of this situation, especially the idea of no presuppositionless knowledge, has made people wary of talking about procedures in terms of what one must do in the name of objectivity. To argue that certain procedures are required would simply pose a contradiction—the attempt to provide a methodological foundation for knowledge based on nonfoundational assumptions. This is why even various strong methodologists, such as Miles and Huberman (1984a), feel it necessary to add qualifiers about the dangers of an "overpreoccupation with method" (p. 28).

On the other hand, however, there seems to be a concern that if certain procedures and criteria are not developed, researchers will be reduced to talking in terms of metaphors rather than in terms of data. For Reason and Rowan (1981a, p. xii), this would leave professional inquiry at the level of naive inquiry—a type of inquiry, laden with subjectivity, that is common to our day-to-day lives. The problem is that in the absence of at least some specified procedures, it may be impossible to establish methodological criteria to judge whether one can accept the results of inquiry as valid, place confidence in any particular finding, and so on. In other words, if methodological formulations do not provide for serious empirical accountability, then there may be no "grounds for accepting a researcher's description and analysis" (Lather, 1986, p. 78). The desire to ground knowledge, coupled with a recognition that there can be no presuppositionless knowledge, has made it very difficult for this position to "epistemologically locate" procedures or to define precisely the role of methods in the inquiry process (see J. Smith, 1984, for an extended discussion of these points).

The third position on the role of methods is very much in line with Gadamer's (1975) discussion of philosophical hermeneutics. In this case the claim is that there are no privileged methods or special procedures that will serve to ground or make universally acceptable a researcher's interpretations. The assumptions of interpretive inquiry—such as a subject-subject relationship and the inseparability of facts and values—and the significance view of ourselves as persons are incompatible with the idea that objectivity can be achieved via methodology. If one conceptualizes hermeneutics as our mode of being in the world, then, as Pearsol (1987) bluntly puts it, the "interpretive perspective cannot appeal to external methodological criteria, like triangulation or trustworthiness, for protection against bias in reaching conclusions" (p. 335).

What is the status, then, of the various procedures such as triangulation, audit trails, and member checks that are so frequently associated with interpretive inquiry? For this third position, such techniques must be seen as activities that researchers may or may not decide important to employ, depending on the context and on their interests, purposes, and values. For example, certain inquirers in certain contexts may reason that member checks are important—but this does not mean that other inquirers, even in the same context, will similarly decide that they are necessary.

Just as a difference of opinion about the interpretation over meanings, intentions, and motives cannot be resolved by an appeal to an independently existing reality, a difference of opinion about the procedures used cannot be resolved by an appeal to what one must do in the name of objectivity. Taylor's (1971) characterization of the hermeneutical circle of explanation can also be applied to our decisions and disagreements about procedures:

> Ultimately a good explanation is one which makes sense of the behavior; but then to appreciate a good explanation, one has to agree on what makes

good sense; what makes good sense is a function of one's readings; and these in turn are based on the kind of sense one understands. (p. 14)

What it makes sense to do in any given research situation depends on one's reading of that situation—which in turn depends on the kind of sense one understands.

This perspective on methods goes even one step further: Method and objectivity are seen as antithetical—just as truth and method are for Gadamer (1975). The idea in this case is that method predetermines our way of approaching the world. A conceptualization of the researcher on one side and the object on the other side, with the researcher calling upon a preestablished, presumably neutral set of methods in order to depict the object accurately, can only lead to the control and manipulation of knowledge. Such a position fails to recognize that we must stand in a dialogical relationship with our subject matter. That is, our condition as finite, hermeneutical beings means that just as the researcher poses questions of the subject matter, so too must the researcher be open to the questions posed to him or her by the subject matter. An objective interpretation of intentions, motivations, and so on, which can only be defined for this third position as what is "agreed upon," can arise only from the dialogue and not from the application of privileged methods.

Thus, the profound difference between this position and the two previously described—as well as the empiricist position—is the issue of methods for minimizing bias, constraining subjectivity, grounding and legitimating knowledge, and so on versus norms for negotiating agreement. This negotiation of agreement, or dialogue, must take place not only among inquirers, but also between inquirers and the subject matter of their inquiry. In the absence of special procedures or methods to ground or legitimate interpretations, the resources inquirers bring to the negotiation process are very much like those employed by laypeople—especially in the sense that the norms that we accept to guide this process are not expressions of epistemological privilege, but are rather expressions of the moral standards we acknowledge in regard to social interaction. This is one of the major reasons why many people refer to social inquiry as moral inquiry.

SUMMARY

There are two different perspectives concerning the role of methods in the process of inquiry. These perspectives reflect and support two different views of researchers as persons and of persons as researchers. On the one side is the representation view, with the idea that we can detach ourselves from the world and "look back in" to assess accurately or objectively how things really are in the world. On the other side is the significance view, which holds that such detachment is impossible and that the world can only be described in terms of the significance it has for the describer.

For empiricism and for some inquirers who place themselves in the interpretive camp, method is crucial for detachment and objectivity. Methods serve to constrain the subjectivity of the researcher and thus allow for valid results, or results in which we can have confidence. For another group of interpretive inquirers the role assigned to methods is somewhat ambiguous. They have held out the possibility of objectivity, as Betti and Hirsch have at the philosophical level, but have not strictly tied this possibility to a set of privileged procedures. Accordingly, they speak in terms of the need to develop procedures—heuristic guides as opposed to things one must do—and the need to minimize bias. Finally, one group of interpretive inquirers argues that there are no particular procedures, that researchers do what they do depending on the particular situation and on their particular interests, purposes, and values.

CHAPTER VIII
Objectivism and Relativism: The Nature of Social and Educational Inquiry

> But at the heart of the objectivist's vision, and what makes sense of his or her passion, is the belief that there are or must be some fixed, permanent constraints to which we can appeal and which are secure and stable. At its most profound level the relativist's message is that there are no such basic constraints except those that we invent or temporally (and temporarily) accept. . . . The primary reason why the *agon* [clash] between objectivists and relativists has become so intense today is the growing apprehension that there may be nothing—not God, reason, philosophy, science, or poetry—that answers to and satisfies our longing for ultimate constraints, for a stable and reliable rock upon which we can secure our thought and action. (Bernstein, 1983, p. 19)

In addition to a summary, this concluding chapter must include a brief discussion of the crucial issue of whether we can realize the objectivist's vision of a secure foundation upon which to build our knowledge or whether we must accept the relativist message that such a permanent foundation is not available to us. Although this issue, as well as its implications for inquiry, has been implicit in the previous chapters, for the most part it has remained in the background of the discussion. This situation must now be rectified because, at its most profound level, any concern over the different approaches to social and educational inquiry is intimately entangled with the issue of objectivism versus relativism.

The fundamental importance of this issue is immediately apparent when one looks at the nature of the major criticism each perspective directs at the other—empiricists at interpretivists, and vice versa, and to a lesser extent, advocates of hermeneutics as a method for inquiry at those who hold to the philosophical version of hermeneutics, and vice versa. For empiricists, for example, the ultimate problem with the interpretive approach is that it leads to an unacceptable and possibly dangerous relativism. This approach offers no secure and stable criteria and, even worse, either implies or directly argues that no such criteria can ever be established to sort out the correct from the incorrect, the well-done study from the poorly done study, and so on. If this is so, then not only are there no grounds for our knowledge claims, there is not much point in even talking in terms of knowledge and truth. The danger is that this approach reduces everything to the level of personal opinion and thus leaves open the possibility of a permanent clash of positions based on nothing more than personal discernments.

For interpretivists, empiricists are naive in thinking that knowledge claims can be grounded, methodologically or otherwise, and that there is a way to resolve our disagreements that stands above and beyond dialogue. The only way our knowledge could be grounded would be to do what is clearly impossible—to abstract ourselves from our place in the world and thereby take a view from nowhere in particular. In other words, objectivity requires that we have independent access to both an independently existing reality and to our own minds. The belief that objectivism is possible simply misses the most crucial point about us as human beings—we are and never can be anything other than finite, historical beings. Thus, it is no exaggeration to say that the differences in the approaches to social and educational inquiry ultimately must be understood in terms of the empiricist vision of objectivism versus the interpretivist message of relativism.

OBJECTIVISM AND RELATIVISM

Clearly the concepts of objectivism and relativism have been present throughout the above discussion of the differences between the two perspectives to social and educational inquiry. The separation of investigator from what is investigated, the role of methods as constraint, the separation of facts and values, and so on are all essential to the empiricist vision of objectivism. Similarly, the ideas of a constructed reality, the inseparability of facts and values, the claim of no special procedures or methods, and so on are integral to the interpretive message that there is no secure and stable foundation for our knowledge claims. What, then, are we to make of this issue of objectivism versus relativism?

The Concepts Defined

As is always the case, a great deal depends on how terms such as these are defined. Even though *objectivism* and *relativism* are used with great frequency, their exact definition in any given situation is often left unclear. For empiricism, objectivism seems most accurately characterized as the "basic conviction that there is or must be some permanent, ahistorical matrix or framework to which we can ultimately appeal in determining the nature of rationality, knowledge, truth, goodness, or rightness" (Bernstein, 1983, p. 8). This conceptualization of objectivism also includes the ideas that reality exists independent of our interest in it and that this reality can be described as it actually is (accurate reflection).

This conceptualization, however, does not hold that certain knowledge claims are completely resistant to criticism. Even the most adamant empiricists seem to agree that there are no knowledge claims that are totally immune from criticism, counterinterpretation, and so on. Thus, the objectivist position goes no further than to hold, very often on an intuitionist basis, that there is a foundation for knowledge and that there are "some fixed, permanent constraints to which we can appeal" (Bernstein, 1983, p. 19) to adjudicate competing knowledge claims. This constraint, of course, is the external referent point of reality itself—a reality that can be described as it is (objectively) given the proper methodological approach.

Relativism holds that objectivism errs by claiming that there is a permanent matrix to appeal to for sorting out knowledge claims and resolving disagreements. For this conceptualization, knowledge claims and, for that matter, claims made in other areas—such as the moral—can only be undertaken relative to a particular conceptual scheme, form of life, and so on. Relativism maintains that

> there can be no higher appeal than to a given conceptual scheme, language game, set of social practices, or historical epoch. There is a nonreducible plurality of such schemes, paradigms, and practices; there is no substantive overarching framework in which radically different and alternative schemes are commensurable—no universal standards that somehow stand outside of and above these competing alternatives. (Bernstein, 1983, pp. 11–12)

Just as the definition of objectivism does not honor a crude absolutism, this definition of relativism does not honor the strong subjectivist notion of relativism that is the basis for the claim "anything goes." Only when relativism is given this strong subjectivist cast does the idea come to the fore that all judgments are reduced to matters of taste, personal opinion, or emotive reaction. The point is that this version of relativism, because it still holds that reason and rationality are crucial (even if only within a conceptual scheme), does not reduce itself to a stubborn clash of opinion or of how things happen to strike people at the moment. Thus, relativism goes no further than to hold that there is no neutral methodology to employ, or "brute data" to appeal to, to resolve competing knowledge claims. The concepts of truth, reality, the good, and so on "must be understood as relative to a particular conceptual scheme, theoretical framework, paradigm, form of life, society, or culture" (Bernstein, 1983, p. 8).

Thus, objective inquiry and objective results are understood in terms of "making contact with reality." The proper application of the proper methods is essential here because it constrains researchers by allowing them to maintain the necessary detachment from what they study. Since this leads to accurate depictions of reality, reality itself can and must serve as the referent for grounding knowledge claims and resolving disagreements. Relativism must be understood as a denial of objectivism or a denial of such a referent point. Every claim made to truth, to the correct and right, and so on must be undertaken as part of a conceptual scheme. As such, there is nothing that stands apart from or beyond reasoned dialogue when it comes to justifying knowledge and resolving differences. However, just as objectivism should not be thought of in terms of an absolutism, relativism should not be conceptualized as "anything goes." For interpretive inquirers, just as for empiricist inquirers, this latter position is a foolish one.

Criticism and Response

Given these definitions of objectivism and relativism, each side must respond to the major charge brought against it. Empiricists, even if they are not absolutists, still must answer the charge that their methods do not prevent interests, purposes, and values from entering the research process. For critics of this approach, this charge is a valid one because, in the end, methods themselves depend on interests, purposes, and values. To paraphrase Hesse (1980), one's interest in the application of a particular theory influences the method used to develop that theory, so that different interests can very easily lead to, if not different procedures in a mechanical sense, certainly different interpretations of the procedures.

Over the last few years various arguments have been advanced in support of this claim: Rorty's (1979, 1982) discussion of a neutral language versus an evaluative language, Hesse's (1980) examination of theory and values in social inquiry, Giddens's (1976) discussion of the permeability of the boundary between lay and professional knowledge, Taylor's (1985) concern over the univocity of data transformation procedures, Putnam's (1981) analysis of Bayesian priors as subjective degrees of belief, and D. MacKenzie's (1981) discussion of eugenics and the development of statistics in Great Britain in the 19th century. These arguments all result in the conclusion that the desire for a formal method, one that is isolated from theoretical concerns and from values, is an unrealizable one. And if this is so, then the desire for objectivism, or for a solid foundation upon which to construct our knowledge, is also an unrealizable one.

The principal charge to which interpretivists must respond, their disavowal of "anything goes" notwithstanding, is that any form of relativism is self-contradictory and thereby self-refuting. This argument can be summarized as follows: If statements can only be relatively true as opposed to absolutely true, why should this condition not apply to the statement of relativism itself? And if this is so,

> then the relativist's position itself is only "relative" and "subjective" and need not be taken seriously by anyone who does not already subscribe to that position. If, on the other hand, the relativist thesis does not apply to itself, then there is something which is absolutely true (namely, the relativist's own thesis), a position which blatantly contradicts that very thesis. (Meiland & Krausz, 1982, p. 31)

Thus, the claim that there is no permanent foundation for knowledge and no permanent, neutral matrix with which to resolve differences poses an absolute statement, thereby violating the relativist scheme—unless, of course, one is willing to tolerate direct contradiction. An empiricist might also point out the irony of ignoring this contradiction: After all, it is the interpretivists themselves who talk of coherence as a possible definition of truth and who focus on reasoned discourse and dialogue—which might easily be taken to mean that one must present a coherent justification for one's position.

Both sides have attempted, of course, to respond to these charges, but a good case can be made that their responses are not yet well developed. Certainly, neither side has been able to present an argument to convince the other. Those who have kept objectivism alive have done so by rejecting substantial aspects of the standard version of empiricism. For example, the security of knowledge claims and the strong distinction between professional knowledge and lay knowledge have been, if not abandoned, certainly modified. On the other hand, however, this group has generally attempted to maintain certain crucial features of empiricism, such as the ability to explain and predict and the idea of inquiry as a systematic, public enterprise.

Among those who have attempted to sustain objectivism as a workable concept in the face of major concessions to hermeneutics are advocates of what is called critical realism and those who, as previously discussed, hold that there is a method for the interpretive approach. However, is making their case for objectivism, both groups have actually attempted to redefine the concept—but in ways that are not completely clear. For example, Manicas and Secord (1983), in adopting a critical realist perspective, say that if objectivity is "construed as warranted assertibility" (p. 410), we can avoid the "morass of relativism" (p. 410). However, just as those who favor a method of interpretation have had difficulty defining crucial terms such as *objectively subjective* and *more or less objective*, Manicas and Secord have not given a clear and precise definition for *warranted assertibility*. As J. Yates (personal communication, May 10, 1986) has so well noted, if the warranties themselves are culturally and historically conditioned, then it is unclear what kind of definition one might give to the term *objectivity*.

A second attempt to recast objectivism is related to the nonabsolutist position noted above. The idea in this case is not that inquiry presents completely objective or accurate depictions of reality, but that objectivity must be thought of in terms of inquiry that presents increasingly accurate approximations of reality. The idea is that over time, inquiry allows us to obtain a "more accurate, though always incomplete or biased, picture of reality" (McClintock, 1987, p. 316). In other words, objectivity must be understood against the backdrop of inquiry as a linear, cumulative process that produces closer and closer approximations of reality. There is, however, the following logical problem with this position: To judge how closely one's version is to a particular bit of reality implies that one already knows that reality—but if one already knew that reality, then there would be no point in bothering with approximations. Although this position may be appealing, it is a very difficult one to bring into focus.

For interpretivists, there are basically two responses—other than completely ignoring the charge that relativism is self-refuting (which is not uncommon). The first argues that critics are mistaken if they assume that the intent is to convince others to adopt a relativist position. The claim that there is no permanent neutral matrix to ground knowledge claims and resolve differences is simply a statement of our human finitude and not an argument to be judged by empiricist and/or absolutist standards.

The second response to this charge is generally in line with the position taken by Gadamer (1975). In this case the idea that relativism is self-contradictory is accepted, but the counterclaim is that this acceptance does not make any difference. Gadamer fully concedes that relativism is self-refuting, but he maintains that this concession does not lead to any insights of consequence. As he puts it, the self-refuting case against relativism, correct though it may be, does not result in "superior insight of any value" (p. 308). For better or worse, there is little interest in directly responding to the self-contradiction criticism—rather, this criticism is either dismissed or bypassed.

Thus, each side has had major charges leveled against it, and a good case can be made that neither side has responded adequately to these charges. Empiricism has unsuccessfully attempted to redefine objectivism; the interpretive approach has attempted either to ignore or dismiss the idea that relativism is self-refuting. This lack of a convincing response is not, however, surprising. As Bernstein (1983, pp. 1–4) so clearly notes, this issue brings us to the very edge of our present thinking—not only in regard to approaches to inquiry, but also with reference to almost every aspect of our intellectual and cultural lives.

The Paradox of Objectivism and Relativism

Each approach to inquiry brings with it its own special paradox, a paradox that in each case contributes greatly to the inability of either side to present a convincing response. The paradox of objectivism is that a truly objective understanding would be possible only in conditions in which objectivity was not a problem (see Bauman, 1978, p. 231). In other words, the only way objectivity could be achieved would be if we could somehow transcend our own finitude—if we could be context-free in our view of the world. But if we could adopt such a "contextless" or God's eye view, then objective understanding would not have been a problem to begin with, and there would have been no need to construct methods or even address the issue of how to achieve objective knowledge.

The interpretive perspective ultimately comes to rest on the idea of conversation or dialogue. Thus, an issue of great consequence to this perspective is how inquiry can contribute to the practical task of establishing and maintaining a free and open dialogue. As will be recalled, this issue is central to interpretive inquiry because our differences cannot be resolved by an appeal to an external referent or to how things really are, but can only be worked out through "debate, conversation, and dialogue" (Bernstein, 1983, p. 223). The paradox here is that the call for reasoned discourse based on a sense of shared community "already presupposes, at least in an incipient form, the existence of the very sense of community that such practical and political reason is intended to develop" (Bernstein, 1983, p. 225). A research community—one that fully realizes that appeals to an external referent are impossible (one that accepts relativism in this sense)—may only be possible when it is not needed; and when it is needed, it may not be possible.

Clearly, no discussion of these two approaches to social and educational inquiry can stray very far from the issue of objectivism versus relativism. Empiricist inquiry has long laid claim to being foundational—that the proper methodology, properly followed, will allow for a depiction of social and educational life as it really is (objectivism). Recently, however, this position has been seriously criticized. Interpretive inquiry is based on the idea that our knowledge cannot be grounded—via methodology or otherwise. There are only different interpretations based on different interests, purposes, and values (relativism), and all we can do is promote dialogue among those holding different interpretations. This position has in turn been criticized as leading to an unacceptable relativism. To date, neither side has produced a convincing response to the criticism directed at it. Although the problems seem clear, what the next stage in our thinking will be and what the consequences will be for the future of social and educational inquiry remain unclear at this time.

IN THE END . . .

In the end, we are faced with two different perspectives on social and educational inquiry. The terms used to denote these different perspectives vary greatly—*quantitative* versus *qualitative, explanation* versus *understanding, scientistic* versus *naturalistic,* and so on. In our case, the terms *empiricism* and *interpretation* have been employed to label these perspectives at the level of the practice of inquiry, whereas *externalism* and *internalism* have been used to refer to the philosophical background or the logic of justification associated with each, respectively.

At the level of the techniques employed in doing research, no great distinction need be made between the two approaches. That each side can "borrow" techniques or specific practices from the other poses no problem of consequence. However, at the level of the logic of justification that supports each approach, there are differences of major importance.

The first major point of distinction involves the relationship of the investigator to what is investigated. The empiricist approach to inquiry holds to an externalist position that maintains that social and educational reality is an existent reality—one that is external and independent of us. The investigator and the process of investigation are thought of as separate from what is investigated. Truth, then, is defined or characterized as the correspondence of our words to (the accurate reflection of) this external, independently existing reality.

The internalist perspective, upon which the interpretive approach is based, holds that social and educational reality is a constructed reality.

We construct reality, as it is for us at any given time and place, through a constant process of interpretation and reinterpretation of both the intentional, meaningful behavior of others and our own intentional, meaningful behavior. There can be no distinct separation between the investigator and what is investigated. Inquiry is not a matter of offering interpretations of reality, but one of offering interpretations that become reality, to the extent they are agreed upon. Accordingly, truth—or what we come to accept as true in terms of intentions, purposes, and meanings—is the result of socially conditioned agreement, arising from dialogue and reasoned discourse.

Empiricist inquirers, in line with externalist assumptions, hold that the realm of facts stands separate from the realm of values. The central claim here is that it is possible to describe "objects" such as intentions or purposes, for example, without appraising or evaluating those intentions or purposes. Even though a researcher's own values pose a constant threat to both the process of inquiry and the accurate depiction of the facts, this threat can be controlled (or seriously minimized) by the proper conduct of inquiry and by an adherence to values of open and honest inquiry.

The internalist position accepts the conclusion that any distinction between facts and values is "hopelessly fuzzy" at best. There can be no facts without values, and different values inevitably result in different facts. The distinction between describing and appraising people's meaningful social action is virtually impossible to make. Moreover, the inseparability of facts and values, although a problem for empiricism, is the essence of interpretive inquiry. This is a major reason why many think that social and educational inquiry should be called moral inquiry.

The intent of empiricist inquiry is to produce empirically verified knowledge. This is knowledge that accurately describes how things really are out there in the social and educational world. Social and educational inquiry succeeds when it is able to explain and predict events scientifically with reference to laws and theory. The latter point about prediction is important because, in the end, one of the major goals of empiricist inquiry is not only an intellectual mastery, but also a practical mastery, of the subject matter.

Interpretive inquiry is concerned with the meaningful behavior of people—their intentions, purposes, motives, and so on. The goal in this case is to make clear what is unclear or not well understood. This process is hermeneutical because interpretations must always be undertaken within a context. The circular process of interpretation between parts and whole has no definite beginning or ending points. Interpretive inquiry succeeds when it produces interpretations that deepen and enlarge our sense of community as social and moral beings.

Finally, different positions are taken on the role of methods in the research process. For empiricists and for some "new paradigm" inquirers who hold that objectivity is the goal of all forms of inquiry, established methods or procedures are essential. Methods are a constraint on the subjectivity of the researcher and thereby allow researchers to maintain the detachment necessary to obtain valid results, or results in which others can have confidence. On the other side, many interpretivists argue that there are no special procedures for the conduct of inquiry. The inquirer does not commence a study with a set of fixed, universally applicable procedures already in hand, but does what seems important and reasonable to do, given the situation, his or her own interests and purposes, and so on. Just as an interpretation can only be justified through reasoned discourse, so it is for the procedures one uses in pursuit of that interpretation.

Do these differences matter for inquirers? Clearly the answer is *yes*. For example, the interpretation given to the results of inquiry differs, depending on the logic of justification one accepts. The phrases "research has shown" and "the results of the research indicate" are subject to different interpretations, given different logics of justification. For empiricists, these phrases are the researcher's claims to have made contact with an independently existing reality, claims that are seen as divorced from his or her particular interests and purposes. For interpretive inquiry, on the other hand, these phrases announce an interpretation that becomes reality—to the extent it finds agreement—as it is for those interpreters at any given time and place, a reality that is very much constrained by values, interests, and purposes.

These differences are also important for how inquirers resolve disagreements among themselves over the process and results of inquiry. If empiricists disagree, they must hold that a further, methodologically proper analysis of the facts of the case will eventually allow them to sort out the problem. There is an external referent—reality itself—to appeal to in resolving disagreements. For interpretive inquiry, disagreements over both the process and results of inquiry can only take place through dialogue because there are no unconceptualized facts, no independent external referent to appeal to. Of course, the most tangible expression of this issue occurs in the all-important area of what gets published and what does not get published in professional journals.

In a final example, these differences even extend to how social and educational inquiry should be classified within the structure of our intellectual life and, by extension, within the structure of the university. As noted by Bernstein (1983) in the opening quote of this book, one can think in terms of a three-part division of the natural sciences, the social sciences, and the humanities, or in terms of a two-part division of the natural sciences and the moral sciences. Put differently, is social and educational inquiry more at home with the physical sciences, or would it be more appropriately aligned with the humanities? Empiricists would undoubtedly opt for the former, whereas interpretivists who perceive inquiry as continuous with literature, art, and journalism would choose the latter.

What does the future hold for this concern over the different perspectives on social and educational inquiry? It seems unlikely that the discussion will end with a victor and a vanquished. The two sides are so significantly different in their positions and, for that matter, in the language they purport to speak—a neutral scientific or value-free language versus a value-laden language of everyday discourse—that debate between them is unlikely to end with one side or the other convinced of the error of its ways. It also seems unlikely that a *via media* can be found between the two positions. Weber's apparent lack of success in finding such a middle ground should pose a serious cautionary tale for those who hope that a blending of the approaches is possible.

In the end, it seems most reasonable to conclude that eventually we must somehow "transcend" this issue and develop new ways to think about the nature of inquiry. However, exactly what it will mean for social and educational inquiry to "move beyond" the issues of empiricism and interpretation, externalism and internalism, and objectivism and relativism is impossible, at this point, to say.

REFERENCES

Abel, T. (1948). The operation called *verstehen*. *American Journal of Sociology, 54*, 211–218.

Ariès, P. (1962). *Centuries of childhood*. New York: Vintage.

Aron, R. (1967). *Main currents in sociological thought 2*. New York: Penguin Books.

Aron, R. (1970). The logic of the social sciences. In D. Wrong (Ed.), *Max Weber* (pp. 77–89). Englewood Cliffs, NJ: Prentice-Hall.

Bauman, Z. (1978). *Hermeneutics and social science*. London: Century Hutchinson, Ltd. (Published in U.S.A. by Columbia University Press.)

Bellah, R. (1981). The ethical aims of social inquiry. *Teachers College Record, 83*, 1–18.

Benton, T. (1977). *Philosophical foundations of the three sociologies*. London: Routledge and Kegan Paul.

Bergner, J. (1981). *The origins of formalism in social science*. Chicago: University of Chicago Press.

Bernstein, R. (1983). *Beyond objectivism and relativism*. Philadelphia: University of Pennsylvania Press.

Betti, E. (1980). Hermeneutics as the general methodology of the *Geisteswissenschaften*. In J. Bleicher, *Contemporary hermeneutics* (pp. 51–94). London: Routledge and Kegan Paul.

Bhaskar, R. (1979). *The possibility of naturalism*. Atlantic Highlands, NJ: Humanities Press.

Blakney, J. (1960). *An Immanuel Kant reader*. New York: Harper and Bros.

Bleicher, J. (1980). *Contemporary hermeneutics*. London: Routledge and Kegan Paul.

Borg, W., & Gall, M. (1983). *Educational research*. New York: Longman.

Brecht, A. (1959). *Political theory*. Princeton, NJ: Princeton University Press.

Church, W. (1974). *The influence of the Enlightenment on the French Revolution*. Lexington, MA: Heath.

Cohen, M., & Nagel, E. (1934). *An introduction to the logic of the scientific method*. New York: Harcourt, Brace, and World.

Cronbach, L. (1971). Test validation. In R. Thorndike (Ed.), *Educational measurement* (2nd ed.) (pp. 443–507). Washington, DC: American Council on Education.

Cronbach, L., Ambron, S., Dornbusch, S., Hess, R., Hornik, R., Phillips, D., Walker, D., & Weiner, S. (1980). *Toward reform of program evaluation.* San Francisco: Jossey-Bass.

Cronbach, L., & Meehl, P. (1955). Construct validity in psychological tests. *Psychological Bulletin, 52,* 281–302.

De Kruif, P. (1932). *Men against death.* New York: Harcourt.

Durkheim, E. (1938). *Rules of the sociological method* (S. Solovay & J. Mueller, Trans., & G. Catlin, Ed.). Chicago: University of Chicago Press.

Durkheim, E. (1951). *Suicide* (J. Spaulding & G. Simpson, Trans., & G. Simpson, Ed.). New York: Free Press.

Ermarth, M. (1978). *Wilhelm Dilthey: The critique of historical reason.* Chicago: University of Chicago Press.

Ewing, A. (1974). *Idealism: A critical survey.* London: Methuen.

Gadamer, H.-G. (1975). *Truth and method.* New York: Seabury Press.

Giddens, A. (1976). *New rules of the sociological method.* New York: Basic Books.

Giddens, A. (1977). *Studies in social and political theory.* New York: Basic Books.

Goetz, J., & LeCompte, M. (1984). *Ethnography and qualitative design in educational research.* New York: Academic Press.

Grayling, A. (1982). *An introduction to philosophical logic.* Totowa, NJ: Barnes and Noble.

Guba, E. (1981). Criteria for assessing the trustworthiness of naturalistic inquiry. *Educational Communication and Technology Journal, 29,* 79–92.

Hanson, N. (1958). *Patterns of discovery.* Cambridge: Cambridge University Press.

Harris, R. (1954). *Nature, mind, and modern science.* London: George Allen and Unwin.

Heidegger, M. (1962). *Being and time* (J. Macquarrie & E. Robinson, Trans.). London: SCM Press.

Heilbroner, R. (1972, March 9). Through the Marxian maze. *New York Review of Books, 4,* 9–10.

Hempel, C. (1965). *Aspects of scientific explanation.* New York: Free Press.

Hempel, C. (1966). *Philosophy of natural science.* Englewood Cliffs, NJ: Prentice-Hall.

Hesse, M. (1980). *Revolutions and reconstructions in the philosophy of science.* Brighton, England: Harvester Press.

Hirsch, E. (1967). *Validity in interpretation.* New Haven, CT: Yale University Press.

Hodges, H. (1944). *Wilhelm Dilthey.* New York: Oxford University Press.

Holmes, M. (1986, April). *Traditionalism and educational administration.* Paper presented at the annual meeting of the American Educational Research Association, San Francisco.

Hughes, H. (1958). *Consciousness and society.* New York: Knopf.

Hughes, J. (1980). *The philosophy of social research.* London: Longman.

Hull, L. (1959). *History and philosophy of science.* London: Longman.

Kaplan, A. (1964). *The conduct of inquiry.* New York: Harper & Row. (Originally published by Chandler, 1964.)

Keat, R., & Urry, J. (1975). *Social theory as science.* London: Routledge and Kegan Paul.

Kuhn, T. (1962). *The structure of scientific revolutions.* Chicago: University of Chicago Press.

Lather, P. (1986). Issues of validity in openly ideological research: Between a rock and a soft place. *Interchange, 17,* 63–84.

LeCompte, M., & Goetz, J. (1982). Problems of reliability and validity in ethnographic research. *Review of Educational Research, 52,* 31–60.

Lessnoff, M. (1974). *The structure of social science.* London: George Allen and Unwin.

Louch, A. (1966). *Explanation and human action.* London: Oxford University Press.

Lynch, K. (1983). Qualitative and quantitative evaluation: Two terms in search of a meaning. *Educational Evaluation and Policy Analysis, 5,* 461–464.

MacKenzie, B. (1977). *Behaviourism and the limits of scientific method.* Atlantic Highlands, NJ: Humanities Press.

MacKenzie, D. (1981). *Statistics in Great Britain: 1865–1930.* Edinburgh: Edinburgh University Press.

MacKinnon, E. (1972). *The problem of scientific realism.* New York: Appleton-Century-Crofts.

Manicas, P., & Secord, P. (1983). Implications for psychology of the new philosophy of science. *American Psychologist, 38,* 399–413.

McClintock, C. (1987). Administrators as information brokers: A managerial perspective on naturalistic evaluation. *Evaluation and Program Planning, 10,* 315–323.

Meiland, J., & Krausz, M. (1982). [Section introductions]. In J. Meiland & M. Krausz (Eds.), *Relativism* (pp. 13–17, 30–33). Notre Dame, IN: University of Notre Dame Press.

Melden, A. (1961). *Free action.* London: Routledge and Kegan Paul.

Messick, S. (1980). Test validity and the ethics of assessment. *American Psychologist, 35,* 1012–1027.

Miles, M., & Huberman, A. (1984a). Drawing valid meaning from qualitative data: Toward a shared craft. *Educational Researcher, 13*(5), 20–30.

Miles, M., & Huberman, A. (1984b). *Qualitative data analysis.* Beverly Hills, CA: Sage.

Myrdal, G. (1944). Methodological note on facts and valuations in social science. In G. Myrdal, *An American dilemma* (pp. 1035–1064). New York: McGraw-Hill.

Myrdal, G. (1958). *Value in social theory.* London: Routledge and Kegan Paul.

Nagel, E. (1961). *The structure of science.* New York: Harcourt, Brace, and World.

Nagel, T. (1981). *Mortal questions.* New York: Cambridge University Press.

Nagel, T. (1986). *The view from nowhere.* New York: Oxford University Press.

O'Connor, D. (1964). Locke. In D. O'Connor (Ed.), *A critical history of Western philosophy* (pp. 204–219). Glencoe, IL: Free Press.

Outhwaite, W. (1975). *Understanding social life: The method called verstehen.* New York: Holmes and Meier.

Outhwaite, W. (1983). *Concept formation in social science.* London: Routledge and Kegan Paul.

Palmer, R. (1969). *Hermeneutics.* Evanston, IL: Northwestern University Press.

Pearsol, J. (1987). Justifying conclusions in naturalistic evaluations: An interpretive perspective. *Evaluation and Program Planning, 10,* 335–341.

Pinkard, T. (1976). Interpretation and verification in the human sciences: A note on Taylor. *Philosophy of Social Science, 6,* 165–173.

Polanyi, M. (1958). *Personal knowledge.* Chicago: University of Chicago Press.

Polkinghorne, D. (1983). *Methodology for the human sciences.* Albany: State University of New York Press.

Putnam, H. (1981). *Reason, truth, and history.* Cambridge: Cambridge University Press.

Reason, P., & Rowan, J. (1981a). Foreword. In P. Reason & J. Rowan (Eds.), *Human inquiry* (pp. xi–xxiv). New York: John Wiley.

Reason, P., & Rowan, J. (1981b). Issues of validity in new paradigm research. In P. Reason & J. Rowan (Eds.), *Human inquiry* (pp. 239–262). New York: John Wiley.

Reichardt, C., & Cook, T. (1979). Beyond qualitative and quantitative methods. In T. Cook & C. Reichardt (Eds.), *Qualitative and quantita-*

tive methods in evaluation research (pp. 7–32). Beverly Hills, CA: Sage.

Rescher, N. (1973). *Conceptual idealism.* Oxford: Basil Blackwell.

Robinson, D. (1981). *An intellectual history of psychology.* New York: MacMillan.

Rorty, R. (1979). *Philosophy and the mirror of nature.* Princeton, NJ: Princeton University Press.

Rorty, R. (1982). Method, social science, and social hope. In R. Rorty, *Consequences of pragmatism* (pp. 191–210). Minneapolis: University of Minnesota Press.

Rossman, G., & Wilson, B. (1984, April). *Numbers and words: Combining quantitative and qualitative methods in a single large-scale study.* Paper presented at the annual meeting of the American Educational Research Association, New Orleans.

Rubinstein, D. (1981). *Marx and Wittgenstein.* London: Routledge and Kegan Paul.

Rudner, R. (1966). *Philosophy of social science.* Englewood Cliffs, NJ: Prentice-Hall.

Russell, B. (1912). *The problems of philosophy.* London: Oxford University Press.

Russell, B. (1945). *A history of Western philosophy.* New York: Simon and Schuster.

Simey, T. (1969). *Social science and social purpose.* New York: Schocken.

Simpson, G. (1969). *Auguste Comte: Sire of sociology.* Westport, CT: Greenwood Press.

Smith, F. (1977). *Pulsars.* Cambridge: Cambridge University Press.

Smith, J. (1984). The problem of criteria for judging interpretive inquiry. *Educational Evaluation and Policy Analysis, 4,* 379–391.

Smith, J. (1985). Social reality as mind-dependent versus mind-independent and the interpretation of test validity. *Journal of Research and Development in Education, 1,* 1–9.

Smith, J. (1988). The evaluator/researcher as person versus the person as evaluator/researcher. *Educational Researcher, 17*(2), 18–23.

Smith, J., & Heshusius, L. (1986). Closing down the conversation: The end of the quantitative-qualitative debate. *Educational Researcher, 15*(1), 4–12.

Smith, M. (1987). Publishing qualitative research. *American Educational Research Journal, 24,* 173–183.

Spencer, M. (1982). The ontologies of social science. *Philosophy of Social Science, 12,* 121–141.

Strauss, L. (1953). *Natural right and history.* Chicago: University of Chicago Press.

Szacki, J. (1979). *History of sociological thought*. Westport, CT: Greenwood Press.

Sztompka, P. (1979). *Sociological dilemmas*. New York: Academic Press.

Taylor, C. (1971). Interpretation and the sciences of man. *Review of Metaphysics, 25*, 3–51.

Taylor, C. (1973). Neutrality in political science. In A. Ryan (Ed.), *The philosophy of social explanation* (pp. 139–170). London: Oxford University Press.

Taylor, C. (1980). Understanding in human science. *Review of Metaphysics, 34*, 25–38.

Taylor, C. (1985). The concept of a person. In C. Taylor, *Human agency and language* (pp. 97–114). Cambridge: Cambridge University Press.

Thomas, D. (1979). *Naturalism and social science*. New York: Cambridge University Press.

Thompson, K. (1975). *Auguste Comte: The foundation of sociology*. New York: Halstead Press.

Trigg, R. (1980). *Reality at risk*. Totowa, NJ: Barnes and Noble.

Urban, W. (1949). *Beyond realism and idealism*. London: George Allen and Unwin.

Warnock, G. (1964). Kant. In D. O'Connor (Ed.), *A critical history of Western philosophy* (pp. 296–318). Glencoe, IL: Free Press.

Wartofsky, M. (1968). *Conceptual foundations of scientific thought*. New York: Macmillan.

Weber, M. (1946a). Politics as a vocation. In H. Gerth & C. Mills (Trans. and Eds.), *From Max Weber* (pp. 77–128). New York: Oxford University Press.

Weber, M. (1946b). Science as a vocation. In H. Gerth & C. Mills (Trans. and Eds.), *From Max Weber* (pp. 129–156). New York: Oxford University Press.

Weber, M. (1947). *Theory of social and economic organization* (A. Henderson & T. Parsons, Trans.). Oxford: Oxford University Press.

Weber, M. (1949). Objectivity in social science and social policy. In E. Shils & H. Finch (Trans. and Eds.), *Max Weber on the methodology of the social sciences* (pp. 50–112). Glencoe, IL: Free Press.

Wheeler, J. (1975). Genesis and observership. In R. Butts & J. Hintikka (Eds.), *Foundational problems in the special sciences* (pp. 3–33). Boston: Reidel.

Wigner, E. (1967). *Symmetries and reflections*. Bloomington, IN: Indiana University Press.

Wilkerson, T. (1976). *Kant's critique of pure reason*. Oxford: Oxford University Press.

Winch, P. (1958). *The idea of a social science and its relation to philosophy.* London: Routledge and Kegan Paul.

Wrong, D. (1970). Max Weber. In D. Wrong (Ed.), *Max Weber* (pp. 1–76). Englewood Cliffs, NJ: Prentice-Hall.

Yolton, J. (1977). *The Locke reader.* Cambridge: Cambridge University Press.

Author Index

A

Abel, T., 10, *175*
Ambron, S., 5, *176*
Ariès, P., 67, 76, *175*
Aron, R., 58, 59, 60, 95, *175*

B

Bauman, Z., 2, 5, 35, 60, 61, 95, 109,
    139, 140, 169, *175*
Bellah, R., 88, 95, *175*
Benton, T., 7, 40, *175*
Bergner, J., 53, *175*
Bernstein, R., 1, 135, 154, 163, 165, 166,
    169, 172, *175*
Betti, E., 6, 136, 140, 150, 151, 152, 153,
    175
Bhaskar, R., 106, 109, *175*
Blakney, J., 51, *175*
Bleicher, J., 141, 153, *175*
Borg, W., 17, *175*
Brecht, A., 90, *175*

C

Church, W., 40, *175*
Cohen, M., 30, 44, *175*
Cook, T., 5, *178*
Cronbach, L., 5, 80, 81, 83, *176*

D

De Kruif, P., 18, *176*
Dornbusch, S., 5, *176*
Durkheim, E., 4, 45, 46, 47, 48, 50, 71,
    78, 79, *176*

E

Ermarth, M., 13, 55, 56, *176*
Ewing, A., 8, 72, *176*

G

Gadamer, H.G., 6, 135, 136, 153, 155,
    156, 160, 161, 168, *176*
Gall, M., 17, *175*
Giddens, A., 4, 7, 8, 12, 14, 37, 119, 124,
    125, 136, 137, 146, 166, *176*
Goetz, J., 4, 157, 158, *176, 177*
Grayling, A., 77, *176*
Guba, E., 157, *176*

H

Hanson, N., 10, *176*
Harris, R., 39, *176*
Heidegger, M., 135, *176*
Heilbroner, R., 63, 71, *176*
Hempel, C., 31, 77, 120, 121, *176*
Heshusius, L., 158, *179*
Hess, R., 5, *176*
Hesse, M., 14, 166, *176*
Hirsch, E., 6, 136, 140, 150, 151, 152,
    153, 159, *177*
Hodges, H., 13, 53, *177*
Holmes, M., 125, *177*
Hornik, R., 5, *176*
Huberman, A., 4, 5, 157, 158, 159, *178*
Hughes, H., 50, *177*
Hughes, J., 55, 125, 126, *177*
Hull, L., 39, *177*

K

Kaplan, A., 4, 88, 99, 100, 101, 102, 103,
    104, 105, 107, 117, 148, *177*
Keat, R., 71, *177*
Krausz, M., 76, 167, *177*
Kuhn, T., 10, *177*

L

Lather, P., 159, 160, *177*
Le Compte, M., 4, 157, 158, *176, 177*

Lessnoff, M., 118, 125, 128, *177*
Louch, A., 12, *177*
Lynch, K., 5, *177*

M
McClintock, C., 168, *177*
MacKenzie, B., 96, *177*
MacKenzie, D., 166, *177*
MacKinnon, E., 73, *177*
Manicas, P., 168, *177*
Meehl, R., 81, *176*
Meiland, J., 76, 167, *177*
Melden, A., 128, 130, 134, *177*
Messick, S., 83, *177*
Miles, M., 4, 5, 157, 158, 159, *178*
Myrdal, G., 88, 103, 148, *178*

N
Nagel, E., 13, 30, 44, 101, *175*, *178*
Nagel, T., 78, 147, 148, *178*

O
O'Connor, D., 38, *178*
Outhwaite, W., 7, 57, 126, 133, *178*

P
Palmer, R., 134, 155, 156, *178*
Pearsol, J., 160, *178*
Phillips, D., 5, *176*
Pinkard, T., 76, *178*
Polanyi, M., 10, *178*
Polkinghorne, D., 127, 128, 136, *178*
Putnam, H., 7, 8, 69, 73, 87, 96, 97, 99,
    104, 105, 107, 108, 166, *178*

R
Reason, P., 141, 157, 158, *178*
Reichardt, C., 5, *178*
Rescher, N., 8, 74, 75, *179*
Robinson, D., 45, 49, 51, *179*
Rorty, R., 9, 12, 13, 34, 71, 72, 79, 80,
    98, 104, 131, 132, 149, 166, *179*
Rossman, G., 5, *179*
Rowan, J., 141, 157, 158, *178*
Rubinstein, D., 7, 113, 114, *179*

Rudner, R., 121, 123, *179*
Russell, B., 38, 39, 51, 77, *179*

S
Secord, P., 168, *177*
Simey, T., 57, 95, *179*
Simpson, G., 13, 41, *179*
Smith, F., 64, *179*
Smith, J., 80, 141, 158, *179*
Smith, M., 2, *179*
Spencer, M., 71, *179*
Strauss, L., 95, *179*
Szacki, J., 41, 45, *180*
Sztompka, P., 47, *180*

T
Taylor, C., 9, 13, 14, 75, 107, 125, 126,
    127, 129, 131, 132, 133, 141, 142,
    143, 147, 160, 166, *180*
Thomas, D., 87, *180*
Thompson, K., 13, 40, 41, *180*
Trigg, R., 7, 66, 70, 82, *180*

U
Urban, W., 69, 73, *180*
Urry, J., 71, *177*

W
Walker, D., 5, *176*
Warnock, G., 51, 52, *180*
Wartofsky, M., 10, 114, 120, 121, 123,
    124, *180*
Weber, M., 4, 60, 91, 92, 93, 94, 95, 101,
    127, *180*
Weiner, S., 5, *176*
Wheeler, J., 11, 66, *180*
Wigner, E., 66, *180*
Wilkerson, T., 51, *180*
Wilson, B., 5, *179*
Winch, P., 11, 12, *181*
Wrong, D., 58, *181*

Y
Yolton, J., 38, *181*

Subject Index

A

Accurate, defining, 82–83
Action, 126–133
Art, 154–155
Astronomy, scientific method and, 26–27

B

Bias, defining, 100
Brute data, 75

C

Childhood, existence of, 75–76
Comte, influence on positivism, 40–45
Conceptual idealism, 74
Covering-law model, 120

D

Dilthey
  contribution to hermeneutics, 134–136
  contribution to social inquiry, 52–56
Durkheim, *Rules of the Sociological Method*,
    45–50
  Comte differing from, 46
  Mill differing from, 46

E

Education, development of, 50
Educational inquiry
  being a person, 141–142
    representation view, 142–143
    significance view, 143–145
  current interest in, 9–12
  goals, 113–114, 137
  practice of, 156–161
  procedural roles, 139–141
  scientific explanation, 114–115, 121–123
    covering-law model, 120
    laws, 115–120
    theory, 123–124

social inquiry compared to, 61–62
  summary of, 170–173
  terminology, 6–9
  unity of sciences and, 12–14
  versus social inquiry, 1–3
    method, 3–6
Empiricist approach
  goals, 137–138
  "mainstream," 127–128
  philosophical background, 146–147
  philosophical positions, 150–156
  practice of inquiry, 147–149
  rejection of, 124–126
  See also Educational inquiry; Social
      inquiry; Social sciences
Encyclopedists, 40
Externalism, 7–8, 69–73

F

Fact, defining, 102–103
Fact-value relationship, 87–88, 111
  inseparability of, 103–109
  Weber's separation, 91–96
French Enlightenment, 40–41
French Revolution, 40

G

Geisteswissenschaften, 13, 134–135, 140
Generalizations, scientific method and,
    28–29

H

Heisenberg uncertainty principle, 10–11
Hermeneutics, 6, 52–54, 56, 133–137
  importance of, 55
  "single," 14

I

Inorganic sciences, 42

Internalism, 7, 8–9, 73–78
Interpretive approach, 124
  meaning and action focus, 126–133
Investigator-investigated relationship, 63–
    64, 85–86
  examples, 64–68
  See also Validity
Is/ought, logical separation of, 88–91

K
Kant, contribution to philosophy, 51–52

L
Laws, scientific explanation for, 115–120
Locke, empiricism and, 39–40

M
Mathematics, use in scientific method, 25
Meaning, 126–133
Method, defining, 150–151
Mill, influence on positivism, 44–45
Minot, George; *See* Scientific method
Moral concept, 132–133

N
Naturwissenschaften, 13
Nazism, 105–106

O
Objective, defining, 9, 78–80
Objectivism, 163–164
  criticisms of, 166–169
  defining, 164–166
  paradox of, 169–170
Organic sciences, 42
Ought/is, logical separation of, 88–91

P
Positivism
  Comte's influence on, 40–45
  logical, 96–99
  Mill's influence on, 44–45
  positions of, 43–44
Probabilistic laws, 117–119

Q
Quantum theory, 10–11

R
Realism, 7–8

Relativism, 163–164
  criticisms of, 166–169
  defining, 164–166
  paradox of, 169–170
Rickert, contribution to social inquiry, 56

S
Scientific method, 17–18
  description of, 21, 24–25
    deduction, 27–29
    induction, 27–29
    measurement, 24–27
    observation, 21–24
    testing, 29–31
  example of, 18–21
  explanation for, 31–32
  laws, 31
  methodological role and, 33–35
  theory, 33
Scientific realism, 73
Social inquiry
  being a person, 141–142
    representation view, 142–143
    significance view, 143–145
  current interest in, 9–12
  educational inquiry compared to, 61–62
  empiricist-interpretive discussion, 4–5
  goals, 113–114, 137
  practice of, 156–161
  procedural roles, 139–141
  scientific explanation, 114–115, 121–123
    covering-law model, 120
    laws, 115–120
    theory, 123–124
  summary of, 170–173
  terminology, 6–9
  unity of sciences and, 12–14
  value-free, 96–99
  values, 99–103
  versus educational inquiry, 1–3
    method, 3–6
Social inquiry; *See also* Social sciences
Social sciences
  development of, 45–50
  empiricist approach to, 38–39
  origins of, 37–38
  positivism, 40–45
    Comte's influence on, 40–45
    Dilthey's criticism of, 52–56
    Mill's influence on, 44–45

Rickert's influence on, 56
Weber's contribution to, 57–61
Standard view, defining, 17
Subjective, defining, 78–80
Subject-object dualism, 63–64, 149–150

T
Theories, scientific, 123–124
Theory-neutral data, 9
Truth, 64
Truth, defining, 5, 8

U
Understanding concept, 133–137

V
Validity

empiricist approach to, 80–81
externalist approach to, 82–83
internalist approach to, 83–85
Value construction, 109–110
Value-fact relationship; See Fact-value
    relationship
Verstehen, 54, 58–61

W
Watson, contribution to psychology, 49–
    50
Weber, contribution to social inquiry, 57–
    61
Weber, fact and value separation, 91–96
Wundt, contribution to psychology, 49